The 1997 Developer's Guide

by Whil Hentzen

Please note that I am not a lawyer, nor have these documents been written or approved by a lawyer. They are not to be copied verbatim, but are provided to help you generate ideas for your own methodology. Please consult a lawyer before writing up and sending out your own documents.

PUBLISHED BY
Hentzenwerke Corporation
735 North Water Street
Milwaukee, Wisconsin 53202-4104

Hentzen, Whil
The 1997 Developer's Guide/Whil Hentzen
ISBN 0-9655093-1-1
1. Computer software - Development

Printed and bound in the United States of America

For further information, write Hentzenwerke Corporation, 735 North Water, Milwaukee, WI 53202-4104, USA, Voice (414) 224-7654, Fax (414) 224-7650 or CIS 70651,2270 or whil@hentzenwerke.com.

To KLN,
Who unknowingly started me on this pair of Chautauquas

Table of Contents

Table of Contents

Table of Contents

Table of Contents

Acknowledgments

Writing one book could be considered a fluke. A second - perhaps it was just a mistake. Doing a third - this is clearly a habit. And, as the psychologists will tell you, habits are a by-product of hanging around certain people. Let's see who we can blame for this one.

First, my wife, my partner, my lover, my best friend - yes, all the same person - Linda. Without her I would be an empty shell.

Second, my kids - Jackie, Alex, and Wolfie. They make coming home each night a joy.

Next, my folks, Bill and (the late) Nancy. Hentzen. If there is an ounce of goodness somewhere in my heart or soul, it came from them. They're the parents every kid would be proud to have.

The crew at the shop have been awesome. Linda "Bo" Boinski and Brenda Rave have worked day and night on this with me - they have converted a series of incoherent tapes and madly scribbled notes into the presentation you have before you.

Shauna Brook and John Wiedemann did double duty - taking manuscripts home at night to review, while cutting code and keeping the customers happy during the day.

And David Gauthier has helped Bo keep the web site up while we've been paying attention to other things.

A few of the FoxForum irregulars have gone way beyond the call of duty in their efforts to tweak, proof, nudge, argue and generally watch over me. Without the help of Barry Lee, Ted Roche, and Paul Russell, I would never have gotten this one out the door. Chaim Caron, Doug Hennig, Barbara Peisch, Ceil Rosenfeld, Steve Sawyer and Eric Tranmal all contributed time well above anything that could reasonably be expected of someone to review and edit parts of the book. Even with their help, any errors in the book are still all *mine*.

I also have to thank J. Geils, despite their busy schedule during the second week in August, 1969.

Finally, again, who kept me up those late nights as this guy was being put together? ZZ Top's Concrete and Steel, Aerosmith's No Surprize, and Warren Zevon's I'll Sleep When I'm Dead.

Software is always better when written at 105 decibels.

About the Author

Whil Hentzen is President of Hentzenwerke Corporation, a 14-year-old software development firm that specializes in strategic FoxPro-based business applications for Fortune 500 firms. Hentzenwerke also produced "The Ultimate FoxPro Reference," a freeware guide to products and services for the FoxPro market, now available on their web site. The company has commercial products and custom applications in use in 42 states and 18 countries. Hentzenwerke also hosts the Great Lakes Great Database Workshop in Milwaukee each year.

Whil's first commercial system was an inventory tracking application for a national supermarket chain, written in dBase II in 1983; he still treasures that 8.5 x 11 gray loose-leaf binder as a bit of Americana-a symbol of a simpler times. He converted to FoxPro with the release of 1.0 and has been a Fox zealot ever since.

He's the author of *Rapid Application Developer with FoxPro 2.6*, published by Pinnacle Publishing and *Programming Visual FoxPro 3.0*, published by Ziff-Davis Press. He is series editor for Pinnacle's "The Pros Talk Visual FoxPro" collection and the editor for *FoxTalk* and has contributed technical articles to a variety of other publication, including *FoxPro Advisor, Cobb's FoxPro Developer Journal* and *DBMS*. He has spoken on FoxPro topics at numerous conferences and user groups throughout the United States, Canada and Europe, including the Spanish National DevCon, Database and Client-Server World, FoxTeach, the Mid-Atlantic Database Solutions Workshop, the FoxPro Users Conference and the Twin Cities Database Fair.

A regular on CompuServe's FoxForum, Whil has maintained a top 25 standing in Calvin Hsia's Most Talkative list since 1992. He also founded the Milwaukee Association of FoxPro Developers in 1993 and maintains MOAFUGL-the Mother of All FoxPro User Group List.

When not injured <sigh>, Whil spends his free time running between 90- and 110-mile weeks in preparation for short distance races. He's logged over 43,000 lifetime miles and is hoping for one more shot at a sub-15-minute 5K before old age shuts the door on that chapter. In the rest of his spare time, he collects race statistics for Wisconsin's largest running club, the Badgerland Striders, and publishes their annual Wisconsin Race Book. He's casually working on his first fiction book, *Will the Aliens Ever Forgive Us For Disco?*

Preface

If you walk into a bookstore, you'll find a zillion books on the latest incarnations of every development tool imaginable. You can also find a number of books that discuss the route towards becoming a "computer consultant." And, tucked away in one of the more obscure corners, are a number of tomes about software development theory that have, for my liking, far too many equations and no mention of the concept of a "customer." Smack dab in the middle of this triangle lies a great big hole. There aren't many books on how to manage the development process.

The chaotic state that lives inside a single developer's head becomes much worse as you try to grow a company. Communication between people becomes exponentially more difficult as the number of individuals increases. The single line of communication required between two people becomes thee lines when a third person is added to the mix, grows to six potential paths when a fourth person joins the fray, and increases to ten with the fifth person. Add to this compounding confusion the rapidly increasing volume of knowledge that we're forced to deal with, and we've got a problem. We've got chaos on top of chaos.

Most organizations will survive, but that's all they do - survive. Every day is a mad rush, trying to stay ahead of the giant rolling ball, like in the beginning of *Raiders of the Lost Ark*. Eventually, many stumble and get crushed.

A methodical software development process is a way of managing this chaos.

The purpose of this book is to provide a manual that fills the void of knowledge between "Starting a computer consulting business" and "How to make a scrolling list box stop flickering between record fetches in VisualMagic" by organizing and documenting this process.

As you'll see, this is not a stuffy, ivory tower type of tome. In fact, we use this text as our company manual. This book documents the current state of our procedures and processes by which we do our daily work.

Processes are not static. They grow, change and adapt as needed. The software development process we're documenting is no different. As a result, this book is not a finished work. It's a snapshot of our current environment, and we're continually improving it.

Where is this leading me? There's a lot of good material in here, and I've already started a file folder for next year's book. But we're not the only ones looking at our processes and trying to improve them. And we don't have a monopoly on great ideas and real life experiences. (I just started writing them down.)

I'd like your feedback regarding what you think about this book as well as what you run into yourself. You can reach me directly on CompuServe at

70651,2270 or on the Internet through whil@hentzenwerke.com. You can also post messages for me in section 3 (Consultant's Corner) of FOXUSER or any number of sections on CONSULT. A complete list of *errata* will be posted on our web site, http://www.hentzenwerke.com.

By the way, you'll find that I'm somewhat, er, well, uh, opinionated - yeah, that's it - *opinionated.* If you don't flinch at least once before the end of this book, you may not be reading very carefully. But the intent is not to offend, it's simply a natural byproduct of passion. And no one will ever argue that I'm not passionate about software development.

Whil Hentzen
Milwaukee, WI
Summer, 1996

Introduction

So what do you have to know before you start reading this book in order to make the most of your time? Who am I directing this book toward, what do you have know about me, and what assumptions am I making?

After I answer the first two questions, I'll discuss the two underlying assumptions of this book: that being able to manage the process of software development is critical for success in the next few years, and that fixed price software development projects are the optimal way to run a software development shop.

Who is This Book For?

This book is for the skilled software developer who is comfortable with the technical part of developing an application - the design and coding phases - and wants to improve how they go about the rest of the software development process.

You should find value if you're (1) an independent developer (the "one-man shop") who is either trying to polish their current process, or trying to grow into a multi-person shop, (2) the owner or a developer in a small (a few to a dozen people) shop, (3) a lone corporate developer, or (4) a developer or project manager in a small to medium size corporate MIS department trying to bring to some order to their group.

If you're in a large development shop or corporate environment, I'm not sure how well the procedures and processes here scale up. Our intent is to grow from a half-dozen people into a 20, 30 or 50 person shop sometime in the future, but until we get there, we won't know what we need. We're trying to put these processes in place now so that we're ready when that seven figure contract knocks on the door. How much of the material will scale to a 20 or 50 person shop? Don't know yet. But we'll find out, and I'm certain the groundwork we're laying now will stand us in good stead down the road.

Boring Stuff About My Shop

I've been writing custom database applications since 1982, first using dBASE and then FoxPro as my only tools. I had a computer training, consulting and programming firm with a half-dozen employees in Cincinnati throughout the '80's, but sold it in order to move back to my hometown of Milwaukee upon the birth of my first child. Until January, 1995, I worked out of my den as an independent. At that time, I hired my first employee and opened an office in downtown Milwaukee. At the time of this writing (Fall of 1996), we're up to six people - three developers, a technical support person who handles testing and other process-related tasks, a part-time Internet developer, and my administrative assistant who doubles as our webmaster and generally saves my butt on a daily basis.

Several years ago, I wrote a book about Rapid Application Development with FoxPro 2.6. Its purpose was to formalize the process of the development of desktop database applications. When a programmer starts out in the business of writing custom programs, they usually start from scratch and build everything themselves. After the first few (or many) attempts, an idea dawns on some people: maybe not all of this has to be invented each time. That reusable code, repeatable techniques, and so on, can be an aid to building applications faster and with fewer problems.

Once the RAD process was in place, the work of building systems was a lot more fun, and a lot more profitable. The boring grunt work of setting up a new system and building the standard "we've done this screen a hundred times" interfaces was minimized, since core foundations and reusable routines that had been built and tested in the past could be plugged in easily, providing error-free functionality quickly and consistently.

As we've grown, one of the recurring themes in our staff meetings (OK, those impromptu chats in the halls) was how to improve the quality of our systems. The programming part was actually pretty easy, but writing the code is just *part* of the job. I stumbled upon Watts Humphrey's *"Managing the Software Process,"* but it was one of those "10 equations per page" types of books. He managed a large organization and talks of "4% of your staff should be dedicated to..." For an independent developer, or a corporate guy who's one of three guys in the MIS department, this is fairly far removed from reality.

Programming is 90% of the job; the surrounding part - selling, writing specifications, design, estimating, coordinating the coding, finding employees, training them, testing (and re-testing), tracking employees activities, tracking bugs, shipping, handling issues after shipping, getting paid, and ongoing maintenance - these all take the other 90% of the time. And that second 90% of the time is the subject of this book.

The Process Is the Key!

In other words, this book is dedicated to the process of software development. Writing code is just one facet of that process. Yes, I know, I know, some people treat the choice of their programming language as if it were a matter of life and death. (And we all know that it's much more important than that.) But, throughout this book, I'm going to treat language as largely irrelevant. The crew in my shop use five to seven different languages, depending on how you want to define "different" - FoxPro 2.6 for DOS/Windows, Visual FoxPro 3.0 and 5.0, Visual Basic 3.0 and 4.0, Delphi 2.0 and a combination of Java and Javascript.

But the process of software development is the key to producing high quality custom applications profitably in order to grow your firm.

There are five reasons that I am as concerned about the process of software development as I am about the nuts and bolts of writing code and shipping EXEs to customers.

1. It's Deja Vu - All Over Again

The first big reason for me is that, as I grow my company, I find I'm seeing the same thing for the third time. I've been here before. Training people is time-intensive, and while I really like it, there are some parts I like more than others. I needed a way to get some of the routine stuff done better. So my training needed a set of common routines as well as the custom stuff.

2. Applications are Bigger and More Important

The second reason is that this process is becoming more and more important. When you were developing applications on a 286 with a local 20 MB hard disk and a network card to a server with a (gasp!) 250 MB main drive, well, the term "mission critical" didn't really pop up too often. These days, even small shops and individual developers have machines with the horsepower that can support large, important, sophisticated applications. The construction techniques you employ to panel your basement need not be nearly as rigorous as those you would use to build an entire house, and a sophisticated house-building process wouldn't be well suited if you tried to scale it to the erection of a 40 story skyscraper. And furthermore, given a bit of common sense, the crew that builds a multi-million dollar office building will benefit from their experience when they tackle smaller projects.

Of course, you may be able to get away with a casual, catch-as-catch-can approach to software development when you're writing smaller applications, but the first time you're asked to tackle a larger project, you'll need a more formal approach to the development process.

3. Revision Cycles are Accelerating

The third reason that process is important to me is that the rate of change is accelerating. (Well, I guess, technically, the rate of change is increasing. The fact that it's increasing means that change is accelerating, right? Nice to know something from college has still stuck around.)

Somewhere in the early '80's, dBASE II came out. I bought version 2.41 in 1982, and the main difference between it and version 2.40, 2.3, 2.2, and so on, were a reduction in the number of bugs and a few new features and commands. dBASE III and dBASE III Plus came out in 1985, and dBASE IV showed up, sort of, in 1988 and 1989. In 1990, FoxPro 1.0 came out, followed by FoxPro 2.0 in 1992 and Visual FoxPro 3.0 in 1995. Visual FoxPro 5.0 was released about 15 months after 3.0, and we'll probably have 6.0 arrive before most people get the plastic wrap off the box of 5.0.

So what's my point? Let's look at the amount of time between releases. It's shrinking rapidly. We had *three to four years* to get good - and to make a bunch of money - with each of the major releases. The next revision to 3.0 (which would be 5.0) came out 15 months later. Yikes! And this isn't the case just with FoxPro - it's happening with Delphi, Visual Basic, you name it. The product cycle is shortened. People aren't frantic about the rate of change anymore. We don't have time to think about it! It was truly frightening to hear an executive from Sun Microsystems repeatedly use the term "perpetual beta" when referring to their Internet products at the 1996 Borland Developers Conference.

4. Applications are More Complex

The knowledge requirements for developing applications now is significantly higher than it was a decade ago. Back then, you wrote a few hundred or a few thousand lines of procedural code, tried not to use the GOTO command too often, slapped in a few token comments, and shot the whole thing into a directory on the customer's machine. If you were sophisticated, you had a mechanism for separating data from the program, and you might even have a set of library routines that you shipped with every application.

In the big, bad world of development in the late 1990's (are we there *already*?), it's considerably more complex. Your application might have to run on Windows 3.1, Windows for Workgroups 3.11, Windows95, Windows NT, Netware, LANtastic, and maybe talk to some Macs as well. Your application has to install itself properly, talk nicely to other applications, be able to share data through OLE, and do a bunch of other nice Windows type things that aren't really that well documented and, frankly, don't always work that well.

You'll need to learn object-oriented programming, how to design classes, maintain encapsulation, avoid multiple inheritance, and handle performance problems that arise when your class hierarchy goes too deep. Your application must communicate with client-server back ends, switch between remote and local data, work with network drives with a variety of different mapping conventions, and deal with WANs as well as LANs. Of course, replication across three continents will have to be built in because some VP just read about this topic in Time magazine and wants their application to do it as well - by next Monday. And all of your applications will conform to the browser interface being fought over by Netscape and Microsoft these days, right?

Doesn't it just make you want to go back and bus tables at Burger Boy?

5. "I Hope You're Teaching Quality"

Finally, according to Dr. W. Edward Deming in his book *"Out of Crisis,"* at least 90% of all defects are caused by process problems. My friend, Mac Rubel, has often stated "Programs don't come with bugs. You have to put them in there." To me, this means that a syntax error a programmer puts in their program isn't a defect. But when the program leaves their arena and goes to testing, the build lab, or the customer, it then becomes a defect. The proper process will prevent the syntax error in the program from becoming a defect.

Delivering high quality software has always been a particular issue with me. Of course, relatively few of you reading this have "We want to write crappy code and just shove it down the throats of our customers" as your company mission. But in the heat of the battle, it's easy to let substandard work get out the door. With the potential for errors increasing as described previously, it's important to buttress the process as well as we can.

This isn't just a good business decision, however. There was a landmark article in the September 1994 issue of Scientific American that bemoaned the crisis that software development is facing, and that it may well be **the** most critical issue facing the industrialized world over the next 10 years. Let's face it. The world revolves around software to an incomprehensible degree. Low-tech devices that have been around for hundreds of years now include microprocessors: a razor contains 2000 bytes of software code and a sneaker has twice that.

Just as pundits are arguing that the world is dividing into two groups - the "haves" being those that have access to the information, and the "have-nots" being those that don't. I would argue that the software development community is going to fracture into two groups. On the one side you have professional developers who understand the process of building applications, and on the other, hacks who go to bed each night and pray that none of their code breaks before morning. The fact that you picked up this book is a good indication that you belong to the first group (hey, even an author can suck up to his readers, can't he?) If you make it to the end of this book before dozing off, then the chances of you staying in the "haves" group is even stronger.

The Pricing Debate

One of the fundamental debates in the development of custom software applications is whether to charge a fixed price or charge on an hourly basis.

I believe that fixed price software development is a better business decision (if, of course, it's done properly) because it is a more profitable method. I also believe that it's a better decision for the customer, since they can evaluate a software project with a specific price and determine if it is a wise investment or not. And furthermore, many companies prefer a fixed price because it allows them to plan and budget for software just like most other "things" that they buy.

However, most developers charge on an hourly basis for one simple reason - because they do not know how to accurately price an application.

This book will show you how to accurately determine your cost of developing a custom application with a degree of repeatability that most developers can not do now.

Let's lay down some background on fixed price versus time and materials methods before we begin.

Why Do Developers Hate Fixed Price Work?

The fundamental reason is the way that developers create the price in a fixed price situation. We've all heard the jokes, you know, "take your best estimate, double it, and then tack on a bunch more." The trouble is these aren't jokes.

The bottom line is that developers are simply guessing. No wonder they hate fixed price work. They don't know how much to guess, and if they guess wrong, they're going to lose their shirt. Most programmers are incurable optimists. The ones who have been around for a while are knowledgeable incurable optimists. They always figure, despite being burned on twenty applications in the past five years, that the next one will work fine, that there won't be any problems, and they'll finally make a buck at it. It's in our nature to guess low to begin with. You never hear of a programmer guessing way too high and the customer going for it, do you?

Let's take an analogy. Suppose you were a grocery store clerk, and the customer walked up to you with a basket stuffed to overflowing. You could charge them one of two ways. The first is to guess how much they've got in the basket. You take a look, think real hard, try to remember what you guessed on another cart that looked like it, and then pull a number out of the air.

Obviously, this isn't a very good method. If it was, we'd all be playing grocery store lottery each week. Now, as bad as this method is, let's suppose that you *never* found out how good your guesses were? That's right, after a customer left the store, you were never able to find out what the actual value of that cart of stuff was. So you'd never be able to determine if you were guessing well, or if you were really lousy, or if, with just one small tweak to your guessing routine, you'd be able to guess right on target.

Of course, there is the ultimate measuring stick. If, at some point, the grocery store manager comes by and says that over the past month, the store's income was lower than the store's expenses and you're all fired - well, that's a pretty bad way to measure. If the manager would come over and say that today's guesses, in total, were lower than today's actual sales, then everyone would make random adjustments to their guesses, but it's still just a crapshoot. What if tomorrow all the customers start putting bottles of Dom Perignon in their basket?

This whole scenario sounds pretty silly, but isn't it what 9 out of 10 programmers do? They take a couple of long hard looks, perhaps shuffle around the contents of the top of the grocery basket a bit, and then - wham! - guess away. There is no allowance for something really expensive that's been hidden out of sight; like a routine that's going to be a bear to code, or a screen that's trivial at first blush, but contains some hidden requirements that are going to be extremely difficult to do.

The second part of this analogy is dead on accurate as well. Most programmers do not have any mechanism for determining how much they "spent" on a project, so they can't tell how good their guess on their last project was. Here we have a recipe for disaster. Wild, random guesses with virtually no logical reasoning behind them, and no mechanism for measuring the accuracy or providing feedback with the intent of improving the next guess.

Rather strange for a profession that relies on logic as its cornerstone, wouldn't you say?

You're probably thinking, "There are a lot of awfully smart people in this industry. If none of them have figured out how to, then it probably can't be done." But if you've lost all hope of ever figuring out how to do fixed price work, let me reassure you. It can be done. It just takes a few tricks and some discipline.

Before we get into the nuts and bolts, let me explain our reasoning for wanting to do fixed price work. This is more work than simply recording your hours and sending in a bill every couple of weeks. There has to be a corresponding benefit to it.

What's the Advantage to Fixed Price Work?

My firm, like most others, exists for one reason: to make money for the shareholders. The owners expect to make a return on the funds they invest in the company just as if they had invested the money in a mutual fund or precious metals. In my firm, there is one investor - me. These circumstances don't change the rules.

Given that a company makes money for the shareholders by making a profit, the mission of the company should be to maximize its profits, so as to maximize the return for the shareholders. I feel that software development firms can do so by doing work on a fixed price basis.

Doing hourly work has a built-in profit ceiling, because there are only so many hours in a day. This argument holds regardless if you're a one-person shop or if you have 50 folk in the office. There is still a maximum profit per "unit of production." With fixed price work, however, the maximum profit, while it still exists, can be significantly higher - to a factor of anywhere from two to ten times as much or more.

The advantage of fixed price development is being able to charge by value, not by cost. Suppose your hourly rate is $75/hour, and an application you're quoting will take you 200 hours. That's a price of $15,000. If, on the other hand, the application is worth $30,000 to the customer, your hourly rate has doubled, since you will spend 200 hours to bring in $30,000. The key is that the application *is worth* $30,000 to the customer, and it's totally irrelevant to them (in fact, it's none of their business) what your cost is.

Let me put this another way. *You do not have to price the job at your cost.* In fact, you'd be doing an injustice to your shareholders if you did so. Microsoft, at the time of this writing, is making approximately 20-30% net profit. This means that they could bring their prices down 10% and still be making a healthy profit. In fact, if it were not due to competitive market pressures, we'd probably still be paying $495 or $795 for Word, instead of $99.

The trick is to know what your work is worth to the customer, and to know what your costs are. Section One of this book will deal with assessing the value of the project to the customer, and Section Two will explain how to determine your cost to produce that project. When the value to the customer is larger than your cost, you both win. You'll make a profit, and the customer will get the project done. You wouldn't do the work if you were going to lose money.

I can't stress enough that your cost doesn't have to be your price. The only reason the cost number is so important is that you don't want to quote a price to the customer that is below your cost. Since most developers guess when putting together prices for applications, it's very easy for them to provide a price that will end up being below their cost. This is what has happened when you hear "I really took a bath on that one - I thought it would take 500 hours and I spent nearly 800!" They simply provided a price that was lower than their cost. Despite common wisdom, you can't make a profit through this method!

We're used to thinking that we should bill by the hour like the other professionals: lawyers, accountants, and so on. But with a properly drawn up specification, you can stop thinking about charging for time and instead build (and charge for) a product.

When Isn't Fixed Price Work a Good Idea?

The one requirement for fixed price work is that the deliverables be measurable. The application must be described to an extent that it is clear to both the developer and the customer what is included and what is not.

This is difficult to do. That's why an entire section of this book is dedicated simply to write a specification. When it's impossible to write a spec, the fixed price path is not a good idea.

Our company will go the fixed price route for new applications, modifications (upgrades, changes) to existing applications, and new modules for existing applications, because we can write detailed specifications from which we can determine our cost. We may or may not be able to provide fixed prices for modifications to another programmer's system. There are some types of work that we won't do on a fixed price basis - ever. Obviously, any situation where the specifications are so vague or incomplete that the deliverables can't be measured, or for work that is time-dependent, but the amount of work is not quantifiable - such as design and analysis, general consulting on application requirements, and debugging or troubleshooting. Most of the time, working with someone else's system falls into this same category.

What About "Not To Exceed" Contracts?

Occasionally you have a request for a contract that specifies actual cost (time and materials spent) but with a top end "Not To Exceed" amount. These are the worst of all possible worlds. The customer is asking you to take the risk - since it's likely that a detailed spec doesn't exist - yet there is no reward for the corresponding risk.

I was once asked to do a project on a NTE basis under the most brazen of pretenses. The customer (or, I should say, potential customer) insisted that I make all my profit in my standard hourly rate. it was immoral of me to expect to make some obscene, windfall profit through a fixed price job. The best part of this? The part that had me laughing all the way home?

The individual in question was a personal injury lawyer. The stereotypical "ambulance chaser" who worked on a contingency basis - netting fees way out of proportion to the time spent on the case.

There are all types in this world, aren't there?

Should a customer ask you for a NTE contract, in the words of King Arthur in Monty Python and the Holy Grail, "Run away! Run away!"

Section 1: Selling

"Nothing happens until somebody sells something." A very wise, very old man told me this one day. He then told me the same thing a few weeks later, and then two days after that, and again, again, again, incessantly. He could get away with it, because he was my dad.

And he was right.

We often don't have to worry about selling. People come to us with a desperate look in their eyes, begging us to save their bacon. It's a seller's market. But there's a difference between scraping by and doing it right. Attention to selling will pay huge dividends - better margins, higher profits, more sleep at night, a day off once in a while, even a chance to go out on a date with your spouse.

In this section, I will discuss the development of a basic marketing strategy. A great deal of a company's success, aside from having the client base, is having a focused point on the horizon to steer by or aim toward. The ability to adhere to this strategy, while still maintaining a certain amount of flexibility to adjust to changes in the business or programming environment, is key.

Let's look at the sales process involved in developing custom software.

1.1 Positioning

- What is Positioning?
- What Do You Sell?
- Why Do They Buy It?
- Why Do They Buy It From You?
- Conclusion

Positioning may seem like an odd topic to start out a book on developing applications. In fact, you may not even be familiar with the concept. Positioning is the placement of your product or service in relation to those of your competition in the market that you are serving. (From now on, I'm going to use the term "product" to mean both "product and service.") That sounds like one of those textbook definitions that you had to memorize in school, and forgot soon after.

In a practical sense, positioning allows you to differentiate yourself from the competition. Differentiation is what gets you the business, lets you charge premium prices, and generally lets you enjoy life. Conversely, when the product you're offering is perceived as "just like all the others" and therefore a commodity, you'll have a tougher time selling. The buyer has no specific motivation to choose you over the other guys.

> If you can't describe your position on the back of a business card, you don't have a clear idea of what it is.

It is not the purpose of this chapter to write a whole book on positioning. You can go to the library or bookstore and find lots of very sophisticated books on positioning. Rather, we're going to broach the subject and discuss how you might take advantage of it in your business. If your interest is piqued, then you can read on.

What is Positioning?

Let's look at a couple of well-known examples of positioning. "We're number two" has been the rallying cry of a certain company for years. You already know I'm talking about Avis. Why would anyone in their right mind boast that they're losing the race? Because it attracts the attention and sympathy of America's Everyman, who loves to back the underdog. It's also a position that no one else can claim. It also stakes out the high ground in an area that's extremely valuable - customer service. "We're number two, so we have to try harder" implies that you'll get better care than by going to the market leader.

Another classic example of positioning is Apple's "A computer for the rest of us." Again, this is positioning for a perceived consumer product. This campaign was targeted at individuals, not corporations - but, surprisingly, a large percentage of corporations have people working with them.

Positioning in a business market works the same way, but perhaps without the goofy cartoon characters and sappy TV commercials. In order to successfully position your product, you need to answer a few questions.

What Do You Sell?

First and foremost, what is it that you think you're selling? A disconcerting number of business people are in the "AFAB" business - "Anything For A Buck." Yes, I know, when the mortgage payment is due in four days and you don't have a lick of work, most anything from installing network cards to changing printer ribbons sounds awfully attractive. Let's assume for the moment that you've gotten past those growing pains and can, to some extent, afford the luxury of choosing what you want to do.

For the purposes of our book, I'm going to assume the answer is some variant of "I write custom database applications." What you do and what your customers buy are two different things. Maybe you've heard the old saw "People don't buy ¼ inch drill bits. They buy the ability to make quarter inch holes." Along the same lines, as much as it might hurt your feelings, people aren't all that interested in buying your software. They've got a problem to solve, and they're hoping, yes, praying, that your custom application will solve that problem.

Why Do They Buy It?

Let's examine the issue of why people buy. Fundamentally, people buy things because they're dissatisfied with the status quo. More succinctly, they're in pain, and they expect their purchase to ease or remove that pain. Money is generally considered to be the scarcest of scarce resources. People are rather particular about parting with it. (Although, when you think about it, you can always get more money, but you can't turn back the clock.)

Think about the last few things you bought. In each case, if you reflect carefully, your purchase was aimed at removing some sort of pain. You were hungry, so you bought a burger and fries at that fine cafe named "EAT." When you were done, you weren't hungry anymore. However, your eye hurt from the fight with the regulars at "EAT," so you bought a bottle of disinfectant. You also found that you were a mite chilly from the new holes in your shirt, again from that fight with the boys from "EAT," so your third purchase, a new shirt and sweater, eased that pain. Get the idea?

What types of pain could someone be experiencing that would cause them to buy custom software from you? Although, as a custom software developer you're probably selling to companies, you really have to convince the people in those companies to sign the purchase order. They won't do so unless they're convinced that your software can ease their pain.

They might have a legitimate business reason. For example, they want to provide IVR (Interactive Voice Response) access to part of their database, and want you to provide the programs that will do so. But, funny enough, people are rather human, and (you can quote me on this), one of the biggest mistakes you can make is to assume that people will act rationally in a business setting.

There are a lot of not so obvious reasons that someone would buy something. They need to get their boss off their back, they want to boast to the others in their golf foursome, they need to impress a customer, they want to keep their budget from shrinking next year; the list is endless.

The one thing people don't want to do upon the purchase of an item is to be even more unhappy afterwards than they were before. Even more than becoming the hero, they don't want to become the goat. So pain avoidance is a significant part of the equation.

How does this insight on why people buy things help you determine what you're selling? We decided that the product (ahem, service) was "custom database applications." It might be more beneficial to realize that you're selling peace of mind, or a week of freedom from the boss, or fewer paper. If you can decide what it is that you really sell, then you're well on the way to developing a position.

Why Do They Buy It From You?

The next question to address is, "Why do people buy from you and not someone else?" In other words, what distinguishing characteristics do you have? You know that you're the worst person to answer this question, right? Partly because it's hard to be objective, and partly because 99% of what you are going to say is something out of a Dilbert cartoon: "Because our quality is better!" or "Because we have the best people!" or perhaps "Because we are focused on total quality management in a team while delivering 100% customer satisfaction."

Unfortunately, the answer to why someone is going to buy from you is much less flattering. More often than not, the answer is something like, "You had the biggest ad in the Yellow Pages", "You were closer than the other guys we called," "No one answered the phone when we called our regular programmer" or even, "You happened to be open."

If you're a developer, how do they tell that you're different than the next developer? Everybody has a beard (well, maybe not some of the women), everybody looks like a geek (well, again, maybe not some of the women), and everybody can recite the top ten inconsistencies in the first episode of ST:TNG (yes, even the women.)

Let me tell you a secret - how we developed an unbeatable answer to this last question. As I mentioned in the introduction, I started developing PC applications in 1982 with dBASE II on a 64K PC. My first company was based in Cincinnati, and we used dBASE for a number of years. I sold that company in the late 80's and moved my family back to my hometown of Milwaukee. When I started up again, I was the new guy in town with a few skills but no contacts and no leads. As a result, the first thing I did was call up each of the current developers in town and ask to subcontract, in order to get started and move some bucks into my wallet.

After making 20 or 30 calls, I came to one incredible conclusion: they were all the same. I couldn't tell one from the next from the third. I'm sure that if any of them are reading this, they're thinking that I probably skipped over their name, but that's OK. The point is that after a week of cold calling competitors in my own business, I couldn't tell any of them apart. And if I couldn't, I knew potential customers couldn't either.

Thus, I could see myself walking into a prospective customer and as soon as I left, they'd forget my name and call the next guy on the list.

My next step was to develop a set of public credentials such as speaking engagements, writing articles, being active on the CompuServe forums, and so on. I did this to be regarded as somewhat of an expert in the language. Admittedly, I've been very fortunate to gain the visibility I have, and a couple of great breaks have fallen my way, but all in all, the positioning was a very calculated move.

Once I achieved that, it was easy to stand out from the competition. More than once I've gone into prospects to discuss potential development, and brought along copies of things I've written. The competition doesn't stand much of a chance when the customer finds out that their other potential software vendor is learning from a book that I've written. Our firm is also able to command higher prices because of the credentials of the "exalted leader."

You may be wondering how writing a book or editing an industry rag translates into respect for application development capability. Everyone says they're an expert and can show off some whiz-bang screen to impress a potential customer. It's different to explain that my code is exposed for the world to see and ridicule. In fact, as a result of publishing articles and books, my work is being used as the foundation of other people's applications. My having produced a couple of publicly-accepted baseline frameworks makes the customer feel more comfortable.

Well, enough of the "I Love Me" story. The point is that positioning yourself in the market - as I did with language expertise - enables you to win jobs and command higher margins than you would otherwise be able to. Let's examine other ways you can differentiate yourself from your competition.

We should address the question already on the tip of your tongue: "You just told us how you did it, and now anyone can do the same thing. Don't you feel stupid for giving away your secret?" The answer to this is pretty easy. It's "No." While developing language expertise in 1991 was a viable method to gain visibility, I don't think it's the answer in 1997. It took a great deal of time to develop extensive expertise in the language, and time is not a resource we have an overabundance of anymore. The frequent revision cycle of our tools makes a large investment in a single application more and more difficult, and so I'm not sure it can be done any longer.

Language specialization. How might you differentiate yourself from the other developers in your area? Although I've just played the doom and gloom guy about developing expertise in a particular language, this area is still wide open. Become the world's best on a particular product, to the absolute exclusion of everything else. Conversely, become comfortable with absolutely everything under the sun regarding that product, so that when the customer calls, you're in a position to do whatever they ask.

Customer service orientation. Perhaps your answer lies in the non-technical arena: 24 hour, on-call service, or offices in multiple cities. What about servicing the rural areas from a metropolitan base? There are lots of large manufacturing companies located in small communities, and they typically "come to the big city" for their legal and accounting help. Why not for their software development services as well?

Vertical market expert. The next possibility for positioning that you could look at would be to focus on customer needs instead of your capabilities. Languages and products come and go, but experts in a specific field can make a living forever. Do you know more about the laundromat or used car or fresh produce business than anyone else within 100 miles? If you know everything there is to know about providing pricing data to manufacturers reps, you're going to be able to go in against the competition who is learning about the business for the first time, and clean their clock.

In fact, positioning yourself as an expert in a specific vertical tool is an excellent idea, because your ability now transcends the requirement of being an expert in a language. You can say, "Yes, I've written 17 applications that deal with pricing data for manufacturers reps," and the competitor is going to stutter, "Yeah, uh, I think I can do one of those."

You may be an expert in Paradox 4 or Visual Basic 5.0, but as soon as the new release comes out, voila! you're a rookie just like everyone else again. On the other hand, if you know tons and tons about medical data, and the new version comes out, you *still* know tons and tons about medical data. (Thanks to my friend Miriam Davis for making this point so clear.) Meanwhile, the other guy is trying to learn the new version like you are and still doesn't have any vertical expertise.

What else can you do to position yourself against the other guy? If the above ideas leave you cold, here's a trick. Take out a large sheet of paper and list one or two dozen characteristics about developers that customers would be interested in (or horrified about.) This list might include professional appearance items like suits or jeans, business cards with raised lettering or with smears from the HP III that they printed them on, fancy offices or someone's garage. Or it may be technical things like presence on beta test teams of current products, access to industry resources, and years of expertise in the field. Does the firm answer the phone within two rings, do they have an after hours number, and do they have a receptionist or a scratchy answering machine?

Then call a dozen of your competitors and find out how they rate - or if they even make the list. Eventually you'll find a number of similarities and a few differences. Finally, rank yourself on the same list (or have some associates do it for you), and see where you stand. If you like what you see, you have just positioned yourself competitively against them. If you don't like what you see, you've now got the ingredients for developing a positioning plan.

Before you get all fired up about trumpeting the differences between you and the other guys, remember that the advantage or the difference that you're trying to project has to be important to the customer. If your primary distinguishing characteristic is that you always wear a propeller beanie when you work, it's entirely possible that not many customers are going to care.

Conclusion

One last word about positioning. Part of the reason for this book is to suggest and publish a standard methodology for developing custom applications. Because there is no standard methodology like those in the medical, legal or financial fields, any one can buy a PC and call themselves an expert. By providing a set of guidelines or generally accepted practices, I'm hoping to create some common groundwork for application development.

So this whole book is a case study in positioning. Think about it.

1.2 Marketing

- Running Ads in the Newspaper
- Yellow Pages
- Direct Mail
- Cold Calling
- Electronic Marketing
- So How Do You Get Business?
- Web Sites
- Company Name
- Rules About Company Names
- Conclusion

If you are reading this chapter in the hopes of finding the holy grail to marketing, the magic answer, the trick to making a million dollars next week, then you'll find it here. No problems. Yeah, Right!

Bob Kehoe, a friend of mine and co-founder of RDI Software Technologies in Chicago has been quoted as saying, "Marketing: nothing works." What he means is that none of the traditional avenues toward marketing - yellow pages ads, newspaper ads, direct mailing, cold calling - none of them work. Custom software is kind of one of those weird beasts. It's not like selling vacuum cleaners or industrial pipe fittings or any number of hard goods. It's more like selling accounting services. You can't just "smile and dial" like a stockbroker. You need to make a lot of personal contacts, collect references, and wait a long time. Don't expect to go into business, run a few ads, and be swimming in business as if you were a pet shop. That's what Bob is saying.

So, how *do* you go about picking up new business? How do companies grow if they don't have the means to market?

Running Ads in the Newspaper

This is frightfully expensive for the small shop. If you're looking at a daily paper in a medium sized city like Milwaukee, Memphis or Oklahoma City, an ad that's 2 columns by 4 inches in the Sunday paper and one day in the daily paper, will run close to $1,000 per week. And that's if you are using a frequency contract, which means you have to commit to a certain amount of inches or a certain amount of dollars. It would be significantly more on an ad by ad basis. If you look in the paper to see who else is advertising, you will see stockbrokers, transmission people, and local computer suppliers like "PC's R US." Not too many service firms.

I guess you can look at the lack of advertising in the paper as being a glass that's either half empty or half full. It's an opportunity because no one else is doing it, therefore you'll stand out. On the other hand, why isn't anyone else doing it? Maybe because it doesn't work.

You need to have a healthy marketing budget to withstand that type of expense. However, you don't have to sell a lot from one of those ads. A campaign that runs $5,000 only has to sell a couple of jobs in order to make that back. On the other hand, if you are an individual or two people, $5,000 is a lot of money if you don't get any responses. And don't expect to have the phone ringing off the hook after your first ad.

Yellow Pages

Not many people look in the Yellow Pages for custom work. Generally, those who let their fingers do the walking either 1) don't have any contacts in the playing field or 2) don't even understand the playing field. They look in the Yellow Pages for a diskette duplicating service or someone to repair their broken driveway. They ask friends and associates about a computer programmer.

> We have run a reasonably good sized ad for years, and we're very clear in our ad that all we do is custom software development. We still get calls from 14 year olds wanting to buy a copy of Doom. Or somebody wanting help writing a WordPerfect macro, and they really think we ought to do it for free because, after all, aren't we the ones who wrote that program?

But once in a while you will pick up a couple customers.

I am sure someone is going to be unhappy with this, but frankly, the Yellow Pages have honed their sales techniques to the extent that a Used-Car salesperson could learn some lessons, and you have to be careful. You can usually work a deal where they will give you the next higher size for no, or minimal, additional costs. The following year, however, they will charge you for running that same size advertisement. Nobody ever wants to decrease their ad size the following year.

What we have done for years is to each year ask for something else free. We were going to pay for bold so we said we wanted extra large type this year. Next year we were ready to pay for bold and extra large type, and said we want a picture now. If our ad size is going to get bigger, we might as well take advantage of the fact that they will do this.

Do not take them up on the "see us in the Yellow Pages" line. Why would you, in your own literature, refer someone to the Yellow Pages where your competition is advertising?

Once you start advertising in one Yellow Pages directory, you'll have to watch out for solicitations from other directories that appear to be the same publication. There are multiple Yellow Pages and when you list in one, they want you listed in all. It is very easy to suddenly get hooked into a bill for several hundred or thousand dollars every month.

Make sure you get a camera ready copy of what they are going to print. They have a tendency to be really lousy at taking what you give them and actually doing something with it.

Nonetheless, we do have an ad in the Yellow Pages every year. Amazingly enough, despite the pessimism voiced in this section, we have, on occasion, picked up a lead that's turned into business. For about $5,000 a year, you can run several reasonable sized ads. You only have to sell one job to recoup that.

Direct Mail

It is very hard to sell professional services using direct mail. Would you buy services from a lawyer that mailed you a letter? We think not. You must have an extremely compelling message and be able to do it over and over again to have a winning record at direct mail. A lot of people figure since they have a computer, they can print out a bunch of names and addresses, slap together something in their desktop publisher and they have a direct mail piece. Unfortunately, it's going to look like they did it themselves.

So now that we're convinced that an hour with Pagemaker doesn't qualify as a marketing campaign, what types of activities are worth considering?

If you have a specialty in a specific industry segment, you can buy mailing lists (or research them yourselves through the public library) and target a mailing to those companies. By explaining precisely what benefits you have provided for other firms in their industry, you can grab their attention quickly. Many companies are starting to consider the replacement of their current systems, given the double whammy of DOS systems not cutting it anymore, and year 2000 problems starting to become an issue.

Again, I'm not saying that finding business through direct mail is impossible, but it's difficult. If you are going to go the direct mail route, either hire a professional or at least get a couple of books on how to do it right. There are ways to make it happen.

Cold Calling

Arguably the single biggest waste of time you could ever spend. You could be giving away money and half the people still wouldn't take your phone call.

Electronic Marketing

A number of developers say that they have received a lot of business by responding to requests for help on CompuServe or the Internet. These messages are usually via newsgroups or bulletin boards.

So How Do You Get Business?

Personal referrals work well. This usually requires a bit of savvy that I don't think most developers have. Professional associations, user groups, being visible in the local marketplace - these are all ideas that have worked for some people. Also, get quoted in the paper. This is more P.R. than marketing. This is something that most software developers are not good at, but some people swear that this as the way to go.

Given all of these things, you may be inclined to put this book down, toss your hands up in despair, and say, "I'm going to go start making bricks." What do you do? The answer is: Do It All. That's a little bit facetious, but you have to be prepared to explore more than one avenue. You are not going to be able to drop 20,000 pieces of direct mail and expect a windfall. You have to do direct mail, advertising, get your name in the paper and so on. You need to be seen in a number of places.

The trick to marketing that most people overlook is consistency. People have to see your name over and over. Who are some of the biggest marketers? Who has the biggest marketing budgets in the world? Companies we all know: Toyota, GM, Coca-Cola, Kimberly Clark, Proctor and Gamble. You would think that Coke would never have to advertise again. It is possibly the best known trademark in the world. Why does IBM have to advertise? Everybody knows who IBM is, but they continue to advertise for consistency.

Web Sites

You're invited to visit www.hentzenwerke.com. (Shameless self-promotion, but go ahead - you might enjoy yourself anyway.)

Two rules about web sites. Rule number one - know why you're doing it. How many people are going to buy custom development work from you because they were surfing around and suddenly saw your page? I'd say approximately zero. However, it is nice that you can direct a potential customer to your web site instead of sending them literature. That is, if they are so inclined. It is easier to update your web page than your literature, so you should use your web page as an extension of your literature.

It's very easy to say, "Hey, I'll just spend a whole bunch of time on this web site because it's fun to do, it's cool, it's intellectually challenging to see what we can do," and so on. Suddenly you've chewed up hundreds of hours and what's the benefit? Where are you going to get a payback for that time? Keep sharp on this one, because it's an easy trap to fall into. Web sites are extremely costly to set up if you want to do it right.

Rule number two - just have fun! Have your web site be rewarding and stimulating. That's what we're doing. We want a lot of people to visit our site. At some point, they may be interested in buying something - perhaps a book or two!

If you want people to come back, you have to keep changing the content. How often? My personal opinion - at least a couple of times a week. But that's a high maintenance task and frankly, is it worth it to you? If you're looking for your site to be an extension of your literature, it's should be updated at least monthly. If you want to have people come back and visit the site over and over again, then you need to have something compelling on the site. And compelling means new.

Company Name

If you're starting to choose a company name, I have one pet peeve. Company names that have System and Compu and Micro and Consulting and other "high-tech" buzz words in there - you can't tell them apart, folks. The other type of name that drives me crazy is ABC Consulting. You know, somebody's initials. Or even worse - AAAAA Consulting. I apologize to those of you have already done this, but I simply can't tell them apart - and so I don't think new customers can either. Of course, if you're already in business, then your customers know you and your company name doesn't really matter.

The coolest name is, of course, mine. Hentzenwerke Corporation. I wanted a name that was different and that people would be able to recognize immediately. I searched for a couple of years looking for one. The image I wanted was a parody of all those great big huge conglomerates where they have giant smoke stacks belching tons of toxins into the air. You know, like Pittsburgh around 1900. All these big companies in Germany and the United States, have names like Cameron Iron Works, the Rouge River Works, etc. I was a one guy computer consultant and thought the use of the same idea would be unique. That's how "Works" came about. In Germany, it's called Werke, so I tied that together with my last name and everyone can recognize this name instantly.

I came up with my company name while I was still working somewhere else - at a large manufacturing company. I had "H WERKE" put on my license plate while I was still employed there. Somebody at the factory asked me what it stood for. I couldn't really tell him that it was going to be my company name, so I created this great big long story, with the advance sell on it that "You're gonna love this, this is a really funny story!" I delivered the punch line and said, "Isn't that great, isn't that too funny?" when in reality, the story made no sense and wasn't funny at all. He smiled half-heartedly and nodded, "Uh, yeah, sure," and quickly walked away. I didn't have to worry about anyone else at the plant asking out what my license plate meant.

Another clever name is Michel Fournier's company name. I was at FoxPro DevCon with Ted Roche in 1992 and Michel was looking for a company name. We we're bouncing back and forth various names, and suddenly Ted came up with the idea of Fournier Transformation, a take-off on the mathematical term. Very clever and very cool.

A couple of other cool names are Toni Taylor's company in Arizona - Taylor Made Software. Then there's a company in California that makes Macintosh software, Abra Macdabra. Is that excellent, or what?

Once in a while there is a chance to have a really cool name. If you have one, it makes a whole world of difference.

Rules About Company Names

A name shouldn't be too long. Nothing more than 32 characters. If it's more, people are not going to be able to print it on a mailing label. Some consulting firms are really famous for doing this. They have five peoples names and then Employment Consulting Inc. They will never be able to have labels printed out correctly because nobody can get the whole name on the label.

Avoid acronyms. MLB Consulting Inc. Who knows what MLB stands for, and even worse, who cares? There are so many of them that nobody is going to take the time to remember what yours stands for. It's also really easy to get confused between yours and another one that is very similar.

Conclusion

So we've done some marketing. If we're smart, or lucky, we've gotten some inquiries back in. Typically, these take the format of phone calls. The red lights start flashing, the bells ring and the sirens begin to wail. We have a hot one!

1.3 Phone Call

- The Initial Phone Call
- What Are They Looking For?
- Their Own Custom Software

The Initial Phone Call

Brrrrring - the phone rings. The guy on the other end says, "Hey, I want to buy some of your stuff." (Surprisingly, most of the time those are the exact words they use!) At this point the trick is to be very, very jealous of your time. People will unknowingly try to take your time from you. Guard your time because it is the most precious resource you have.

The first thing to be aware of is that people don't know what you are talking about. They don't understand the business you are in. They don't know how to describe what they are looking for. They might not *know* what they are looking for. You need to be able to determine this quickly and efficiently without making anybody mad.

Make sure the person calling has been identified by name, company, position, phone number, address, and where they heard of you. We keep small, half sheet forms underneath each of our telephones for filling out this information. The single most overlooked piece of information during the initial phone call is where they heard of you. If you just shelled out $9,000 for a series of ads, wouldn't it be nice to find out if they are working?

Some people will resist giving you their name and number. They will tell you their name but refuse to tell you the name of the company. It is my inclination to kiss them off. This is a partnership relationship. If they are not at least willing to identify who they are, this bodes poorly for a trusting relationship.

Once in a while, people will resist because they think that you will call them back and hound them until the world ends. Simply tell them, "We don't work with people we don't know, so I am sorry I am not going to be able to help you out." Let them come back and offer their name.

After finding out their name and company, you should quickly find out what their company does. It never hurts to read the business paper in your town so that when they call, you can say, "Oh, you're from BLX! You just bought this other company, right?" They will feel comfortable and happy because you have paid attention and you know about them. People like to feel important and if you can make them feel like they are, you will establish a good rapport right away.

Be certain to get their last name. I have yet to figure out a good way to drill people around here to get people's last name. It's just hard to do. Now, of course, in a big company callers will most likely give you their last name. In a small company of 19 people, "There's only one Helen here." You should still get it.

If you can, and sometimes it's a delicate question to ask, try to establish the position within the company of the person who's calling and where they are in relation to the problem. Sometimes the person calling is the one with the pain;

at other times, they're simply doing legwork for someone else. Furthermore, if you end up arranging a sales call, you'll need to meet with the decision maker or at least someone with sufficient authority to carry decision making information to that person. You don't want to make an in-person visit only to find out you're dropping off literature. Thus, you need to find out who that person is.

Also, get their address. Some people refer to their company by a set of initials that can't be found in the phone book, and other people who contact you may just be starting out and aren't listed in the phone book. Much better to ask.

What Are They Looking For?

They are going to have to tell you what they are looking for, and they need to be able to get that out in two to four sentences. I ask them right away, "Are you looking for somebody to write a program or modify an existing program for you?" If they say, "No. We want someone to show us how to use Microsoft Word." I can end the conversation right here. Refer them so someone else if you can, but get them off the phone.

Sometimes people don't know what they want. They don't have an idea of what that concrete solution to their problem is, and will go off on tangents over and over again. I have found that if they can't state their problem distinctly right away, you need to drill them until they can state it right away. The issue here is their pain. What is bothering them and what do they want fixed? This is the most important question you've got. Ask this and listen carefully to the answer. You could propose the wrong solution or end up doing the wrong thing. A lot of times they won't answer you directly because they do not know the direct cause of the pain.

Again, you are trying to weed out people who are not appropriate for your business. All of this should only take the first three or four minutes. Once in a while, they are really going to yak your ear off. Stay in control of the conversation. Get them back on track. Here are some questions you can ask them to get them on track:

- What packages do you have now?
- Do you like them?
- What are you doing now?
- What kind of operation are you trying to change?
- How do you foresee changing it?

Once you have identified their pain and determined if you can help them out, you need to find out what their financial expectations are. Why am I going on and on about this? Because it is really easy for them to tell you their pain and how they want it remedied, then find out that they are expecting you to sell them an existing package for $59 and probably spend a couple of hours doing it, too.

How do you turn them away if you can't provide the services they are looking for? Simply tell them that is not what you do. If you know someone else who provides the services they are looking for, you can maintain a bit of goodwill by sending them a list or a referral.

Their Own Custom Software

Once you have determined that custom software is the answer, there are a few more questions to ask. Is this a new system? Modifications to an existing system? A rewrite of an existing system or just add-on to an existing system? Those are the four choices, and what you are going to do depends greatly on what answer they give you.

If it's a new system, then the issues you will have to deal with are:

- What do they want it to do?
- Do they have a preference for the language or tool?
- What OS and hardware environment do they have?
- How many users do they have? Total people in the company?
- What are their plans for future growth?
- How critical is this system? Will their company rely on it or is it somewhat off to the side of their main line of business?

If it is modifications to an existing system, a rewrite, or an add-on, you'll also want to ask:

- Who did the original system?
- Why aren't you using the original developer?

What answers are good for this last question? The developer left town, went out of business, died, was only part time, whatever. You'll want to find out why they are not using the original developer - it may help you avoid the pitfalls the last developer may have had and will tell you something about the customer as well.

1.4 Literature

- **Literature**
- **Business Cards**
    - **What Do You Put on Your Business Cards?**
    - **Titles and Logos**
    - **Flip Up Cards**
    - **Material and Color**
    - **Orientation**
- **Brochures**
- **Non-Traditional Types of Literature**

Literature

Everybody has literature. Everybody has a business card or something to hand out. A lot of it looks pretty amateurish. It's better to go subtle and subdued. Meaning, you don't have to spend a fortune on your literature. Why? No one will read it anyway. It's boring to most people. There is not a lot you can do with computer consultant literature that's going to make it jazzy. You can't put a lot of pictures in it that people will be real interested in. However, you do need some supporting materials. Let's take a look at what these are.

Business Cards

You can buy a little piece of software to print your business cards from your laser printer. They usually look pretty bad. This is not the first impression you want to give somebody. It costs $40 to print 1,000 one color thermographed business cards. Have a graphic designer set your fonts for you if you're not comfortable doing it yourself. If you pay a graphic artist $150-200 (that's high) to do it once, you will never have to do it again.

Make your cards look professional. Some people like to write a short story on their business cards. Other people like to use five colors. Others put a dozen logos on their card.

How do you determine when you've crossed the line? Try this trick. Collect business cards from other people - continuously. (I have never in 20 years thrown out a business card.) Then scan through other people's business cards and you will be amazed at the junk people hand out. Pretty soon you'll be horrified, "Oh my God, I was going to do one of those - it looks so trashy!" You want a card that suggests professionalism and a solid company. I look at the big companies like IBM, Arthur Andersen, EDS, Westinghouse, and Exxon. These are the professionals. You can learn a lot by examining other people's business cards for a half an hour.

A rule of thumb for a business card; you should be able to put a quarter on the business card and not obscure any important information. You may catch the corner of a logo or something but the idea is "White space is your friend."

What Do You Put on Your Business Cards?

You don't write a novel. Instead, just the facts. Include your logo if you have one. It's a graphic and catches people's eye. The second thing to put on is your company name and address, home address, PO Box, whatever works for you.

Identify the voice and fax numbers, including area code. (Yes, I've seen more than one business card without an area code.) If you have a direct dial phone number, put it by your name. You can also squish it in the corner and say

"Direct Dial." Make sure if you do, that you have the proper facilities for picking up that phone. If they direct dial and nobody's there, well, that would be bad, wouldn't it?

You are a computer geek, so why in the world would you print a business card and not include your E-mail addresses? Wait, you don't have an E-mail address because CompuServe at $9.95/month is too expensive? Ummm, well, hmmmmm. If you don't have an E-mail address, get one.

Whil Hentzen
CIS 70651,2270
whil@hentzenwerke.com

Hentzenwerke
CORPORATION

Hentzenwerke Corporation
735 North Water Street
Milwaukee, WI 53202-4104

Voice 414.224.7654
Fax 414.224.7650

Titles and Logos

I guess titles go on your business card. I personally don't like titles so my employees don't have them. But if you have one, it would go under the name. You have a logo, name and address of company with phone numbers and direct dial numbers, E-mail addresses. Then you have the name and title of the person on the card. It's getting crowded, isn't it? That is why we opted for our choice not to have titles and put the E-mail address with the name so we still have some white space.

If you have authorization or certification logos from other companies, include them. But you'll want to be careful. Suddenly a card with "Authentic Certified Whatevers" from Microsoft, Borland, Sun, IBM, Novell, and Autodesk becomes an advertisement and not a business card.

Consider putting them on the back. They're worth using if they set you apart from your competitor or establish an expertise in any given area.

Flip Up Cards

These are those cards that expand to twice their size when you open them up. I have always been intrigued by them but never got around to doing one. I just didn't feel the need to put a brochure in someone's hand every time I met somebody. The ones I've liked have come from retail stores. On the front they talk about what they do. On the inside they give pictures of things, hours, catchy descriptions, a map of their locations.

Material and Color

Can you believe that I could write this much just on a business card? And that I'm so opinionated about the most trivial of points? Well, there's still more. Let's talk about the physical card itself. You can make your card any color you want as long as it is bright white. It should be a linen finish and classy looking. The linen finish is the one where you can see the lines of threads up and down. They look good, solid and established.

The difference in cost between a boring, badly done card and a high quality card is just a few dollars. Spend it here. It's the difference between wearing a dark gray suit, white shirt, and tie or wearing a wide lapel suit that went out of date two years ago, a dark shirt, and a tie that doesn't quite match. It might have been trendy a few years ago but not anymore.

Probably the coolest card I have ever seen was the card of a guy who worked with grain elevator operators. He was dealing with people who were basically filthy all of the time because they loaded trucks, barges, and other transportation vehicles. He needed to get his card in people's hands, but many times, the recipient would just stuff a card in a pocket and forget about it.

That night, Bessie would wash the clothes and the card ordinarily would have become a little ball of fuzz. But the cards were made out of a velum material, like the material they made drawings out of in the old drawing board days. These cards could not be destroyed! The one downside was you couldn't write on this material. So if you were talking to him and wanted to jot a note down, his card was not the place to do it. I'm sure a lot more of his cards made it through the wash and spin cycle than of his competitors!

Orientation

Do you print the card vertically or horizontally? You can do some very nice, good looking things with horizontal cards, but people put cards in a box or Rolodex and page through them. If yours is horizontal it won't match up, and won't play well with the other boys and girls. You may think it will stand out, but I've found that people will say, "Oh, this guy! I hate his card!"

Brochures

Here's the bad news: no one will read them. Pages and pages of tiny text telling the world how great you are. They won't read it. They will look at it, and as long as the front page doesn't have any typos, they will put it aside. Is it really worth it to do a ton of work on your brochure, and spend thousands of dollars for a big fancy four color job? Maybe not.

Our guiding principle has been to make sure literature doesn't put the customer to sleep. We don't want it to be boring. A lot of firms make their brochures look like lawyer brochures. A bunch of guys in suits sitting at a large table with stacks of books behind them. This doesn't tell me why these people are better than everybody else. What is the problem they can solve?

You can't put any of those "We're dedicated to quality" phrases in. "Our people are our best asset. We invest in our people" and all of those platitudes. Everybody puts them in there and nobody believes them. Don't try to sell your products and services directly in your brochure.

So, how do you distinguish yourself? What is it that you do that no one else does? This has to be a measurable item. I just spent a chapter on this topic - use your brochure and other materials to document your distinctive competence. If you have expertise in a specific industry, it's a good idea to have a page dedicated to describing the applications you have done. People will read that because they can relate to it. If you have specific skills, again, that will sell as well. Instead of using a traditional brochure, consider using a "fact sheet" or "case study" of past jobs and projects.

Finally, don't forget your call to action. In other words, tell them what you want them to do, such as call or write.

Non-Traditional Types of Literature

These days you can buy a CD-ROM writer for $1,000. This means that instead of sending somebody some literature, you could send them a CD. Isn't that a cool idea? One of these days, as soon as the rush to produce this book is over, I will cut a CD that gives them a tour of our company. It will show the people in our company, the way we go about things, and the way we write applications. With 650 Mb on a CD-ROM, we can actually include demo applications in multiple languages. So what if the run time for a video tour takes up 12 Mb, no biggie.

We're eventually going to do this ourselves, but right now, we're using our web site as a trial balloon. We're testing out a look and feel for the tour. We're collecting statistics on which pages people are visiting and how often.

1.5 Sales Call

- Purpose
- Where To Meet
- What To Wear
- What To Bring
- The Sales Call Game Plan

  Reiterate the Purpose of the Meeting
  What Is the Pain?
  What Do They Have?
  What Do They Want and What Do They Expect?
  What Tools Do They Have to Go From Current to Desired?
  What Is Their Budget?
  What Is Their Timeframe?
  The Sales Pitch
  Who Else Are They Talking To?
  Who Is The Champion?

- Watch Your Gut!
- The Next Step
- What's The Decision Making Process?

Call me old-fashioned, but I still think software development requires face to face contact. This endeavor is hard work, full of stress, and can be touchy work. Having a face to attach to a voice - the personal contact - makes getting through those tough times a lot easier.

Purpose

The purpose of the sales call is not, as the sales guys would argue, to get the job; rather, it's to determine if you want the job, and if so, then to get it. This is called "qualifying the prospect." Custom software is in high demand and the available suppliers are scarce, so it's not difficult to find people who want the product you supply. Finding people who have reasonable expectations, who are going to be good to work with, and, yes, who have money, is not quite as easy.

You've already weeded out those folk who are obviously not a match during the phone call, but due to the ethereal nature of our business, it's not possible to winnow out everyone. This is the first thing you want to do in this visit. As my friend Ed Leafe has said, "It is better to be sad that you lost the work than be sad that you got it." The gain you realize from a good job is not equivalent to the loss you can get from a bad job - much like short selling in the stock market has significantly more risk than simply buying stock. The most you can gain from a good job is a healthy profit - but if a job goes south, you can lose your company. It pays to be very careful when doing the initial courtship with a new customer.

Once you've got the handle on them, it's your job to show them that you can do the work they want done. Set expectations so that they are not disappointed in the long run. Remember, most likely, this customer has not bought custom software before, so they may well have a set of expectations that are unreasonable or impossible. And no matter how skilled you are, or how good a Joe they are otherwise, if they leave this meeting harboring a false set of hopes, the relationship can turn ugly in short order.

You are trying to sell them on doing a specification, not on the whole programming job. If they like the spec, then the development will come naturally. Don't look so far out in the future that you lose sight of the short term goal.

Where To Meet

As much as it is a hassle for you, the sales call should always be made at the customer's location. There are three reasons for this. First, it's a natural courtesy, and most people expect it. Second, many times, the customer will want you to look at files, programs, printouts, and so on. There is usually no practical way to do this if they have to pack up everything and bring it to your office.

Furthermore, you may need to (or they may want you to) meet with other people who don't have be available for the entire meeting. It's terribly inconvenient for them to bring additional people along in this situation.

And the third reason is that you need to scout out the territory. There's a lot you can learn from the digs a customer resides in. First of all, by visiting them, you'll find out a lot more clearly how big the company is, or how small they are. You will also find out the general atmosphere of the company - are they just basically nice people? I learned a long time ago that there is a percentage of people in the world that simply aren't very nice, and I decided not to do business with them. Let them make the lives of our competition miserable, not ours.

Next, does it feel like the company is on solid ground? Do they have a frugal image, or have they spent enough money to make their people reasonably comfortable? If people are stacked two to a cubicle (no, that's not just in Dilbert's imagination) and the building is in disrepair, could the company be in financial trouble, or are they just grossly stingy with funds? If so, could this be a sign that they're going to try to nickel and dime you? If a company is going to spend $10,000 or $25,000 or $50,000 on an application, a cheap mentality isn't going to be conducive to a good working relationship.

You'll also get a feel for how the company operates. The reason you're there, generally, is because they've got a problem and they want you to solve it. Is it possible that the problem is not one that the implementation of a software application will fix, but rather that it's an operational problem, and that automating it will simply make the mess in a shorter period of time?

Is your contact prepared? Are they organized with the materials they said they'd have on the phone? Do they get constant interruptions? Do they have to look up information, call other people for additional information, or hunt through stacks of paper, mumbling, "I know it's in here somewhere"?

The computer environment is another aspect of the company that you'll be able to see with your own eyes. They may have described that they've got "pretty much new computers" with "a brand new network" but then you see network cabling strung across hallways, machines with filthy keyboards and opaque screens, no-name system units with the covers off, and a laser printer balancing on a stack of books - well, you get the picture.

What To Wear

One of the longer threads in recent memory on CompuServe's FoxUser forum was entitled "Dress for Client?" in which the poster asked whether it was necessary to get dressed up to go to a client for a ten minute visit which consisted of picking up a new set of data files and installing a new report. Of course, as many threads on CompuServe do, this one eventually degenerated into unrelated topics, such as the discussion of what men keep in their pockets that women keep in their purses (one friend said he kept a comb in his left rear pocket, to which I replied "Braggart!"). But the gist of the thread dealt with whether or not a suit and tie were required, recommended, or superfluous.

I have two very strong opinions on this subject. The first is that I very much want to convert the entire world to a casual dress code. More important than this goal is making the customer feel comfortable. If the customer could possibly feel uncomfortable if you were to go on a visit in casual dress, then get dressed up. They, themselves, might not care, but what if their boss happens by? Better to err on the side of caution.

The second opinion entails "what constitutes 'dressing up' for the customer." To my way of thinking, you can wear anything you want, as long as, for men, it's a dark suit, white shirt and conservative patterned tie, and for women, it's essentially the same, a suit with hose and pumps, and white or light colored blouse. Perhaps you could break these rules if you were in Hollywood (flashy suits and fast cars) or Miami (Hawaiian shirts and fast cars), but not in the rest of America. The point in dressing up to see a customer is that what you wear should not detract from the message that you are delivering - in fact, what you wear should be invisible to the customer - so they can concentrate completely on the content of your message.

Again, this is my opinion. Your mileage may vary.

I went to visit a long-time customer. They indicated that I didn't have to get all dressed up in a suit just to see him, even though the meeting was going to be at HQ. I explained that I had two modes of dress - suit and tie, and jeans and sweaters. He hesitated a bit, feeling that jeans and a sweater wasn't going to cut it at HQ. He offered, "Well, be sure to bill me for putting a suit on, OK?" In one of those "I wish I had done this" moments, it occurred to me later that I should have sent him an invoice for $1,000,100, with the accompanying detail lines:

Put a suit on $1,000,000
One hour meeting at HQ building $100

and then include the explanation that "Well, you said I looked like a million bucks."

What To Bring

You may want to bring a computer to demonstrate some of your applications, but don't get sidetracked showing all the cool things you can do. Customers want to talk about themselves, not you. And they probably won't understand much of what you show them anyway. They're probably going to still be staring at that little red thingy in the middle of the keyboard.

Don't forget to bring business cards, additional literature, and note-taking material. Consider a standard "Things to take to meetings" file folder and checklist and keep these materials in there.

The Sales Call Game Plan

It's probably a good idea to prepare an agenda for the meeting. Faxing it off to the folk you're meeting with is an even better idea. The rest of this chapter deals mainly with the agenda.

They'll want to show you what they've got. You'll have some questions. They'll want to talk for hours. The conversation could range all over the back 40. There isn't a single cookbook approach to making this an efficient, purposeful meeting, but the key issues to resolve include:

- Reiterate the purpose of the meeting
- What is the pain?
- What systems do they have?
- What do they *want* and what do they *expect*?
- What tools do they have to go from current to desired?
- What is their budget?
- What is their timeframe?
- The sales pitch
- Who else are they talking to?
- Who is the champion for this project?

Reiterate the Purpose of the Meeting

This is a sales call - so that they can feel you out, you can see what they've got cooking, and to see if there's possibly something that can be worked out between the two of you. This is NOT a problem solving session - that's what you get paid for!

Depending on the nature of the company and who you're meeting with, you may want to tour the office, meet some people and so on.

Section 1.5 Sales Call

What Is the Pain?

This was briefly discussed in the previous chapter about the phone call. Again, the most important thing you can do is to define or pinpoint exactly what is causing them pain. If they can't describe it succinctly, do not let go until they can. This is your ultimate benchmark for determining whether the final product is a success.

Along these same lines, ask yourself, what is the customer's biggest fear, and what can you do to alleviate that fear? They really aren't all that interested in computer code or cool development tools - they've got a business to run and they want their problems solved. Computer programmers are weird and scary. What can you do to put their mind at ease?

What Do They Have?

You'll need to check out both current software, current hardware, and the ancillary things like manuals, source code, documentation, and so on. Yes, you've been over this on the phone, but it's easy for them to make assumptions about things during the "heat of the phone call" or to make mistakes. They may tell you that they have Windows95, but, in actuality, they've got the box, but it's only installed on one laptop. That kind of puts a damper on the possibility of writing with a 32 bit development tool, doesn't it?

As the military's credo went, "Trust, but verify."

What Do They Want and What Do They Expect?

Let's talk about what they want. In short, are they expecting a miracle? When I leave the sales call, we might be in the position to start work on a functional specification. The customer is going to want to know how much this costs, and while you can't give them a fixed price, or, probably, even a reasonably close estimate at this stage, they're still going to want one.

What we do is sketch out, at the sales call, a list of components that the application could contain. We actually go through and list the screens, reports and processes that they want, by name. From this list, we can roughly size the application, and give them a ballpark figure.

Naturally, this will change during the specification process, but what we've done is put a stake in the ground, so that when the scope of the project changes and they see more dollars than originally estimated, you can explicitly explain why. "We started out assuming a system with 10 primary screens, 15 supporting screens, 6 lookup screens, two dozen reports, and two posting processes. It's now grown to 23 primary screens, 31 supporting screens, 8 lookups, three dozen reports, and still two posting processes. This is why we've exceeded over our initial estimate."

You need to keep them informed along the way about how the bill is growing. The point here is that by documenting, right from project inception, how big the system is, you have a baseline that you can refer to later on.

What Tools Do They Have To Go From Current To Desired?

How prepared are they to begin the design of a specification? Do they have a list of desired functionality? Sample screens? Report layouts? Descriptions of processes, operations, flow of work through the system? Or are you starting out with a blank sheet of paper?

What tools do they have? Are they going to have upgrade existing hardware, buy new hardware, upgrade versions of software, install a new operating system, put in a better network?

What kind of shape is their data in? Can it be used as is? Converted from an existing system? Can the existing systems be used in any way? How might they go about a transition from the old data to the new data?

How rigorous are their current MIS procedures? Do they have the ability to audit the information they produce? What are their alternate plans for disaster recovery? Do they perform regular backups? Have they ever done a backup? Do they know what a backup is? Can they spell "backup?"

What Is Their Budget?

They need to give you some sort of idea about what they might want to spend or be able to spend.

If they say they don't have any idea, either they don't know what they are doing, or they are lying. A lot of people feel that that by giving away a budget number, somehow, magically, the price of the project will be just a little bit over the budget number. So I don't ask them what the budget is, but if they've got a budget - and what ballpark they're working in. If they say they don't know what their budget is, then I suggest that they define the problem very carefully and figure out what the solution to that problem is worth to them.

Maybe you could offer to help them develop the budget, for a price, since they have no idea or aren't "current" on hardware pricing and software development. If they balk at your hourly rate for doing this, then it's definitely time to put on the track shoes. If they don't balk, this will go a long way toward cementing their relationship with you, much like the immediate "bonding" that occurs between mother and child at birth.

As far as the ballpark, if they're not willing to provide even a rough idea, then I tell them that it's going to be more expensive in the long run. If I have to create something without knowing what parameters I'm working with, there's going to be some missteps as we discover where we want to head.

You wouldn't build a house without telling the builder what dollars he's got to work with, would you? You can go to that builder with two approaches - either give them a dollar figure and ask for as much house as possible for that number, or tell them your requirements and don't be surprised when the result is much more expensive than you thought it would be. In either case, you'll spend additional time moving from that first pass to something more in line with your expectations.

If they still refuse, then run away. They probably don't trust you and it does not bode well for a good relationship. Or they may have good intentions but are so ignorant of the process and unwilling to take your advice that they'll be nothing but headaches.

What Is Their Timeframe?

The most important thing to realize about timeframes is that they are almost never as ironclad as the customer makes them out to be. At the same time, the customer almost never realizes this. I recall reading about a group of consultants brought in to finish a job and they were given a drop dead target date by which the system had to be up and running.

Upon starting the project, the consultants found that this deadline was the third such "non-negotiable, drop-dead deadline" for this particular project in the past year.

Most deadlines are arbitrarily imposed because someone somewhere wants the project done before they go on vacation.

Furthermore, most deadlines are usually unreasonable because they were imposed by someone who does not understand the scope or the complexity of the system. There are physical limits to the amount of work that can be done. Some people feel that by adding developers to a project, it can be done sooner. Generally, adding more developers to a late project only serves to make it later. See Frederick Brooks' *The Mythical Man-Month* for a complete discussion of this issue.

Nonetheless, you will have to deal with unreasonable expectations that are apparently clad in stone. The key is to manage and mold those expectations as early on in the project as possible - and the sales call is the best place to start.

A lot of times, instead of slapping your knee and laughing like that cartoon "You want it WHEN?," you can help form a more reasonable expectation for delivery by playing detective about the initial request for a finish date. What is so important about this date - why does the project need to be done? Perhaps it's only part of the project that needs to be finished, or it has to be demonstrated, or an interface needs to be defined and complete, so that another project can be started.

Many times people will make assumptions, thinking that they know all there is to know about a system, when in reality, they're providing yet another example of how to spell "assume."

The Sales Pitch

At some point, it might be a good idea to talk about who you are and what you do. Naturally, you're going to want to spend the whole meeting along these lines, but, while it's fascinating material for you, the customer really doesn't care all that much. Sorry, but that's life in the big city.

You need to boil down your sales pitch into a couple of paragraphs, highlighting the key points that are going to be of interest to the folks on the other side of the desk. You may be impressed with yourself that you wrote a book on the newest snazzy development tool, but unless that has specific bearing on the customer's situation, it's not worth more than about a sentence, primarily to illustrate that you are considered, to some extent, as an expert in the field.

The big part of the sales pitch is listening to them, asking the right questions, and taking care to make them feel comfortable that you can solve their problem. If you can show a little evidence along these lines, you'll be well off.

Who Else Are They Talking To?

Believe it or not, you're probably not the only developer on the planet that the customer is talking to. Better to find out who your competition is than to wander around blindly in a fog. You may wish to tilt your message depending on whether your competition is the owner's nephew or Arthur Andersen.

Who Is The Champion?

A champion is the person at the firm who pushes the project along, ensuring that the rest of the company will buy in. This person should have fiscal responsibilities so they can authorize the funds. If that's not plausible, they should at least be knowledgeable about how much the company wants to spend on the project. If you don't have a champion, you don't have a prayer.

Watch Your Gut!

By now you've acquired a fair amount of information. This is not like selling a car or a printing job - where multiple sales calls are required to get the business. Your time is your most precious resource, and they need to decide whether they want to go to the next step. You can't afford to visit again and again. At some point, they have to bring you on board to start doing work. This doesn't mean that once they go with you that they are committed for the rest of their life, simply that they need to start paying you for your time.

At the same time, you need to decide if you feel you are appropriate for the job and whether you feel comfortable with the company. You've listened to them for perhaps a couple of hours, asked questions and gotten a feel for what they're looking for and what they're expecting.

Watch your gut! If the little voice inside you is saying "Oh, I don't know, there's something that feels bad about this" then pay attention! The worst thing to do is realize two months (and three overdue invoices) too late that you really shouldn't have taken this job.

The Next Step

The optimal closing for the meeting will be a request by them for an engagement letter in order that you can start performing work for them. This engagement letter will include a ballpark estimate for the specification work, and, since they're now into the phase of spending money, they may have to get approval. It is a good idea to find out what hoops have to be jumped through at this point in order to get the engagement letter signed.

It's aggravating to find out how little many people in larger companies know about the approval process for spending money. We've had a surprisingly large number of people tell us with a straight face "The money's already been approved" or "I can sign off on this" or "My boss said he'd sign it immediately" only to find out the proposal has to go before some committee and it's going to be three months before you hear anything. Be skeptical.

What's The Decision Making Process?

Depending on the size of the application, there will likely be several layers of approval to go through before the application gets approved. There may be several layers of approval needed to even go ahead with the specification work. Your closing for the meeting should determine whether they want an engagement letter or if they have to get approval first.

1.6 Auditing an Existing Application

Section 1.6 Auditing an Existing Application

It happens to everyone...

Purpose

Often times when you go in for a sales call, they'll want you to take a look at an existing application. This is the time that you go in and investigate a few things and solemnly pronounce, "Yes, it will have to be rewritten." This is said in the same tone of voice used by McCoy when talking to Kirk: "He's dead, Jim."

They are going to look at you as the expert. You're going to go in and take a look at somebody else's work. This is a tough position to be in. I mean, are you just going to go in there and take a look at it for five minutes and say, "Well, this certainly stinks, doesn't it?" Even if they've been complaining about this ever since you walked in the door, it's still theirs. To quote the line from Ferris Bueller's Day Off when he's talking about Cameron's car, "It may be a piece of crap, but it's better than what I got, because I don't have anything!" Besides, you don't yet know who wrote it. It may be the owner's son. Tread carefully.

Another reason to be wary about criticizing the existing work is that they've probably spent money to get the app written. By slamming what they've spent money for, you're indirectly criticizing the people who okayed the purchase, the people who monitored the progress that was made, and possibly countless others. They may tell you, "We didn't know what we were doing." A man can make fun of his kids or his wife, but you can't do the same thing. It's just one of those invisible lines that you can't ever cross.

The Checklist

How do you appear objective auditing an application when you're in the business of making money writing it's replacement? In these situations I go in with a game plan that was prepared before I saw the software. This means that I can't tilt our judgment one way or another based on what I see down the road. Let's say you see a customer's app and the Browse button is on the bottom of the screen. If you say, "Oh, that's bad, that's really bad" with no apparent justification, your judgement will appear to be arbitrary.

However, if you go in there with a preprinted checklist and on the checklist it says "Deduct 7 points if the Browse button is on the bottom of the screen," then you look considerably more impartial.

What are some other benefits of doing this? You're probably going to do a better job. You won't forget things. It's very easy in the heat of the battle to get sidetracked and then skip a few items on your mental checklist. forget to look for things. If you have a checklist, you know were you left off when you got interrupted. Furthermore, your checklist becomes more robust each time you do an audit. You add more things and it becomes a better tool.

Another benefit is being able to use this to position yourself against your competition. If they're looking at having this application rewritten, they're could well be talking to some other people as well. They may ask a couple of other people their opinions of this application, too. That's only natural. Now, you go in with a checklist of 26 things to check. The other firm goes in with an attitude. The checklist makes you look prepared and professional. It says that you've done this before. Furthermore, since you have the checklist and they don't, your checklist becomes the standard against which their work will be measured. People like things written down. People like things on paper.

When the other developer goes and just peeks around and does things mentally, the customer will ask "Where's your checklist? Why didn't you check this? What about that?" The other developer is going to have much more difficult time winging it successfully. Your checklist says to the customer, "These are the rules by which we are going to play." The other developer now has to play by your rules as opposed to theirs, and it's always easier to win a contest if you get to write the rules.

What Goes on the Checklist?

Even I'm not above trying to put a few easy points on the board early in the game.

Documentation. Ask to see their documentation of the existing system. This is a killer. When have you ever seen an application that had documentation? That had specifications? That had change orders? That had comments in the code? (I will discuss these things in Section 3.) Right away you set the stage by saying, "How am I to know what this system is supposed to do if no one has written it down?" Yes, there's word of mouth and the stories that have been passed on from one user to the next, but those are called legends. And while most legends were originally based on fact, a good deal of it is closer to mythology.

Asking for documentation also implies that you're going to provide specifications and documentation if you do the application. At this point, they are probably going to say, "You know, we really should have done that. That makes sense." This makes you look good.

Someone once asked me, "What if the customer claims that they have all of the documentation already? They don't want to pay to answer all of these questions again." I have only one thing to say to that. In 14 years of business, I have yet to see a customer who has complete documentation.

Clean Data Directories. Along those same lines, I look in the data directories where the files are, and try to determine how much junk is laying around. An analogy I've used before is when you go into a restaurant or a hotel, the experienced visitor will immediately check out the restrooms. If the restrooms are spotless, you can pretty much figure that the rest of the place is going to be in pretty good shape too. On the other hand, if the restrooms are a pit, doesn't it make you wonder what the kitchen is going to be like? While having filthy restrooms doesn't necessarily mean that the kitchen is a pit, having clean restrooms will make you feel more confident that the rest of the place is been cleaned up as well.

I look for TEMP.DBF and TEMP1 and TEMP2 and TEMP2X and a bunch of *.OLD and *.BAK and other junk. I recently worked on an application with 426 files. The best part? They weren't in a sub-directory. They were in the ROOT! They were within 100 files of crashing the system because their operating system wasn't going to be able to support more than 512 files in the root directory.

It appears that the previous developer didn't clean up their files or didn't have a mechanism to keep things organized. I wonder what that code is going to look like? Do you think they were perfectly fastidious about the code if they haven't even taken the time to delete a bunch of old junky files? (This is a rhetorical question, by the way.) Again, this is another easy win because this happens an awful lot.

The other thing this tells me is that the coding practices inside are probably not real solid. Why? Some of these files have likely been left around from the running of the application and were never cleaned up afterwards. You know the first rule about going into a national park? Take nothing but pictures and leave nothing but footprints. Your application ought to clean up after itself. It shouldn't leave garbage around.

Application Structure. The next thing to look at is the structure of the application. Did they throw the program and every single data file in the entire application into one directory? In the days of DBASE II or III you could probably get away with it. These days, sorry. When I talk about testing later, one of the prime ways of being able to test properly is being able to restore an initial robust data set from somewhere. If they have a bunch of junk files out there, it's going to be harder to restore the test data, clean out the old data, put in fresh data, etc. People are going to be less willing to back up things if they feel it's too big and never changes.

You also have performance problems if you have huge numbers of files. Not only is it difficult to test with fresh data, but also performance testing is difficult.

Version control is difficult if you have data files and program files in the same directory. Do you see a lot of programs like PRG1, PRG2, PRG3? Are these the same programs with different revs or are they different programs? Are they just throwing new programs on top of old ones and hoping they're OK?

What else do you look for during an audit? These are mostly specific to FoxPro, but you can apply the ideas to other languages:

- Is there source code? Does the customer have it? If they don't have source code, stop here and go to the next section!
- Is there a project file? Did they use a .MAK file or just build things from scratch?
- Do they have a set of common libraries, routines and third part tools that they're using or did they write every single line of code themselves from scratch?
- Did they use proper design techniques? Did they use the proper tools for the version of the product they were using? For example, in FoxPro 2.x, did they use the menu builder, the report writer, the screen builder, etc., or did they hand code everything? In Visual FoxPro, did they use classes, the form builder, data environments, DBC's?
- Does the basic application look like it was written by the same person?
- Does it look like somebody could use it? Can the user use it without having to read a lot of books and manuals. Visual clues should be prevalent and consistent. It should be obvious what you can and cannot do. You may not understand *why* you are only able to post after you've entered a field, but that this rule is in place should be *clear*. If the application doesn't give you visual clues, that's going to be tough for anybody to learn.
- Does the application have a single look and feel - do things operate the same way each time?

The other thing I try to do, even though I hate to admit it, is try to make our applications look like they were written by Microsoft. In other words, it's consistent, it's comfortable, and if they've used a Windows application before, they feel that they can probably use ours also.

Other general things to look for that are not language specific:

- Is the data structure documented? Is it normalized?
- Did they use the same types of fields in different tables to mean the same thing? I saw places where an ID was numeric in one table but character in another table.
- Do they use single keys or compound keys?
- How do they handle deleted records?

- Do they have lookup tables and are the tables overloaded?
- What kind of utilities have been provided in the event of data corruption?
- Can you archive and pack?
- Can you delete?
- How are keys implemented and documented?
- How is performance handled in large tables?
- Do they have audit fields?
- What kind of indexing routines are being used and are they being used properly?
- Does the application even work? That sounds like a silly question. But you'd be surprised at the list of functionality the user expects to have and when asked about says, "Oh, that function never actually worked."
- Do you get the big red box of death showing up every once in a while? Is there error handling in this application?
- Do they track errors?
- Has the developer come up with some incredibly arcane way of handling menus or some other part of the interface to the detriment of the rest of the application?
- Can you maintain users or have multiple levels?
- Do you have multiple levels of security that allow access to one part of an application and not others? Of course, do you have to do detective work to find this out or could you, gasp, look at the on-line help facility.
- Is there on-line help? Is it up to date? Is it full? Does it work?
- Is the system multi-user? OK, it's 1996, so you're thinking this is a stupid question. *It's not that stupid.* I'm shocked at the number of applications I have seen in 1996 that were written in the last couple of years that are still single user. Or that are supposed to be multi-user but do not work because the developer doesn't really understand how multi-user works.
- Has the developer documented how contention is handled?
- What kinds of things can the user be expected to have happen.
- Do they lock and unlock in one place?

Each one of these questions is on this list for a specific reason - because I've seen an application that had problems due to a lack of attention to the subject.

Conclusion

There isn't necessarily one right or wrong answer to each of these questions. The issue is whether they have dealt with the question professionally and consistently. A lot of people will write an application, get it to work once and say "OK, it's done, great, I'm outta here!"

An audit is billable work. This is your time and your experience. and They should be paying you for this. If they think you should audit their application for free, then thank them for their opinion and be on your way. If they don't feel your auditing has any value to them, then you might demonstrate to the client how he/she will benefit, monetarily from such an audit in the overall scheme of things

1.7 The Engagement Letter

- **Contents of the Letter**
  - Format
  - What are We Going To Do?
  - Describe the Company and the Pain
  - The Application
  - The Development Tool
  - Fixed Price Jobs Require Detail!
  - Payment Methodology
  - How to Determine an Initial Estimate
  - Describe the Payment Method
  - The Attachment
  - Call to Action
  - The Close

- **The Attachment**
  - General
  - Services
  - Support
  - Ownership
  - Confidentiality
  - Customer Representative
  - Disputes & Liability

- **Customer Set-Up Form**

- **Various Scenarios**
  - Aborted Confidentiality
  - Resistance to Signing the Letter
  - Their Contract
  - Additional Meetings
  - The Missing Engagement Letter
  - Overcoming Resistance to Paying for Design

Contents of the Letter

The purpose of this letter is to describe to the customer the types of services we are going to provide, and make it clear that from now on they will pay for what we are doing. The sales call was free. During the sales call, I inform them that I do not work without a signed engagement letter.

See Appendix for full text of Engagement Letter

Format

I'm old-fashioned, very conservative, and I want our image to reflect this bent. I want it to look like we've been around for 100 years. I do enough "far out" things (seen our web site yet?) that being solid, conservative is appropriate for the foundation. I need to give people a subtle level of comfort.

That's why I make all of our printed literature - business cards, brochures, flyers, and so on - look very conservative. The message I deliver may be radical, but the clues that the message is coming from a solid, fundamentally solid firm also show. Some people may argue that that's a mixed metaphor and that I don't know what we're doing. Argue away. Marketing is not exact. I prefer to think of it along the lines of that I am providing somebody with a conservative business foundation yet, where it counts, I will be creative. The customer gets the best of both worlds.

```
April 1, 1997

Michael Austin-Thor
The Very Large Manufacturing Company
The Very Large Office Building
Milwaukee WI 53202-4104

Dear Mike,
```

What Are We Going To Do?

This only takes two short paragraphs. You're trying to sell them on something, and their attention, at this point, is tentative. Get to the point immediately. If it takes you a whole letter to describe what you are going to do, you don't have a clear idea.

```
I am pleased to present this letter of engagement regarding
custom database software development services for your firm.
The ultimate intent is to completely replace and
significantly enhance the functionality of your time and
billing database system with a new one written in Visual
FoxPro 7.0. For the purpose of this letter, this new system
will be referred to as TABET (Time and Billing Entry and
Tracking).

The purpose of this letter is to outline the functionality
of the system and describe the services we propose to
provide toward the development of the system.
```

I tell them that this is a letter of engagement for services and describe what those services are. Usually, we're going to create a new application (or significantly modify an existing one). In either case, we're going to need to do a design first, and that's the purpose of this letter - to describe this design phase.

The end result of this set of services is a document - a blueprint - that describes the final product they're interested in.

Describe the Company and the Pain

The "pain" we talked about during the phone call and the sales call need to be stated in the letter as soon as possible. This puts that stake in the ground by which we're going to measure the success of the project.

While you and the customer both know the context in which the pain is being described, it's often useful for others to see the relationship between the company and the pain spelled out clearly. These others include co-workers in the customer's company, or employees in your company who are going to do some of the work.

```
The Very Large Manufacturing Company is in the business of
design, development and installation of automated
manufacturing software. The Very Large Manufacturing Company
has offices throughout North and South America and does
business throughout both continents and the Pacific Rim.

The current time and billing system is an antiquated DOS-
based application that has a number of deficiencies in its
multi-user and multi-tasking capabilities. The purpose of
TABET is to provide a simple, "on-demand" tool for employees
to enter time spent on various jobs, and to provide
automated billing and management reports across multiple
offices. TABET will be completely multi-user across LANs and
WANs and will be a completely native Windows application so
that the user does not have to exit their current work in
order to access the time and billing functions.
```

Again, conciseness here is a virtue. You don't have spell out reams and reams of information. Just show that you weren't nodding off during the sales call. You also need to be able to identify in one or two sentences why they're spending all this money with you, and what they expect to get for their bucks.

Describe a bit about what their company does so that you can reference this system in that context. This gives them an idea of how important the system is and what role it plays. There are two kinds of systems; 1) ones they have but would rather not and 2) ones they like because it helps them do their job and crush the competition.

A payroll system is rather boring but is a must have (sorry if I've offended all of you accounting types.) An example of the second type of system would be one that allows them to pull up the order history of a customer in a nanosecond, something no other firm in the country can do. Therefore they can provide better customer service - and the computer thus provides them with a competitive advantage.

The Application

The customer is generally not very interested in buying software. They're much more interested in buying functionality. They want to be able to do something that they can't do now. These may be new functions, or existing functions, except that they work faster, more efficiently, or with more features.

So let's tell them what they'll be able to do. (If you're having a hard time envisioning this, picture the announcer from The Price is Right exhorting someone to "Come On Down!")

```
Specific functionality includes the ability to:

•   For an employee to record time spent against
    Customer/Project/Module/Task and Activity.
•   To maintain Customers, Projects, Modules, Tasks, and
    Activities.
•   To create Invoice Master and Invoice Detail output.
•   To create Backlog and History reports against various
    entities (Company, Customer, Project, Employee).
•   For an employee to track their "To Do" list.
•   To track and compare time spent against time estimated
    for entities down to the Task level.
```

This can be rather tough to pull together in a short period of time. It's even tougher if the customer has been yakking up a storm for hours about all the things they've had on their wish list for the last five years.

A trick I use is to pretend we're issuing this software in shrinkwrap to sell at 'Puters-R-Us. What are the ten bullet points on the back of the box that the user is going to read and then exclaim, "Oh! I want *this* one because it does X and Y!" Your customer is going to take this list of "things it can do" to their boss or to their users and say "See! See all the cool things it can do for us? Isn't this going to be great?" Those are the items that make up this list of bullets in your engagement letter.

The Development Tool

Next, we'll need to tell them how we propose to do this. Be reasonably straightforward, but you can slide a bit of salesmanship into this area if you like.

```
The system will be written using Visual FoxPro 7.0, will
include a multi-user, security-enabled foundation and
menuing system, maintenance (add/edit/delete/search) screens
for each table and data structure, a flexible reporting
utility for user-configurable reports, on-line help for each
function in the system and system and maintenance utilities.
The system will be developed using industry-standard, state
of the art software development techniques including data
normalization, professional code documentation and discrete
alpha and beta testing to assure the production of a solid
application that will require minimal maintenance.
Installation and training at The Very Large Manufacturing
Company will be included.
```

Some people do not know what development tool they're going to use at this point. By all means, feel free to delete this section if this is the case. You may want to include some sort of description about when you will decide and how the decision will be made.

The Software Development Process

The people who are buying this custom software from you could very well be new at it, and they're almost certainly new at doing it correctly. Thus, you have to educate them about how to go about the process. This next set of paragraphs describes the steps, from writing a specification to actual implementation.

Since they're going to be spending a lot of money for an extremely intangible item - a specification of software - it's important to give them as much information as possible about "what they're going to get."

Development of custom software applications is done in two stages. The first is the system analysis and design, with the resulting product being a Functional Specification and an accompanying prototype. The Functional Specification is a written document that serves as the"blueprint" of the system. It consists of the following items:

Overview
- Purpose of the entire system and how it integrates into the business
- Description of the functionality of each module in the system

Technical Specifications
- Application Architecture (Directory structure, Original Data, Logon and Security, Interface Mechanisms and Maintenance Screens)
- General Interface (Maintenance Screens, Common Buttons, Toolbars, Listbox Controls, and Notes Buttons)
- Screen descriptions (Purpose, Access, Objects and Usage)
- Report and output layouts ((Detail entities, Detail fields, Calculate fields, sort orders, grouping)
- Data Structure (data dictionary, entity relationship diagrams)
- Test Data Set Requirements
- Data validation rules
- Throughput analysis (for example, how many transactions would be entered into the system on a daily basis, how many users, etc.)
- Environment and system requirements (definition of the network, what hardware and software the system will be working with, and what, if any, additional hardware or software will be required)

Implementation
- Installation
- Deliverables
- Testing methodology
- Test plans
- Modifications
- Milestones and Delivery

Are they going to understand all of this? Do you understand all of this yet? Some things may be new or may be phrased in an unfamiliar manner. Not to worry. The purpose is to reassure the customer that you are organized and thorough. They are buying your expertise as a project leader more than as a programmer at this point, and that's what you want to sell them on.

Development of custom software is done in two stages - the system analysis and design with the resulting product being a functional specification and prototype. This tells the customer right away that the end product of these services - what they're going to get - is a written document that describes what this system does.

It also tells them that there is a value to this. I are going to design this and engineer that and these services are not trivial or inconsequential.

I then talk about the different components in the specification. There is no single commonly generally accepted format for what a specification looks like. To one customer, a specification means a page and a half of scribbles they did at 6:15 one evening; to another, it means three binders of unreadable documents that were probably assembled by a committee. What I want to do is to tell the person what they can expect in our specification.

I want to give them enough detail so they understand this is not a trivial undertaking. I want to give them enough detail so they can understand the benefits of what this is going to do and will be detailed enough that there are going to be lots of fun things they will want. On the other hand, I don't want to give them such a huge outline that they basically have gotten the benefits of our knowledge without paying for it. I would like them to hear the sizzle and smell the aroma, but I don't want to give them the steak for free.

Fixed Price Jobs Require Detail!

Some customers will try to avoid making the big decisions, and will delegate responsibility. Part of this avoidance includes the assumption that "You know what we want - just make it happen!"

I talk about the fact that this is a fixed price job, and that it is very important to spell out things clearly. Sure, I can figure out things as I go - but not for a fixed price!

I can't give you a fixed price if I don't know what it is that you're buying. If you have a full grocery basket and you only allow us to peek into one corner of the basket, I can't tell you how much it's going to cost.

The other benefit is (and I will say this a dozen more times) is that I can't test something if I haven't specified what it's going to do. I need to be very clear up front.

```
It is important to note that this Functional Specification
will contain a fixed price and delivery quote for the system
as described in the Specification. Thus, it is important
that the Specification clearly describe the functionality
and operation of the system as The Very Large Manufacturing
Company requires. Changes to the system after the completion
of the Functional Specification may result in additional
costs and delays in delivery.
```

```
The second stage is to use the Functional Specification to
code, test and install the system. The Functional
Specification will cover this process in detail.
During the development of the specification, I will meet
with you and other members of the firm involved with the
system multiple times in order to determine the specific
requirements (functions, data elements, operational
procedures, user access, etc.) of the system. We'll outline
the rules for data importing and validation, create
prototypes of the menus and screens, and mock up the reports
that make up the system. At each meeting we will review the
progress made and view prototypes as they've been developed.

The development of complex software systems is an iterative
process through which discovery of new requirements is a
normal and expected part. As a result, the scope of the
system will change during the specification process.
Accordingly, it is not possible to provide a fixed cost or
even a reasonable timeframe at this point.
```

The next stage in this process is to actually do the work described in the specification. Since the spec is a finished product, I tell the customer that they can take this spec to other places and have them bid on it as well. The idea behind this is that the customer will takes our spec to another development house and get an outrageous number and a shaky feeling from them. After all, we've spent the time getting to know the customer's business, and have a methodology for costing accurately. While we've documented the application thoroughly, we've still got an advantage over the competition by virtue of all of the face to face meetings.

In order to go about this process, I have to meet with them and several other people many times. Each time we'll build more material out of the prototype and flush more material out of the document and so on. Tell them that this iterating process is normal, because again, these people may be new to this. They may not understand and expect a miracle - a complete spec after a single meeting. In fact, they most likely will!

It's kind of like the pregnancy preparation book that has been so hot for the last ten years - *"What to Expect When You're Expecting."* Software development, while not the same as creating a child, is still maybe a somewhat of a scary process. It's complex, and there are a lot of twists and turns on the journey that you may not be able to predict. A lot of this has to do with people's desires and wants or expectations. People are human so they change their minds. I tell them and make it clear to them that this is a normal state of affairs. It's an iterating process because to iterate is in our nature. Therefore, I am comfortable with that process and I move with the current instead of fighting it.

Payment Methodology

Just like everything else in the engagement letter, we've already discussed how we're going to charge, but it's a really, really, really good idea to put this part in writing. I particularly like being explicit about the "extras" that will show up on the bill besides straight time.

> Development of this Functional Specification is done on a time and materials basis. Rates for various Hentzenwerke personnel range from $<rate> to $<rate> per hour, depending on the experience of the individual. My time is billed at top rate; other developers range from $<rate> - $<rate> and administrative and testing personnel cluster at the low end. Time includes time spent meeting with you and other members of your staff and other firms involved in the production of the system, preparation for meetings and work resulting from meetings, including the design of the prototypes, and travel and phone time. Materials include straight reimbursement of long distance phone charges and mileage between Hentzenwerke's offices in Milwaukee and your offices at the standard IRS rate. All billable personnel track their time against specific modules and invoices reflect this level of detail.

I try to be very clear about what we're going to charge, and how, so that there are no misunderstandings down the road. Of course, there always will be misunderstandings. Mainly because the customer didn't read this as carefully as they should have, or because they forgot - but I have it in black and white.

It's easy to deal with one of these situations "How come you're charging me for travel time?" You can simply say "Ummm, that should have been covered in our engagement letter. Let me pull it out to make sure that we didn't forget our standard lingo about travel time."

Of course, you know you didn't forget, but it's an easy way to point this out to the customer without being abrupt or "in your face." The customer, in this case, has made a mistake - the last thing you want to do is make them feel bad about it. This is a good way to allow them to save face while still making sure that you get the point across.

Describe the Initial Deliverables

One of the questions they're always going to ask is "How much will this cost?" (If they don't ask, be afraid. Either they're not serious, or they don't care - and in the second case, that's probably because they're not real worried about paying you.) It's pretty hard to give them any kind of reasonable answer unless you have some sort of idea of what it is they're going to buy. I do this by listing the basic components of the system.

If I can, we'll go to the extent of listing how many screens, processes, and reports are, at least initially, envisioned in the final application.

```
At this point, the proposed deliverables include the
following items:

Screens

•   Customer maintenance
•   Project maintenance
•   Module maintenance
•   Task maintenance
•   Activity maintenance
•   Application Feedback maintenance
•   Change Order maintenance
•   Invoice maintenance
•   Developer maintenance
•   Common Lookup maintenance
•   Time Entry
•   To Do list maintenance
•   Herman (current billings)
•   WIP (work in progress)

Reports

•   Invoices
•   Daily/weekly To Do List
•   Outstanding work/customer
•   Outstanding work/developer
•   Cumulative billings
•   Change Order status
•   Application Feedback status

I estimate that, based on these deliverables as well as our
experience with other systems of similar magnitude and
scope, the development of the Functional Specification will
take between 120 and 150 hours and the Implementation of the
system will take an additional 800 and 1000 hours. Please
note that this time estimate is framed in terms of working
hours and not in calendar terms.

These figures are estimates, not caps. However, you will be
informed in writing should it appear likely that the
estimate will need to be exceeded in order to finish the
development of the specification.
```

While this isn't carved in stone, it's a benchmark from which I can measure deviations.

Of course, I discuss the fact that these are estimates, but no matter how well you cover the topic, 99 out of 99 people will remember the number you provide as an estimate and somehow forget that it was "an estimate." If the design goes over the estimate, they'll generally be upset. It's a lot easier to explain why the initial estimate was for $5500 but the final price for the spec ended up being $8200 - it's because I started out with a spec for 12 screens and 4 reports but the final design has 19 screens and a half-dozen reports.

Another advantage to starting out with a list of actual components is that you can quickly tell (or find out) if you're off track. Nothing is more frustrating than to spend hours and hours (Days and days? Months and months?) on a spec only to find out that you've gone down a blind alley or missed a critical turn way back there.

How to Determine an Initial Estimate

Bet you thought I was going to gloss over this one, didn't you? How did those magic numbers appear? We've taken our historical costs for design of applications, and come up with an average per screen and report, and use those as rough estimates. Yes, this is really crude, but over a period of several years, we've found that -for estimating purposes - it's reasonably accurate. No miracle, just looking at what you did before and using that to forecast the future.

Describe the Payment Method

Now let's get down to the good part, how are you going to get paid? There are two basic methods - either get paid up front, or get paid after the fact.

```
Option I

An initial retainer in the amount of <Amount> is required to
start work, time will be posted against the retainer as
noted above, and monthly statements will be rendered.
Invoices will be used for replenishing the retainer as
necessary.


Funds remaining at the end of the development of the
Functional Specification will be returned to The Very Large
Manufacturing Company or applied toward the implementation
of the system as requested by The Very Large Manufacturing
Company The Functional Specification and prototype tables,
menus, screens, and report layouts are the property of The
Very Large Manufacturing Company as delivered.
```

```
Option II

You will be invoiced every two weeks for work completed to
that point; invoices are due in 10 days. Work will be
stopped in the event an invoice becomes past-due. The
Functional Specification and the prototype tables, menus,
screens & report layouts [but not the supporting libraries
and design tools] become the property of The Very Large
Manufacturing Company upon payment. We can begin work
immediately upon of receipt of a signed copy of this letter
and the attached customer set up form.
```

Retainer. If you choose to require payment in advance for the work you do, this is called a retainer. As the language in the letter shows, you request funds in advance, and do work that draws down those funds. When the funds are low or depleted, an invoice is sent in order to replenish the retainer.

Invoice. If you wish to invoice the customer after doing the work, the appropriate language is provided as well. Don't think that you have to invoice after the entire job is done - invoice on a regular basis or after you've completed identifiable tasks.

The decision, of course, is which method to use. You can talk to twenty developers and get thirty opinions. Some refuse to do any work without a retainer; others have worked successfully for years on an invoice basis. As much as I'd like to be able to provide guidelines for when to go which route - I simply can't. There are too many variables to create a set of fixed rules.

A small company may be perceived to be more risky. It seems that it would be easy for the owner of a small firm to get all hacked off for one reason or another, and simply announce one day, "I'm unhappy and I'm not going to pay you." Once you have a PO from MegaCorp, it would seem a lot harder for an individual to arbitrarily cut you off.

On the other hand, larger companies treat their payables as simply another business issue, and if cash gets tight, it's no problem for the board of directors to unilaterally declare "All invoices will be held for 60 days from now on." And one or two large companies have been known to go bankrupt, leaving their creditors with tears and bad memories.

Meanwhile, most small business owners treat their payables as an extension of their word - and regardless of their financial position, they will pay what they owe - period.

There are no rules - you need to decide for yourself. The only advice I have is to listen to your gut. Every time we've been burned by a customer, hindsight shows us that we really should have seen it coming. This is a business decision, and not a developer's decision. Put on your businessperson's hat. A fifteen day billing cycle may work out well for Acme Large Manufacturing, but a firm with a lousy credit rating may need to work on a deposit basis. You may need to make this call on a case-by-case basis and not set one absolute rule. Follow your gut and common sense.

The Attachment

Then we discuss the attachment included with the engagement letter. I don't think I have been beaten around the bush in the past, so don't beat around the bush now. There are a lot of hacks and amateurs and "I want to learn on your nickel" folks out there. And since I don't have any single accreditation requirements or professional society that requires membership, there aren't any standardized practices for doing things in the software development world.

```
The terms in this engagement letter are good for 90 days as
of the date of this letter. If this letter is not accepted
in this period, we reserve the right to requote.

Software development is a complex process that, due to the
ethereal nature of the product, lends itself to
misunderstandings and miscommunication. Attached to this
engagement letter is a document that describes my view of
the software development process and explains how we handle
issues that typically arise during the custom software
process. If you have any questions or differences of
opinion, please feel free to bring them up with me.
```

What does that mean? That means that customers don't know the questions to ask - they don't know what to expect - and they are at the mercy of their computer consultant.

This is not good for the customer so I want to provide them with a better set of expectations. This attachment gives them a baseline from which they can begin. I explain about our business practices in this industry, and how our company in particular operates. If they need more information, great. If they want or need changes made, that's OK too. The bottom line is to bring forward these issues and explain how I usually handle them.

The contents of the attachment are contained in the next section of this chapter.

Call to Action

As any good sales manual will tell you, always close with a call to action. Don't just wait for the customer to "get it" because they might never do so. Prompt them - make it easy for them to figure out what the next step is. And, as the sales manual also says, "Ask for the order." Ask them to sign this letter and get rolling!

I've included two ways to word this, depending on if you're going to use a retainer or an invoicing scheme.

```
Option I

To confirm that these arrangements reflect your
understanding, please sign one copy of this letter return to
me together with the attached Customer Information sheet and
the aforementioned retainer in the amount of <amount>.
```

```
Option II

To confirm that these arrangements reflect your
understanding, please sign one copy of this letter return to
me together with the attached Customer Information sheet and
a company purchase order if required.
```

Finally, I close the letter and allow a place for the customer to sign and date in order to signal their acceptance.

Note that I am asking the customer to agree that "Yes, this is what we talked about." If they have differences, they're more than welcome to give me a call and discuss what changes they want made.

There shouldn't be any substantial modifications, since we've already discussed these things at our sales call, but you need to be ready just in case.

The Close

I'm particularly picky about the close of a letter. It's just one of those things I have an irrational desire to perfect, and there's no arguing with me.

```
We can begin work within a week of receipt. We're all
looking forward to working with your company. If you have
any questions, please call me at your convenience.

Sincerely,
Hentzenwerke Corporation

Whil Hentzen
President

______________________________________   ________________

Accepted by                                          Date
```

The letter is from the company, so the company signs it: Sincerely, Hentzenwerke Corporation. However, you're acting as a representative, and so you sign underneath, with your title as related to the company.

I also make sure the customer signs and dates the letter. We'll get to the various scenarios later in this chapter.

The Attachment

General

The purpose of spelling this out is for legal reasons. In the event of an IRS audit, it's clear why the other company is contracting with us. Later on we'll spell out the relationship, right now we're just laying the groundwork.

```
Customer: The Very Large Manufacturing Company, Inc.
Vendor: Hentzenwerke Corporation
Custom Software Development Issues

General

The Very Large Manufacturing Company, Inc. ("Customer") is
looking for a vendor that will perform software development
services for internal computer systems that will run on a PC
platform due to the shortage of time and personnel at
Customer, and has approached Hentzenwerke Corporation
("Vendor") to do so.

The purpose of this document is to spell out the terms and
conditions of this working arrangement to ensure that the
expectations of both parties are understood up front.
```

Services

The purpose of this section is to spell out, as best I can without hiring a $500/hour lawyer, that we are an independent contractor doing a work for hire - not an employee. The IRS has created a set of "20 questions" that they use to determine whether a consultant is acting like an employee. In this document, I explicitly address a number of those questions.

```
Services

Vendor agrees to perform for Customer services ("Services")
to generally include, but not be limited to, design,
development, coding, testing, documentation, installation,
training and maintenance of software programs ("Programs")
as specified in this or a future Proposal.

Customer is hereby contracting with Vendor for these
Services and Vendor reserves the right to determine the
method, manner and means by which the Services will be
performed. Vendor is not required to perform the Services
during a fixed hourly or daily time or at a specific
location. If any or all Services are performed at Customer's
premises, then Vendor's time spent at the premises is to be
at the discretion of Vendor.

Vendor shall take appropriate measures to ensure that its
staff who perform Services are competent to do so and that
they do not violate any provision of this agreement or
subsequent Proposals.

Vendor shall supply all equipment, software, peripherals,
and supplies required to perform Services, with the general
exceptions of installation and training, and when requested
otherwise by Customer.

Vendor represents that it is an independent contractor and
as such agrees to indemnify and hold harmless Customer from
any and all liabilities for claims, judgments, or losses and
all lawsuits including the costs, expenses, and attorneys'
fees of any judgment for injuries to or property damage of
any person or persons including parties hereto and their
employees or agents, and third parties, arising from or
caused in whole or in part by any operation incidental to
the performance of the contract performed by Vendor for
Customer under the terms described herein.

As a condition of this contract, Vendor agrees to carry the
statutory Worker's Compensation coverage on any employee
engaged in work on the premises of Customer within the
purview of this agreement.
```

Support

One of the biggest fears of customer has hiring a developer who disappears, leaving them hanging with a system that is badly (or un) documented, buggy, and hard to maintain. Almost as bad is the developer who, once having developed the application, holds the customer hostage, demanding unreasonable sums to make the most trivial of changes.

I explain how we're going to support their application to help alleviate some of these fears.

<u>Support</u>

Vendor will make its best effort via alpha testing, integration testing, beta testing and Customer testing to provide a bug-free application. Customer is responsible for providing a Test Suite of Data (with the assistance of Vendor) that accounts for all scenarios and cases of data that the system may process.

Vendor warrants that Customer will not be charged for fixing "bugs" that slip through the testing phase. A bug is defined as an operation that does not perform as specified in the written specifications and/or change notices, or an error that causes the program to stop and display an error message that says "An application error has occurred" and must be reproducible. Non-inclusion of options, behavior not specifically delineated in the written specifications, and operating system and environmental problems are not considered to be bugs. If the problem can be resolved without changing application code, if it is not reproducible upon demand, or if it occurs in a module which has been working for three months and which has not been changed, then it is not considered to be a bug. This does not mean that Vendor will not resolve these issues; this means that Vendor will not resolve them without charge. Note that Vendor reserves the right to interpret interface and performance issues that are not specifically described in a written specification as it sees fit.

Customer will be charged on a time and materials basis at Vendor's rates then in effect for time spent to investigate perceived bugs and to repair the problem if indeed the problem is not a bug as defined above.

Customer will be charged on a time and materials basis at Vendor's rates then in effect for services outside the scope of the proposal, including but not limited to:

- Additional training,
- Modifications to the system, such as screen or report layouts, after they've been accepted by Customer personnel,
- Modifications to formulas or calculations to account for scenarios or cases that were not part of the proposal or Test Suite of Data,
- Any services relating to modifications made to the application by non-Vendor personnel.

The most important thing is to define what a "bug" is. A ton of credit goes to Pat Adams for her wonderful description of a bug: something that does not perform as specified in the written specifications or change orders. We rely on this definition all the time.

The key part about defining what constitutes a bug is that we will fix bugs for free for the life of the application, but we will charge to do work that is not a "bug fix." Since the issue of money has been raised, it's important to be clear about what is a bug and what isn't.

Note that a bug must be reproducible. It's extremely annoying to go on a bug hunt with a customer only to find that they can't show you what's happening in person. "I swear this happened to me five times yesterday," they wail, but as you and I know, we can't fix what we can't see.

We'll be happy to sit with them for days and days (well, maybe "happy" isn't quite the right adjective) and work with them to find out what is happening, but if it's not reproducible, that time is billable.

This helps the user focus on defining what the problem is - filling out our bug report forms, being clear in their descriptions and so on - if they think that by doing so, they might get the problem fixed without charge.

We've found that we like to reserve the right to charge for bugs after a certain period of time. It's possible that the user hasn't really tested the system, and then, at year end or just before plant shutdown, they run into something. That's pretty annoying and while we might give them the benefit of the doubt, we'd like the option not to.

Ownership

This is usually the first, if any, issue that is raised by the customer. Who owns the code? People want to make sure that they are not liable to you for the rest of their lives. They want to have freedom to do what they have to do in their business. So there are actually two concerns that people can raise here.

The first is whether or not somebody else can come in and modify the code that we've given them. Our answer is "absolutely." We retain ownership, but they have a license that lasts forever. They can use it for any reason, but we must retain ownership of it.

The second issue is pure ownership of the code - for whatever reason, they feel they have to own the code outright. For example, they may have a custom product that this code is incorporated into, or they may have licensing restrictions that require absolute ownership, or maybe they just like to play hardball. Our short answer here is that we have invested thousands of hours in creating common code that we use across many applications, and if they must own all of the code in their application, we're going to have either rewrite all of this common code for them, or that we'll have to sell them our libraries for an amount that will pay for us to be able to rewrite them ourselves.

Do they really want spend the money for thousands of hours of work if there isn't that much benefit to it? Probably not. In the event that you are writing a custom app for anther company who intends to resell it, it might be worth it to them, but that is a business decision that they have to make.

You want to protect the customer's interest, but not to the point of relinquishing your best interest. This is how we've decided to make this a win-win situation.

```
Ownership

Except as specifically set forth in writing and signed by
both Customer and Vendor, Vendor retains all copyright and
patent rights with respect to all materials as described in
"Deliverables" developed under this Agreement and all
subsequent Proposals to Customer. Therefore, Vendor grants
to Customer a permanent, non-exclusive license to use and
employ such materials within their business. Customer
further agrees to execute a non-exclusive license agreement
should Vendor deem that said execution is necessary.
```

We declare that we own all source code, but that we provide a non-exclusive, perpetual license for the customer to use that code in their business. Let's look at each of the points raised here.

Non-exclusive. We reserve the right to use our code again and again. We are able to provide robust, feature-rich, bug-free functionality at an inexpensive price because we reuse code that we've written for other applications. If we were to write their application from scratch, it would cost a fortune.

We must have the ability to continue to reuse code in the future, and that includes items that we specifically wrote for this customer. Note that this is subject to the second paragraph in this section.

Perpetual. They have this right forever. They don't have to pay an annual maintenance fee or be subject to any other requirements down the road.

Use in their business. They can use this code in their business, but they can't resell our code elsewhere. They can't go into business to compete with us, nor can they resell the application outside of their business without talking to use first. Of course, if the definition of the application is that it is to be distributed as a product or service of the customer, then this doesn't apply.

They can also have others come into their company and modify our code, but those individuals are not allowed to use our code outside that customer's business. As a matter of practicality, this is unenforceable. We've found that the issue of someone coming in to take over for us hasn't been a big worry either.

Common code. It's important for the customer to understand the benefits that they realize from our use of our common code libraries - and so that they can then make a wise business decision depending on their needs. But the company that requires complete ownership without paying for it is being unreasonable and that spells problems for the entire relationship down the road.

Confidentiality

If the customer is really concerned about this, they may well ask for their own confidentiality agreement to be signed. We just want them comfortable that we're not going to poach on them.

```
Confidentiality

Each party shall hold in trust for the other party, and
shall not disclose to any nonparty to this Agreement or
subsequent Proposals, any confidential information of the
other party. Confidential information is information which
relates to research, development, trade secrets or business
affairs, but does not include information which is generally
known or easily ascertainable by nonparties of ordinary
skill.
Vendor acknowledges that during the performance of this
Agreement, Vendor may learn or receive confidential Customer
information and therefore Vendor hereby confirms that all
such information relating to Customer's business will be
kept confidential by Vendor.
```

Customer Representative

One uncomfortable situation that sometimes occurs is that of being bounced around from one person at a company to another. Eventually you get caught in the middle. This paragraph simply states that there will be one person with ultimate authority.

```
Customer Representative

Customer shall designate one employee to represent Customer
during the performance of this Agreement. Said employee will
be the primary contact for this Agreement, and will be
authorized to make financial and legal commitments on the
part of Customer. No other Customer employees will be
authorized to act in such a capacity unless such
authorization is made in writing to Vendor.
```

Disputes and Liability

This is where the lawyers start to salivate. The fundamental rule here is to keep them out of the picture. Once lawyers get involved, the only people who win are the lawyers. Keep your customer happy, and if they ask for something that is unreasonable, part ways.

Customer Setup Form

This is an attachment to the engagement letter, and must be filled out just like the engagement letter must be signed and returned.

```
                    Customer Setup
1. Please provide the name and address where invoices should
be sent:

Name ______________________________________________________
Company ___________________________________________________
Address ___________________________________________________
City/State/Zip ____________________________________________

2. Please provide the name and phone number of the person to
contact in the event of a question regarding an invoice:

Name ______________________________________________________
Phone _____________________________________________________
Available Hours ___________________________________________

3. Is a Purchase Order Number required on invoices?
___ Yes   ___ No

If Yes, please provide the PO # for this project:

________________________

4. Work is invoiced every two weeks and our terms are net 10
days. Work will be stopped in the event an invoice becomes
past due.

5. Our Federal ID # is <number>. We are a Wisconsin Corp.

__________________________    ______________________
Authorized by                        Date
```

This makes sure we know how to handle getting paid properly. Small company owners will occasionally look at you funny, saying, "Well, duh - send everything to me" but in general, people look at this form favorably - noting that we seem to have our act together.

With larger companies, it's important to find out exactly where invoices should be sent.

Just as important is the name of the Accounts Payable person - and when they can be reached. This way we don't run into the situation where the invoice is due Thursday, you call them on Thursday afternoon - only to find out out the accounts payable department is only open Tuesday through Thursday, from 8-3 p.m. You don't want to have to wait until the following Tuesday to follow up - that's an additional five days - and when your terms are net 10 days, another five is an eternity.

Also find out if you need a PO number. Once in a while someone at a larger company will try to get the project kick-started - that is, begun without the paperwork having been approved. We've had enough projects get postponed or cancelled that we won't risk spending time on it until we get the official OK. Of course, this doesn't prevent the project from being cancelled later, but at least you have a better chance at getting paid for the time you have already spent.

Finally we tell them the terms and that work will be stopped if invoices go past due, and have them sign this. It's a simple matter to have problems with an invoice and suddenly be waiting for that $7900 check a lot longer than your cash flow plans had anticipated. We tend to get payment problems resolved quite quickly once they hear the magic words, "Can we pick up a check today or should I have <name of developer> stop work until you can send the check out?"

This is the most valuable form that we've put in place to ensure that we don't have problems down the road. If somebody is going to take advantage of you, you can have them fill out forms for the next three days and you're not going to get around it, but in order to solve ordinary misunderstandings, this seems to work out quite well.

Various Scenarios

Aborted Confidentiality

We agree not to resell or duplicate the work that we've done for the customer to a competitor. They're spending a lot of money to build custom software, it would be wrong to go and approach a competitor and do the same thing. That's all there is to it.

There is a touchy issue here. We are more than happy to sign a confidentiality agreement. However, what's going to happen if we start with somebody, we sign a confidentiality agreement and begin work, but two meetings later, they bail. Is that confidentiality still valid? I'd love to hear a lawyer tell me the answer to that question because right now I'm not too comfortable with it. I think it's unfair for a customer to expect you to keep confidentiality on only an hour and a half of information. At the same time, you do want to respect their needs.

Resistance to Signing the Letter

One of the most important things you can do is to make sure they actually do sign the engagement letter and send it back. Without them doing this, you are just opening yourself up to a world of hurt. There is no good logical reason that somebody can't fill this form out. However, there is one very large emotional reason - someone doesn't want to open their wallet quite yet - they'd like to get "some more stuff" for free. As a result, it's not uncommon for people to try to avoid signing the letter and beginning work on an billable basis. Let's look at some of the situations you might find yourself in.

Their Contract

Occasionally they'll want you to sign their contract instead. While this may be OK, it's good to be aware of a few things. First of all, their contract is to protect their interests, and isn't written by software development people, so their lawyers aren't aware of the issues specific to software development. Oftentimes, there are items in their contract that are totally irrelevant or just plain wrong.

Instead, offer to add their clauses to your contract. Bottom line - their contract can't be as effective as yours because they don't know as much about software development as you do.

Second, remember that your "contract" (the attachment) is not a device for providing terms for a lawsuit; rather, it's simply to bring up issues and document them so that you can avoid misunderstandings down the road. You want to show them that you are professional and that you mean business. If the deal goes to the lawyers, you'll lose because you don't have pockets as big as them.

We were once asked to sign a contract of a customer before beginning development. The general manager, new to the firm, apologized for the hassles that their legal department was putting us both through, but kind of made a mistake when he explained, "Evidently we like to be able to sue the people we do business with."

I never got around to returning their calls after that.

Another key point to remember is that contracts can always be negotiated. Each item in a contract has a price; if they want something in a contract that you don't, you can include it for a high-enough price. I mean, for a price of ten million dollars, you could put most anything in a contract. If they insist on having everything in the contract but don't want to pay for any of it, that's pretty much the same as wanting the app for free, right?

Additional Meetings

You can think of a hundred scenarios where the customer would like more information and they don't want to pay for it.. They want to decide if they should do it is DOS or Windows. They want to determine if they have enough capacity or if they have enough hard disk space and they want you to come in again for free to do more analysis before they start paying for your time. Well guess what? That's knowledge and that's your time they're asking for. You are not giving that away for free. Repeat after me - you are not giving that away for free! They want you to evaluate something. They want to you look at something. They want your opinion - to bounce a few ideas off of you. Again, these are services that you provide on a professional, for hire basis. Would your customer expect to be able to call a lawyer and say, "I would like your advice on something" without getting billed for it? If they would expect it for free, perhaps they're not your kind of customer.

What types of 'scams' might someone try in order to pick up some free services, and how might you answer them? Here are some typical lines you might hear:

- "We need to have you come in and talk to our manager before you start anything."
- "We would like to see more examples of your work."
- "We would like your opinion on this before you start"

The initial meeting was set up to handle this situation. If they didn't have the decision makers at the meeting, then that was their mistake, and they'll need to pay for it. (Well, you may not want to say that too sneeringly...) Be selfish. They could spend your time for a half-dozen meetings under the guise of "talking to key personnel." You need to cut that off right away. You're happy to talk to them, but the meter starts running after the sales call. If it's "just one more meeting" then they shouldn't have a problem with a couple hundred dollars, should they?

The Missing Engagement Letter

Just for fun, let's walk through a situation where the engagement letter mysteriously disappears yet you are expected to start cranking out work. How do you respond?

The call came in on Tuesday. They need some work done, and they'd like to see you next Monday morning. Sounds good. You explain the way you do work, and fire off an engagement letter.

Friday's mail comes, and no EL has been returned. You don't know these people, but have heard a rumor or two that they might play a little fast and loose on occasion. And the situation that you're being called in on sounds like it might be indicative of poor management as much as anything else.

Call your contact up - lo and behold! They're not in today! But they'll be back Monday.

What do you do? Blow off the appointment since you don't have a signed agreement? Or place your trust (naïve and foolish as that may be) in humankind once more and make your visit on Monday morning? We trust our fellow man, and barring any other unusual circumstances, keep our meeting on Monday.

But before we hung up the phone, we've left a message gently asking about the engagement letter. "You may not have been able to get to it before the end of the week, no problem. I can pick it up on Monday." Again, don't blame, don't accuse, but make the point that you do expect it to be ready when you show up on Monday.

Come Monday morning, the first question is to double-check on that engagement letter. "Did you get that EL I sent you last week? Just wanted to keep our paperwork in order." 9 times out of 10, your contact will have it on his desk, waiting for you. But what about that one other time?

Our answer is to treat this as an extended sales call. If you end up getting burned for a few hours of work, well, that's the breaks. But generally you can provide some help, generate some goodwill, but also be sure to get that letter immediately. Let's look at some specific situations that may raise a variety of red flags.

"I need someone to check it out/my boss to sign it." The response is to explain that you can't do the work without the paperwork. If they couldn't get their end of the paperwork done, then they weren't ready to have you come out to see them. Treat this as a sales call to determine in more detail what they're looking for.

"I lost it/never got it." You should have a second copy of the letter right there for them to sign. If they can't sign it, see the previous response.

"It's in the system but we're really in a hurry - we need to get started today!" "Great! We want to get going too, but we never start work on a job without the paperwork in place. We've found that if we start work without the paperwork, we end up forgetting and then it comes to invoice and we can't and then we have to stop work and it delays everything. Let's plan out what we're going to do and investigate what we'll need to do first."

"I don't see why I have to sign this. I'm good for the money." Here, the funny feeling in the pit of your stomach grows. Ask them if there is something objectionable or unclear. If the answer is no - but they still resist having to sign something, walk away. The person you need to watch more than anyone else is the person who has to tell you how honest they are.

"We need to get a PO number for you, but we're in a real hurry." Again, see the previous argument. Every time I've been coerced into doing something because they were in a hurry, I've regretted it. Every single time. And if their company needs a PO to get started, then shouldn't we wait?

Overcoming Resistance to Paying for Design

We've not seen it much anymore, but you will occasionally run into people who don't want to pay for the design of an application - you're supposed to "get paid" for it through the coding of the application itself. I guess that works in some industries, but not in ours. Here are some of the scenarios you may run into, and how to respond.

"The design is sales work - we don't pay for it in our industry, and we won't pay you for it either." "The first visit was a sales call - but the rest of the work is professional, technical work. Just as the first visit to an architect or a lawyer could be considered a sales call, but from then on, you would expect to pay for their services. The expertise you're paying for here is the ability to design a system specification for your system.

"We don't need your expertise to do this." If you have the expertise in-house to do the design, and it makes sense for you to do the design in-house, then by all means, go for it! However, if you want us to provide a fixed price quote on the final spec, then it will have to be in a format that we can use - and we use a specific methodology that requires a large amount of information described a certain way." Then, list **some** of those items, and see how quickly they decide that they don't have the expertise after all.

"We need to know how much the specification will cost before you begin. We understand that the specification will have a fixed price, but we need to know how much the specification will run." "The price depends on how long it takes to determine what you need. We can't tell you how much it will cost because the specification process is an iterative process - we are discovering your needs and requirements. The quicker we can complete that discovery, the sooner we'll be done and the lower the cost will be, but we can't tell you how long because we don't know how much we have to do.

"What we can do - right now - is write out a rough draft of how many screens, processes and reports you have, and then we can provide an estimate of how big this specification will be - and how much it will cost. But please note that there is still a lot of room for unknowns.

"For example, suppose you need a screen to maintain information about doctors. Depending on your needs, we may be able to spec this out in an hour -

because it's a simple screen with name, address, specialty, medical school attended and a couple of phone numbers, and this is all raw data entry.

"On the other hand, it may take us several days because we need to be able to maintain multiple addresses - home, a couple of offices, several hospitals, and an office in another state. Furthermore, we need to track what days the doctor is at which address. And we have many phone numbers, and we need to track which are active and at what time. And we need to be able to dial the phone by clicking on any phone number. And we'd like to be able to drag a file from a pick list onto the phone number and fax that document when applicable.

"Furthermore, the specialties vary from hospital to hospital. We also select the hospitals from a pick list - instead of just typing in the name in a non-validated field. And once we've figured out all this, the specification for this screen has to be approved by someone else, and they see some things they want changed, so we go through another round of changes.

"Thus this doctor maintenance screen could take anywhere from an hour to several days, and we don't know this up front. We can make estimates, but until we're done, we won't know.

"Finally, our business is to continually ask you questions so that you consider things that you may not have thought of before - that's our job and we've seen things like this before. We can give you an estimate based on the number of screens, reports and processes, but it's just a rough idea. "

If they are persistent, then ask them to specify, exactly, how many screens, how many reports, and how many processes there will be in the system. Then have them assign a complexity from 1 to 5 for each. Finally, have them guarantee that they will have all the answers to our questions in one iteration. Then we can give them a fixed price for the specification.

"The price of the specification will be folded into the app, right?" We explain that the specification is a separate product with a separate price. They are not required to buy the app from us - and, in fact, are encouraged to shop around to make sure they are getting the best price on the app that is described in the specification. But the fact that the price of the spec is separate is spelled out in the engagement letter.

"This is such a big job, we want a volume discount." This one is remarkably easy to counter. The job is bigger, yes, but it also requires more skill because it's bigger. It takes more skill to build a skyscraper than a doghouse, and the rates charged for those higher level skills are higher. Furthermore, there's more to a bigger project than just "more hours." A skyscraper that's 100 stories doesn't cost 10 times more than a skyscraper that's 10 stories - it's more complex to build and the building process is more involved as well. So while you could well expect a volume discount on the bricks and steel you'll use to build that 100 story skyscraper, you'll also have to pay considerably more for the know-how to do so.

Section 2: Designing

At this point, you have a signed Engagement Letter that asks you to develop specifications - blueprints - for the system. Now that you've got the job - to develop the spec, that is - you have to do it. That's what this entire section is about - putting the specification together.

We produce a single specification for the entire system that contains both a description of the functionality that the users see, as well as technical information that will be used primarily by the developers and technical support people.

This section discusses the creation of a specification and determining the cost. If you don't already have a formal specification yourself, this may provide the framework you need to put yours together. If you've delivered a number of specs, our methodology might not surprise you, although I hope you'll pick up a few tips along the way. However, I expect that our approach for accurately determining a cost for the system based on our Action Point Counting technique will strike you as fairly radical - and hope it's and useful.

I don't discuss the actual design of the system much, as that is the province of the gazillion books on application development that already exist.

2.1 The Process of Developing a Specification

♦ Gathering Information

Be Prepared

A Word About Customer Management

Ask Questions

Design Meetings

Document the Meetinging Results

Acceptance of the Specification

♦ More Customer Management Techniques

Call the Customer First!

Gathering Information

Be prepared

During the initial sales call you gathered some basic information - enough to let you determine if you were interested and able to do the job and hopefully to quote them a cost for the development of a Specification. As we have already discussed, in a fixed price situation, a solid, tightly defined specification is critical to the success (and profitability) of the project. Half the work of the spec is done before you write a single line. It comes in doing your prep work for the spec.

You will need to gather a lot of information, so it's important that you plan your attack.

First: Start off by using a generic specification template to guide you through. Use it as a questionnaire.

Second: Plan x number of meetings to get the information and create a preliminary meeting schedule.

Third: Break out the topics to be discussed each meeting. Develop your agendas.

A Word About Customer Management

Although you need to be a good listener, this doesn't mean be passive. For this project to succeed, *you* - not your customer - have to drive and manage it.

This means, in addition to setting the meeting schedule and agendas, you should also specify who should be at the meetings. Share the agendas with them ahead of time. This gives them a chance to prepare.

Ask Questions

During your meetings, make sure you get the answers you need. If not, keep asking. Hopefully, if you prepped your clients beforehand you have a better chance of getting all your questions answered.

If you don't understand what the customer is trying to tell you, most likely it's because they're not doing the explaining correctly. That doesn't mean they don't know what they're doing (well, OK, maybe that's a wee part of it <grin>). It's just that they aren't skilled at delivering complex, methodical explanations of their work.

The worst thing you can do is pretend to understand something that you didn't quite pick up on.

I once had the delightful experience of watching a fraternity brother of mine drive an insurance salesman absolutely mad. The insurance rep had stumbled upon the idea of hitting on the seniors at the local fraternity houses, but unfortunately picked our house as his first target.

Rich (my fraternity brother) was one of those people you simply detested because he was so bright. Three degrees and 280 credits in four years - carrying a 3.8 GPA - and *he never studied.* He just sat around the house shooting hoops and talking to his girlfriend. So when the insurance guy came a'calling, Rich was available.

Having something of a mind for math, Rich started asking about how this life insurance thing worked. He asked some more - and a few more questions. "And one more thing I don't understand."

The insurance rep didn't realize he was in over his head, and first tried to bluff his way through a couple of answers. Then he deferred a few more questions, saying that he'd be back the next day with the answers. Then he gave half-hearted responses to the last batch of questions.

The next night was considerably worse. The insurance salesman had prepared, or so he thought. But so had Rich. This time, Rich wasn't quite as gentle. "If you're selling this product, shouldn't you know the answers to these questions?", "I thought you were going to find out about this - didn't you wonder about this part?" and "Is there someone at your office who I could talk to that knows what they're talking about? What's the name of your boss? Or do you have to get back to me on that too?

Whenever Rich ran into something he didn't understand, he simply asked - and the insurance fellow never once felt that Rich was stupid for asking the question.

Fundamentally, *you can't bullshit a program into working*. You can't fast-talk your way past one of those big red error message boxes - it's obvious to everyone around that something bad happened. Ask questions - because you can't make the application do what it's supposed to do unless you understand what it's supposed to do.

Design Meetings

First and foremost, at the beginning of each meeting, quickly review your agenda. As they say - plan your work and work your plan.

It's very easy to get off track or wander onto other topics that seem important. It's up to you to keep them on target. This sounds easy enough, but let's face it, we've all had it drilled into us that the client is always right and if they want to discuss XYZ, it's not always easy to persuade them otherwise. Let's say two of your clients start discussing a topic which is important, but not on the current agenda, or you realize this is an issue they still need to spend more time defining, suggest they take it off line - either bring it back to the next meeting - or if you can't wait that long on it, take a ten minute break and see if they can make some headway and give you an answer when the meeting resumes.

Document the Meeting Results

As soon as possible after the meeting, rewrite the notes you took during the meeting and sending a copy of the highlights - to all parties concerned. Include a listing of the topics discussed witha brief description of the conclusions you reached. Also list open items - and who is responsible for them. These become item #1 on your next agenda. Do be sure to point out the project that you've made and thank them for sticking to the tasks at hand.

Acceptance of the Specification

Finally, after the meetings and note taking you will actually produce a Specification for their project. Your goal all along has been to *get them to buy it!* (How many of you are, right now, visualizing Ferris Bueller as he stares into the camera and says "They bought it!"?)

As you're developing the spec, writing the proposal and demonstrating the prototypes, watch them to see how they're "taking it." The idea is get approval for the job while you're working on it, so that by the time you've finished the specification, they know what it's going to do (and not do), how much it's going to cost, and what time frame it's going to take. The idea is that the customer doesn't get any surprises. By the time you deliver a final specification, it's already a "done deal" in that they've cleared the way with their management, gotten the price approved, or at least are comfortable with it, and have achieved some level of user buy-in.

The one thing you don't want to do is drop a bound specification on their desk (or mail it to them) and then have them upset about the contents: "We had no idea it would be this much!", or "What do you mean you didn't include the XYZ module?"

If you've worked with them on the assembly of the specification, you'll avoid another problem - that of expecting them to read and comprehend a 40 page technical document from cover to cover. Even the most conscientious of customers simply aren't going to stay awake through the whole thing. This doesn't happen, however, if you've built the specification with them, and reviewed each part as it was finished. You can get most anyone to really get their arms around a specification as long as you cut it up into small enough pieces and give them enough time to digest it.

More Customer Management Techniques

> "Customers, in the same way that animals sense fear, sense desperation in a developer."

You are the expert and you control the process of designing the application. The customer is there to provide input about what they want, but you are the one doing the work. If they don't want to take your professional opinion, then why are you there in the first place?

Unfortunately, your customers may not realize this. We're talking about money now, and some customers aren't shy at all about bludgeoning you about the head and shoulders in order to win a better price. Here are some typical situations that come up during the design and acceptance phases, and how you might deal with them.

Call the Customer First!

Cardinal rule #1 in dealing with customers: always call them first! It doesn't matter if you haven't done a thing since you last talked to them. If they have to call you to get updated on the status of the project you're working on, you've just taken two steps backwards. This is true even if you've been doing nothing but grinding out material for the project. If you have to say "I was just going to call you," you've lost credibility.

Of course, you can regain some of that credibility by explaining very matter-of-factly where you stand, showing that you've got plenty of stuff done since you last called, and that you really weren't ready to touch base with them because you weren't quite at an appropriate milestone, but be cautious here.

One of our customers got rather used to having us work on projects during the weekend due to a series of very tight deadlines. We realized that we had erred in admitting our propensity for working seven days a week when they would call on Friday afternoon with a list of things to do, and then call again on Monday morning, expecting the list to be finished. We asked them if they had accomplished anything on their part of the list since Friday, and, of course, they responded, "Heck no! It was the weekend!"

If you call them, even if it's just to say that you've been backlogged or out of the country or simply goofing off, they'll appreciate that you're still thinking of them and that you're keeping them in the loop.

Finally, following are some common issues or objections that customers may try to raise and some hints for dealing with them.

"We need to see the algorithms and formulas you used to calculate this price."

We simply explain that our "weights, price/point, and algorithms are proprietary company information" just as I'm sure that your costing formulas are confidential for your company. They may counter with an argument that the price is too high and they need to shave some dollars off, and so they want to do some "what-ifs" for various pieces of the app. We answer that we can provide module by module breakdowns, but that the algorithm that builds the price for even a single screen is too complex to provide the ability for breakdown that is any more granular. In other words, they can't simply say "If I take this list box off the screen, will I save $50?" If they insist, walk.

Another reason they may give is that they want to make sure that they're not overpaying, or that you've done the calculations correctly, or some such business. Again, in this case, we offer to provide a module by module breakdown (if we haven't already), but indicate that the pricing mechanism past a module is far too complex.

If they continue to get insistent, you might try the analogy to a grocery store - you can add up the grocery bill yourself - but the numbers you're adding up are prices - not costs - of each specific item. Similarly, you're more than happy to provide the prices for each module. But you can't break down a form or a report into prices for single components.

"How many hours does this dollar figure equate to?"

The trick is to distinguish what they're asking - 'when can you deliver' or 'how many hours does this equate to'. We answer the first, but explain that we don't price on an 'hourly' basis. The salaries of our developers are part of the cost, to be sure, but we have a lot of other factors that make up the cost as well, just as if we were building widgets. The hourly rate of the factory worker is one cost, but there's a lot more than just his hourly wage that goes into the cost of a widget.

"We really can't quite afford that. Can you come down a bit?"

Several different scenarios can occur here, but let's look at two in particular. In both situations, we play just like the copier salesman - offer to take away features that would be 'nice to have' but aren't absolutely essential. But there are variations on how to do it.

The first is when we have a cost of $30,000 and for whatever reason, believe they have a value attached to this for $45,000, so we price at $40,000. But wham! The customer comes back with the statement that the app is too expensive. Perhaps they mean it (we might have made a mistake hearing $45,000), perhaps they're just trying to bargain. In any case, they're not going to buy at $40,000. Obviously we don't want to lose the job, but we also can't just say, "Oh, gorsh, since you're such nice folk, well knock $10,000 off!"

Say they say they've only got $35,000 in their budget. How do we come down since we've got the extra margin, without appearing to be open to negotiation? The answer: We take something really simple/trivial off but claim that it was really expensive to do, so we give them virtually the same app but knock off most of the money.

The second possibility is that we priced the app at pretty much our cost, and it's still too expensive. In this case, we also need to find out what they perceive as being less important, and work with them until we get the price down to an acceptable level.

"We don't have time to go through all this song and dance with a specification. Just tell us how much it will cost!"

There's always the arrogant, rude, abrasive prospect who won't want to spend the time working on a spec. Instead, they'll insist, "You're the programmer - you should just know how much it costs!" and fold their arms across their chest.

There are two things this person might be doing. First, he might be irrational, fully expecting you to price a three to six month application based on a 40 minute phone conversation. There are a lot of them out there.

In this situation, you'd be best served walking away from this person. They're the same person who is going to insist that he told you that the application needs to run on a Mac and a Sparcstation as well as the creaky old 386 in the corner, and he's going to sue if you don't spend the next three months making it do so.

On the other hand, the customer may simply be naïve, not knowing that write an industrial strength custom database application is not the same as a really long WordPerfect macro.

But before completely giving up, remember that they might be having a bad day, or testing you to see if you've got some backbone. We explain to the customer that we deliver production quality, ready to run applications, and that in order to do so, we also need to test the applications. If we don't have the rules of operation for the application written down, we're not going to be able to test, and that will prevent us from delivering a complete application. We can deliver one, but we will not guarantee a bug-free product, since we can't define what is a bug and what isn't. A lot of folk really like the sound of "All bugs are fixed for free" and will then go along with you.

"Why did you charge us for a meeting we canceled at the last minute?"

It's the rare consultant who doesn't show up for a meeting at a customer's office only to find out that the meeting has been postponed or canceled due to some event outside of the consultant's control. Some customers will not expect to be billed for this time, since nothing was accomplished. However, unless the customer's office is down the hall, you still have to take the time to prepare for the meeting, don a suit (some of us don't work in a suit all day long), drive to the customer's site, wait around, and then drive back. Explain that the work you are doing is on a time and materials basis. You had to spend your time on the meeting, even if the body of the meeting didn't take any time.

"Wow! From the looks of this prototype, you're just about done with the app. Why are you telling us you're only 20% finished?"

We run into this question an awful lot. It's usually posed out of naiveté, not malice. Bringing up the imagery of the old Wild West (which may be more appropriate in our industry than one would care to admit), with the grand, multi-story buildings on the main street usually does the trick. "The prototype you're seeing is constructed just like these buildings - an impressive facade, but nothing behind them. "

If they still resist, arguing that the prototype appears to operate as it is supposed to, I further bring up the minefield analogy. "There is a very limited amount of functionality in this prototype - and I know what works. I'm stepping very carefully to avoid pressing the wrong button."

"We've gone through this with a fine tooth comb and it looks great."

Once in a while, you'll come across the customer who swears that they're memorizing your every word. Yet you can tell that somewhere inside the company, you're not getting any cooperation.

If this is happening, I have a trick to focus the customer's attention to the point that reading and understanding the spec is important. In two or three parts of the document, I will deliberately put errors in the spec - major errors, things that are pretty clearly wrong or missing.

Then, upon meeting with the customer for final sign-off, I'll direct their attention to a couple of these points. A blank look or some fancy footwork tells me that they've never seen this page before, and I can suggest that maybe they might want to re-read the spec before signing off completely.

You can't make them read it, but if you find out that they're not cooperating, you may reconsider taking them on as a customer.

2.2 Contents of a Functional Specification

- **Executive Overview**
  - General Description
- **Functionality**
- **Special Terminology**
- **Technical Specifications**
  - Application Architecture
  - Directory Structure
  - File Structures
  - Original Data
  - Logon
  - General Interface Notes
- **Maintenance Screens**
- **Main Menu**
  - File Menu Options
  - Process Menu Options
  - Report Menu Options
  - Utilities, Developer & Help Menu Options
  - Data Structures
  - Test Data Set Requirements
  - Environment
  - Throughput Analysis
- **Implementation**
  - Installation
  - Deliverables
  - Test Methodology and Plans
  - Modifications
  - Milestones and Delivery
  - Conclusion

Section 2.2 Contents of a Functional Specification

What goes in a functional specification for a custom application? Let me make one thing clear at the outset. This is a functional description, not a technical one. You'll see some technical details included, but the target audience of this document is the end user who has helped you design the system. And they want to know what the system is going to do - not some arcane technical details about optimizing keys or overloading tables or overriding subclassed methods.

They want to know what this thing they're buying will do, how it will solve their problems and ease their pain, and what the impact on them will be - what they have to do and what the schedule is as it relates to them.

That is all. So let's provide them with this information as easily and succinctly as possible.

While this particular example is biased toward a database-oriented application, many of the pieces apply regardless of what you are building. The most important aspect of a functional specification is to thoroughly document *what the system does*. If you have done so, the rest of the job becomes considerably easier - you can determine the cost, you can turn over the production (the coding) to someone else, and the application can be tested. Without detailed specs, you're shooting in the dark.

Executive Overview

The executive overview contains several pieces which are basically a big picture view of the system and what you're going to be able to do with the it.

General Description

First, we have a general description. This description is the piece you would give to somebody else in order to explain to them how the whole process is going to work: what the system is, what the pain is, and how the application will ease the pain. Whether or not this project is a success and meets the needs of the customer is measured by how much pain it relieves.

```
The purpose of TABET is to provide a centralized repository
for time and billing records for all employees at the
company that will be used for billing, backlog projections
and "To Do" list maintenance.
We propose to provide a multi-user database system that will
replace the current paper-based systems being maintained by
various individuals and the administrative personnel at the
company. In addition, TABET will create a database of data
points of actual time spent to produce application
components. This data will be used to fine-tune future
project cost analysis.
```

You and I know that we are writing a custom database system. So does our primary contact at the company. But someone else who has to get involved with the system - a user from a different department, a high-level management person, someone's mom - they could be coming in cold, and they might not be quite sure that these computers are a good idea. We need to give them the big picture idea, and this description does so. Don't let them assume anything.

Functionality

What specifically will the customer be able to do? "You can do this, you can do that, but it will not pull really long umbrellas out of a itty bitty handbag. Only Mary Poppins software can do that."

We need to be able to explain to them that they will be able to maintain customers, post transactions, print landscape reports, and back up their data on to CD-ROM's.

```
The major functions of TABET include the ability:
♦   For a developer to record time spent against
    Customer/Project/Module/Task and Activity.
♦   To maintain Customers, Projects, Modules, Tasks, and
    Activities.
♦   To create Invoices Master and Invoice Detail output.
♦   To create Backlog and History reports against various
    entities (Company, Customer, Project, Developer).
♦   For a developer to track their "To Do" list.
♦   To track and compare time spent against time estimated
    for entities down to the Task level.
```

How detailed should this section be? One page is sufficient - no one is going to read (or remember) more than about a page. You want a digestible chunk of information.

If it is absolutely necessary to have more than a page, break it into groups, modules or other categories, or combine multiple types of functionality into the same description.

The other way of thinking about what types of things go into this section is to pretend you're writing the copy that goes on the back of the box of software that you'd pick up at Egghead. You're providing the description on the back of the box that's going to help sell the software.

One last tip - when writing a description, make sure that you phrase each bullet point in the same way - noun/verb/object, or verb/object, or whatever style suits you best. If you are inconsistent, the customer will be confused.

Section 2.2 Contents of a Functional Specification

Special Terminology

In many industries and companies, there is a whole suite of terminology that is particular to that industry and/or company. We want to make sure that we define these terms so we are on the same wavelength as the customer.

A couple of years ago, we had a customer that was using the term "parts" one way when we were using it another. This was causing a lot of confusion in trying to create the data structures because we thought "parts" should be placed at one level of the hierarchy but they kept trying to place it at one end. We assumed they were trying to play Monday Morning Programmer when they didn't have the skills, when in fact they were correct. We simply didn't understand the relationship of "parts" to the rest of the data set. Once we defined the terms, their attempts at data design made a lot more sense.

It's best to describe each one of these terms and what they mean. Don't just use a description of that term, provide live examples. This ensures that you really do understand what they mean and you're not making incorrect assumptions.

Suppose you're describing an entity that receives medical care. If you simply describe that entity as "people" or "patients", you've not made clear a possible distinction between insured individuals and dependents of an insured individual. However, if you then provide an example of an individual and their entire family as making up multiple records in the table, your intent and plans for overloading the person table with both insureds and dependents becomes obvious.

Technical Specifications

The technical specifications provide a description of how the system will be put together, what each function or operation will do, and how the user will use the system.

Application Architecture

We're going to be installing the application onto some sort of computer. Since we're now invading someone else's domain, we like to describe what impact our application will have on their property. We also get a chance to tell them how wonderfully brilliant we are.

The majority of the cost of a custom software application is not in it's initial price but in the maintenance costs over the life of the system. Maintenance costs of 400% of the initial cost are often quoted in industry literature. Accordingly, a basic tenet of the design of this system is keeping maintenance costs down by providing user configurability and data-driven functionality whenever possible. A well-designed, maintainable system will provide substantial benefits over the life of the system.

Directory Structure

We need to explain to the customer how we are going to set up the application architecture and how it is going to reside on their hard disk. This helps the MIS folks understand the requirement and demands we will place on their computer system. The other advantage is that we get to do a little bit of the sales job because most developers are, shall we say, not so sophisticated when it comes to handling application architectures. In other words, many developers throw everything in one directory and walk out the door.

```
In order to avoid the difficulties encountered by having
hundreds of files in a single directory as commonly
practiced, the files for this application are broken out
into multiple directories by function.
TABET will be loaded onto the network in a series of
directories structured like so:
FPAPPS
 COMMON27 <Hentzenwerke-designed system-wide files>
 THIRDP27 <third party system-wide files>
 TABET
  <TABET executable files - production version>
  APPFILES <user-modifiable data-independent files >
  MDFILES  <data dictionary - not modifiable by user>
  SOURCE  <source code - used during testing>
  TESTDATA <data set used for testing>
  LIVEDATA <production data set>
```

A healthy application has a number of requirements. For ease of maintenance, upgrade and being able to keep things straight, I feel it's important to keep your program, meta data and data into different directories. Depending on the size of an application, you may even want to do that for performance reasons.

Naturally, we put all of this information into on-line help. Later, when we are asked, "What does the stuff in this directory do?" (or, more likely, "Were the files in the MDFILES directory important? We deleted that directory but now your application won't run."), we can say, "Well, let's call up Help (or look at our specification) together and find out".

File Structures

Even the most technically challenged customer is highly interested in their data and how it's going to be organized. However, trying to explain proper data normalization is sometimes difficult. We found the customer understood the description of a table when we explained it the following way:

"A table is essentially a spreadsheet in which every row contains one example or instance of whatever it is that the table is representing, and every column represents a single piece of information about that instance.

"If your table contains pets, you might have a single row for each living or dead pet. Columns would be: name, type of animal, type of species, date of birth, date of death, date and type of immunizations and sex. "

When you describe each table, it's really important to provide an example of an instance within that table. For example, "If you have a pet goldfish, is it possible that your whole tank of goldfish is really considered one pet? In that case, you will have to design your table differently because within that whole bowl of goldfish there are probably some male and some female."

This way, the customer understands the kinds of data that will go into the table. By explicitly saying that each instance of a pet has to go in one and only one row, you avoid the people who suddenly don't think linearly and think they can use three rows to describe a pet, because that's the way they would actually just type it in themselves if they were entering it into 1-2-3 or Excel. By giving them this visual conceptualization of a spreadsheet, they can help identify what is in the table in terms of rows and columns themselves.

```
The primary entities of TABET consist of a parent-child
hierarchy chain of tables. The top-level entity is a
Customer. A Customer is a physical billing location. If
invoices are sent to more than one location or individual of
a company, each is set up as a separate Customer.
A Customer may have one or more Projects. A Project is a
discrete entity that is billed against; typically, each
Project for a company will have it's own PO Number, as well
as additional attributes such as PO amount and time-to-date
hours and dollars.
```

The complete contents of this box are in the Appendix.

The other thing that we must do is describe the relationships between the tables. "If you have a bunch of people and a bunch of pets, how do you identify which pets belong to which people (or in the case of cats, which people belong to which pets?)"

It's pretty straightforward to make sure that we have an owner key in a pet table that ties that pet record back to the owner - but we have to verify if the key is one that the user sees. We use surrogate (hidden) keys for all of our work, but in some cases, the user also wants to see a physical attribute that ties the two tables together.

The other piece of information you have to discover about relationships between tables is *how many*. For example:

- **Does every person have to have a pet?** Possibly not.
- **Can an owner have more than one pet?** Only if the pet allows it.
- **Can more than one person own the same pet?** Possibly - in the case of children, more than one person may be listed as being attached to the pet (so that each kid could take the pet to school for Sharing Day.)

As you know, in the case of many-to-many relationships, a third table is required to join them. While you and I know how to do this in terms of relational theory, it may not be necessary to describe the underlying concept of how this works to the customer. Still, it is important to document that there is a many to many relationship. When your are describing file structures, you may also want to provide some examples of typical data.

Original Data

This is really an important point but most developers either don't think about it or forget about it. Hopefully, this tip will be enough for you to feel it was worth the price of the book alone.

If you don't identify where the data for the system is going to come from, the customer is going to assume something very bad - they are going to assume that it will just magically show up. The customer assumes a replacement system will come with the data from the existing system. After all, what good would an accounting system be if you didn't have any data in there? You couldn't do comparisons or postings. And the customer is not about to enter all the data from scratch. It is imperative to tell the customer how you will handle the original data

```
TABET will initially be populated with the test data that is
described later in this Specification.
```

What are your options? The first option is leave the tables empty. And this is OK, as long as you have told the customer up front (and reminded them several times) that this was going to be the case.

The second option is to provide a bare minimum data set - possibly some look up tables and a few minor entity tables - but the guts will be empty. When the customer adds a new invoice, they can select an existing customer, but the system will not be loaded with the invoices dating back from 1931.

The third possibility is to convert all of the existing data from the old system. Unless the old system uses the exact same data structures (fat chance!), you will have to describe how you are going to convert the data.

If a customer has a boatload of information they want converted over to their new system, we need to provide a mapping of how that is going to happen and who will do what. Ordinarily, there is a lot of manual labor associated with this kind of thing. Why? One of the reasons an old system is being replaced is because it doesn't work well. One of the prime reasons a system is deemed as not working well is that it doesn't care for the data very well. Therefore, the data that you moved from old system to the new system may not be very good.

People don't know their data. They do not understand what is in their current data, they do not know what holes exist, and they do not know if there is corrupt data in the system. Repeat after me: People don't know their data.

Never assume that the data will come over flawlessly - no matter what the customer tells you. I don't think I've seen a flawless conversion in the last thirty systems I've done. You may get lucky, but if you assume that their data is good, you're going to be unhappy. Make sure you describe what needs to be done to convert their data into a format usable by the system you are proposing.

Furthermore - and this is the important part - you'll have to describe what's going to happen if the conversion doesn't go smoothly.

There could be missing records, invalid entries or holes in the data. Perhaps they are missing all of July's records. (Where *did* they go?) This would be a good time to ask if they really need the July transactions. Perhaps they should reconstruct the July transactions now so that you can get those records into the new system and allow the users to start off with a new robust set of data.

There could be invalid data. For example, the valid codes are A, B, C and D. For some reason, there are a thousand records with a "7X" in that field. Why is there a 7X? If you're lucky, you'll find Ed down there in the bowels of the accounting department saying, "Oh, I remember what a 7X was." But that's if you're lucky. Otherwise, well, you'll need to have a plan for what to do when you run into unexpected data.

Thus, be sure to specify the rules used during import and conversion routines. You will need to do this in your specification so the customer understands what will be done and what will be left undone - and what they'll have to do after conversion.

Logon

How is the user going to get into the application? Do they just have a username or will they also be required to have a password?

```
In order to access the system, the user will select an icon
in Windows to load the application. The user will enter
their logon name and password. If the logon parameters are
valid, the application will load and display the TABET main
menu. If the parameters are not valid, the user will have
two more attempts and then will be returned to Windows. In
order to enhance security, the user will not be informed
which piece of data is incorrect.
```

At this point, we're starting to show screen shots - pictures - of the application's interface. They won't remember the demonstration of the prototype five minutes after you leave their offices - but they'll refer back to the spec to look at the pictures over and over.

General Interface Notes

This section describes the general look and feel of the application. This is very similar to the very first few pages in the Windows manual that describes what a command button is and what happens when you hit a spinner. Standard stuff that operates regardless of what Windows application you are running or who you are working for.

```
The following rules apply to the entire application.
Exceptions are noted in the particular screen, process or
report.
All screens are set up to be equally friendly to the
keyboard and mouse users. For example, all objects can be
operated with a keyboard shortcut as well as the mouse, the
focus is automatically moved to the next appropriate object
when a field is left, and so on.
```

The complete contents of this box are in the Appendix.

There are a number of advantages to having this section.

- You don't have to repeat this information every place.
- It's good to document it somewhere
- It fattens up the specification by a dozen pages or so, and this makes the customers who want to pay for their specification by the pound happier.

As customers ask more and more questions, and as we add more and more standard features, this section grows. Over the past year, we've added the last paragraph that indicates our care and feeding for Year 2000 issues.

```
All dates are stored internally in CCYYMMDD format so that
dates after the year 2000 are handled correctly. Dates will
be shown on the screen with the century (for example,
07/27/1996), but the user need only enter the year (for
example, 07/27/96) for dates in the twentieth century.
```

Maintenance Screens

A lot of our screens have the same look and feel. They have the Next, Previous, First, Last, Search and Find features. It's efficient to describe key functions in one place. Furthermore, since all of this functionality is part of our foundation, describing all of it raises the bar for competitors. Suddenly they have to duplicate all of this functionality - and most likely have to write a fair amount of it from scratch.

We are not saying all of the functions described are included in every application, but if the user sees a multi-column list box, they can find out how it works in the description here.

```
A maintenance screen is used to add, edit and delete data in
a specific table. A maintenance screen may also be used to
access child records related to the parent table in a
parent-child relationship.

All maintenance screens have similar functionality; instead
or repeating the same information for each screen, the
following describes the common functionality across all
maintenance screens.
```

The complete contents of this box are in the Appendix.

Since we basically include all of this in every spec, it's a simple cut and paste (oh, to have inheritance in your word processor!) operation, and this saves the customer money. They don't have to pay to have every word of the spec customized.

Main Menu

The next section of the technical specifications goes through the entire menu (we always use a standard CUA menuing system that appears after a successful logon) and describe what happens with each menu option.

On some systems, the user may see a pick list that allows them to choose a subsystem which is then used to create a subsystem-specific menu. This is becoming more common as our systems are getting bigger, but it still fits in with our general paradigm.

The menu should be comfortable and familiar - they should expect it to behave just like every other Windows application. They will expect to see File, Edit, Help, Utilities, Tools, and each option should work the way they have been conditioned to expect it to. They know Ctrl + X, Ctrl + C and Ctrl + V work for cut, copy and paste. They know they can do a Find and a Find/Replace, and that Exit is found under File.

This next section will be somewhat specific to the way we design applications. I am presenting this as one possible way to do it - you are welcome to present the information to your customers differently. Nonetheless, you will need to, at some point, define the specific functionality of your application and what the operating rules are for each function. If you don't, you're not going to be able to take advantage of our pricing methodology later in this section, and that would be a shame.

File Menu Options

Underneath "File" we have menu options for every data-centric form in the system. These forms visually or mentally tie to a specific table or set of tables - the invoices, the parts, the transmographers (it's a technical term - don't worry about it unless you're a six year old kid with a tiger named Hobbes) and patients that the application handles.

These kinds of things basically map to forms they use in their business to do work, whether they enter a customer, discharge a patient, fill out shipping label information, update transaction dates, and so on.

For each form, we show a screen shot of the form and describe what the form is, how it works, and how they will use it. This is were the rubber meets the road. If you scrimp here, you are going to be one seriously unhappy camper down the road. There is a ton of work to be done when describing each screen, but doing the work now will pay you incredible benefits in the future.

The Screen Shot. The screen shot should be a picture of the form as it appears in the prototype that you're building - and, if you can, populate the prototype with real customer data instead of Bugs Bunny and Daffy Duck. You obviously need the customer's cooperation to get that information, but this act significantly enhances communication about how this form will look and act.

Purpose. This one people forget all the time because it's obvious after you use the form for about 10 minutes. But if you haven't used the form, it's pretty useful. Remember how confused you were when you had to first turn on a computer and didn't know where the "ON" button was?

What will the form allow the user to do? What is its mission in life? This doesn't have to be a long section. It's not a tutorial, simply an explanation of what they can do with it and why it's important.

```
The customer form allows you to add new customers, edit
existing customer data and delete previous customers.
```

Access. How does a user get there and who can do so?

```
This screen is accessed by selecting the
File/Transmographers menu option. This menu option is
available to people with a super duper user permission
level.
```

Form Objects. Next, we get into the meat of the form - a description of every "thing" on the form. The most interesting objects are those that perform actions, i.e., push buttons, data entry fields, drop down list boxes, and so on.

Every object on the screen that is not a dumb label, shape or graphic image needs to be described. In order to make sure that there is nothing extra happening on (or behind) the form, we add the following most wonderful phrase:

```
"All fields are editable and no validation is performed
except the following:
```

If we have a text box in which the user can enter 26 characters, no description is necessary. The data dictionary listing (later in the spec) shows that this field is 26 characters long. The user should expect to be able to enter all 26 characters in any form that this field appears on.

However, if the data in that text box has to be converted to capitals automatically, we explicitly say that. If a red dot is supposed to appear if the data entered is invalid, we say that. If the text box holds more characters than can be displayed on the form, we say that.

The key is to ensure that the customer understands how the form works and what the validations and rules are behind the scenes.

There are a number of objects that have a relationship with particular sets of data that may or may not be evident. For example, a list box may be populated from a table but the records that appear depend on a rule, such as who has access to that table, or whether a flag was set elsewhere in the form.

You need to explicitly identify how each one of these works and how it will be presented. For example, "List box A displays the last five transactions for this customer. It will be sorted by transaction date, and then by transaction code within transaction date. If the customer doesn't have any transactions, the list box will display <None> in the first row." This makes it clear what will happen. The user can choose to change the contents of this list box, but that request is definitely a change order.

Another example would be a radio button populated by the contents of a field. What happened if the contents of that field are empty? Do we have a radio button that says "None" or do we leave all of the radio buttons unchecked? The key here is that these rules are tied to a specific object and thus belong in this section.

Form Level Rules. There are several types of rules that are tied to a form. An example is the enabling of one control based on the user changing the value of another - selecting a certain radio button enables a text box elsewhere on the form. Another example would be special record level validation upon saving a record. You could argue that this rule would actually be a data engine validation, or a trigger. It might be, if any type of save function on that table required the rule to be fired. But it might not be a trigger if the rule was specific to this form, or if the development tool you were using didn't know what a data engine or a trigger was.

Two benefits of describing your rules in this manner are that not only does the user have a checklist of what is going to happen during the operation of the screen, but your QA group (or person) can use this guideline to test.

Usage. Finally, tell the user how the form works and how they are going to use it in their day to day work. In order to perform function X, you must do Step 1, Step 2, and then Step 3.

Not only have you just described how the screen works in terms of describing to the user what they can (and can't do), but you've also written a complete description for the programmer . Furthermore, this description is also good for testing because now the QA people know what the form is supposed to do, and what it may not do.

Finally, we now know what makes up the form. We know how many things (labels, text boxes, spinners, list boxes) are on the form and how many things (validations, rules, triggers, function calls) are attached to the form. We're going to use this information to cost out the application. If we start with bad data, we might as well go back to throwing darts at a dartboard.

Process Menu Options

The "Process" menu contains menu options for functions where the primary motive is to do data manipulation that doesn't require much, if any, user input, and may involve tables and processes that the user in not aware of.

Examples of processes include import and export routines, transaction updates, posting processes, and calculation type operations.

It is significantly more difficult to explicitly describe a process. Therefore the Processes part of the specification contains a wider margin for error. Some people might even argue that it's impossible to define a process well enough to be able to determine a fixed price for it. It's easy enough to see all the objects on a form, and to count the number of rules attached to the form. But a process can be anything. It would be impossible to categorize a routine into a discrete set of objects like a form can. Let's take a look at how we might approach "what goes into a process."

We have figured out so far that there are perhaps a dozen types of operations that go into a process. These operations are the building blocks that go into various types of processes. The ones we've identified include:

- **Create temp files.** This is the operation that either creates a temporary text file, a temporary table, or a cursor that will be used during the process. Typically, you'll have a generic function to handle the dirty work for you, so this would often be a simple function call or a small number of lines of code.
- **Delete temp files.** Why are they called temp files? Because they're not permanent - and that means that you'll often have to take care of cleaning them up - either deleting off of the disk or simply closing the cursor.
- **Match two files.** In many processes, you'll need to look for the key of a record in one file in another file.
- **Update one file with data from another file.** If you are successful in the aforementioned match, you may overwrite one file's data with the information in the other one.

- **Assign data values with a calculation.** A process often updates a file with a value that is calculated. This value may be calculated any number of ways - a combination of fields, fields and memory variables, or even with standard "magic numbers."
- **Add a record to a file.** If the aforementioned match wasn't successful, the solution is to often add a new record.
- **Set a flag for later use.** When handling validation, you'll often need to "keep your place" and refer to that place holder later.
- **Set up a countdown.** If you're ripping through a file, it's often polite to let the user know how much processing remains. We often do this through a simple countdown window in the corner of the screen that tells the user how many operations needed to be handled and how many are left.
- **Write a record to an exception file.** If you found a match when you weren't supposed to (duplicate records) or didn't find a record when you thought you would (missing keys), you may want to record this information in a file that the user can later access.
- **Write an alert to the user for immediate processing.** If something Very Bad happened, you might want to stop processing until a user can intervene.

Now that we've defined some of the building blocks, let's determine how we might describe the process that uses these building blocks in order to accomplish something useful for the user.

We don't have a foolproof way to make sure we catch every step of a process (if we did, only the fools would use it, right?), but we do have a set of questions that tend to catch most of the "what if this happened" events.

One of the things we do most often is handling things that go wrong - in other words, validation. Most processes can be handled with reasonably straightforward procedural code - until you start considering what could go wrong.

- What's the purpose of the process?
- How many tables are involved?
- How many tables are updated (as opposed to being used as read-only lookups)?
- What actions (update, append, exception) must occur during each operation?

Given this description, we can begin to identify each of the types of building blocks that are needed at each stage. That's what we'll need when we determine the cost for this app.

Report Menu Options

We use a third-party tool that provides a lot of our reporting functionality for us. We describe output knowing that we are going to use this tool to do so. Fortunately, many of the techniques we use and assumptions we've made are equally valid in other environments, or can be adapted to your specific requirements.

We build a single flat file that contains all of the data we need for creating the report, and then run that file through a report form that formats the data as the user wishes to see it. Thus, there are two steps to building the report - creating the file and creating the report form.

The Report Form. A report form has "things" on it just like a screen - and so they can be defined and counted. The things are somewhat different in nature, but they can be discretely defined just as well. These things include:

- Labels - either text or graphical.
- Fields - straight from the data file.
- Calculated Fields - a combination of one or more fields from the data file in concert with other operations.
- Group Bands - a feature specific to our report forms, but that has a similar feature in many other reporting tools.
- Subtotals - either in group bands, page bands, or title/summary bands.
- Rules - we don't use them often, but we can even attach processing rules that are fired when the report is executed.

Each of these things plays a special role in handling the data file that is sent through the report form.

The Data File. Now that we've got a report form - a skeleton through which we can throw data - we need to get the data itself together. Typically, a data file consists of fields from at least one if not several tables. When we join the tables, we have to apply a variety of filters, specify the order in which the result is created, and perhaps create calculated fields or group on expressions in order to create output data at the appropriate level. Each of these actions also represents a "thing" that we can count:

- Data Items - these are fields, combinations of fields, or user-defined functions that create a value that can be placed on a report as a field.
- Joins - the definition of how two tables in the report are joined.
  Filters - expressions that select only certain records.
- Group By Expressions - key values that create aggregations of data.

Now that we have a data file with a certain number of "things" and a report form that also has a definable number of "things", we have done two things. First, we have explicitly described what the report is going to look like and what's going to be in it to the user. Second, we can determine the cost of this report.

By the way, this method of describing out put can be used regardless of the destination of the output - the screen, a printed report or a file.

Open Task List By Customer:
Purpose: This report will list all tasks for a specific customer which are to be completed within the user specified time frame.
Detail Entity: Tasks
Filter: Tasks for a user-selected customer with due dates that fall within user-defined date range and that have not been finished.
Order/Group: Group by project, then module within project, then due date within module.
Fields: Customer, Project, Module, Task Description, Task Due Date, Task Scheduled Date, Developer Responsible.
Calculated Fields: None.

There is one very important paragraph to include in the report section. Since we are specifying a fixed price application, we want to limit (or prevent) the number of iterations that the user performs on the final deliverable. There will always be a few tweaks that we throw in for free - moving this field over there, changing the name of a menu option, and so on.

But reports are one of those things that can be tweaked forever, and that can break you if you're on a fixed budget of time - as we are. Our reporting tool includes a mechanism for allowing the user to modify the appearance of reports we've already set up, so we include the following wording to limit the number of tweaks that they expect of us:

```
Since the appropriate appearance of reports is a highly
subjective and personal matter, it is possible to make
modifications to reports ad infinitum. Since this is a fixed
price proposal, we will create data items for the detail
fields listed above, produce the data file to populate the
report, and mock up a sample report layout based on the
examples provided. Additional modifications to reports can
be made by customer through the Foxfire! utility or by
vendor at additional charge.
```

I should also mention that our reporting tool also handles printing automatically - so we never have to worry about specifying a certain printer or handling weird print setups. The tool is configured for these cases automatically. It also allows us to set user permissions on a data item or report basis by flipping one switch.

Utilities, Developer & Help Menu Options

We have a number of standard functions in our foundation that are included with every application as part of the package. We've written it once and we don't touch it - the options that need to be configured for each application are all data driven, so there's no work involved at all. However, we do describe how it works in the spec for two reasons. First, this is a description of how the system works and what functionality it possesses for the user. Second, if the customer should send this spec out for competitive bid, we've just raised the bar because now the other companies will have to match this functionality - and they likely do not have the same capabilities built into their systems. Another advantage is that even if a competitor could come up with a competitive bid, we've been using our utilities for years. Which do you think is more bug free?

Data Structures

There are two parts to this section. The first is to describe our naming conventions for databases, tables, and fields, so that the reader can more closely understand the technical detail to follow.

```
Identical field names indicate the same attribute (data
element) in different tables. For example, the CIDFa field
in the FACILITY table represents the same data element
wherever CIDFa is found.
All fields that begin with "CID" are unique, primary keys or
foreign keys. All keys are system generated and hidden from
the user.
All fields that are named "NLMOD" or "CLMOD" are audit
fields that track the date and time of the last edit of the
record.
```

The complete contents of this box are in the Appendix.

Then, we list every table in the system, except the meta-data tables, and describe what every field is going to be. This is one of those CYA kinds of things - nothing is more aggravating than having a customer who, upon final delivery, produces a list of changes to the tables - field lengths, types, and so on - and expects you do so for free.

```
DEV.DBF

Field Field Name Type     Width  Dec  Description
  1 CIDDEV    Character   5      PK
  2 CNAF     Character   10      First Name
  3 CNAL     Character   15      Last Name
  4 CINITIALS  Character   3       Initials
  5 NRATEDEV  Numeric     6   2  Rate/Hour
  6 LISACTDEV  Logical     1      Is Active
  7 CIDA_US   Character    5      FK to A_USER
  8 CLMOD    Character   10      User stamp
  9 NLMOD    Numeric    15   2  Time stamp
** Total **            71
```

Hopefully, we have gotten the table structures from the user. They should specify if the customer number has to be seven characters long and the PO number has to be 14 characters but sometimes they don't, therefore, we have to make it up. If the customer comes back with a set of requests like "Oh, that has to be another character wider." Or "This has to be numeric", they're going to expect the change to take ten seconds. However, it's a lot more work than that, because you have to change the actual table, the data dictionary, your screen, reporting meta data, and possibly other things.

We'll be happy to do so, but we are going to charge them for that. Therefore, we document what we are going to provide and should they need a different type of mechanism, we will provide that mechanism for a fee.

Test Data Set Requirements

The customer will provide the following data sets. Want a surprise? They never fill this in. They never provide test data. I had one customer provide me with a good set of test data but then that person was fired from their job. (I swear I am not making this up.)

```
Customer will provide the current live data from their
current application to use for testing.
```

Having test data provided is rare, but we do address it if for no other reason to indicate that the customer isn't going to do it and therefore the application will cost more because we will have to do it. (Our metrics assume that we will be generating test data ourselves.) Regardless, it needs to be done. What might go into a test data set requirement description? Here are a number of check-off items we use:

- How to populate minor entities and look-ups.
- How to populate the original tables in terms of having single records, 10 records, and 100 records.
- Where will data come from - manually entered or converted from data provided by customer?

If at all possible, we would like to have data from the customer. Yes, we can put Bugs Bunny and Road Runner into a customer name table but it just doesn't seem to be taken as seriously as if we had actual live data from the customer. Furthermore, you can write up test plans that demonstrate examples that they would be familiar with if you have actual data available.

Environment

We have run into problems when a customer takes an application and decides they are going to run it somewhere we did not anticipate, has problems and then expects us to fix it free of charge. We need to inform the customer what it should run on and how it will work. We also do a little CYA.

```
If the system must run on 16 bit operating systems, FoxPro
2.6 will be used. If the system will only run on 32 bit
operating systems, FoxPro 5.0 can be used if desired.
This system will be written entirely in FoxPro for Windows,
version 2.6, and will be compiled to a runtime .APP to run
under FoxPro on the LAN. However, it is advisable to have
FoxPro installed on the LAN during development instead of
relying on run-time files. This will provide for easier
debugging and other modifications that could be made on
site. Third party software is limited to JKEY, an
incremental search routine for use within Browse windows,
Foxfire!, a reporting utility, and KeyMask, a password
masking utility.

Operation of System will be performed on equipment
purchased, owned, and maintained by Customer. The system
will run on Novell Netware 3.1x, DOS 5.x or later, and
Windows 3.1, Windows for WorkGroups 3.11 or Windows 95. The
workstations will be IBM PC compatibles containing a minimum
of 486 processors with 8 Mb. Machines with less than 16 Mb
may not work reliably as far as moving data between System
and other Windows applications.
```

For example, in the olden days, we stated that "FoxPro for Windows would not run reliably with less than 8 Mb memory. If you want to run more applications, you would need more memory". Nowadays, in late '96, we are starting to come into the situation where the developer tools are not always compatible across all operating systems. For instance, Visual FoxPro 3.0 will run on Windows 3.1, Windows 95 and Windows NT. Visual FoxPro 5.0 is a 32 bit only tool which means it will not run on Windows 3.1. We need to specify that. They can not take this Visual FoxPro Application and run it on the old clunker in the corner with 8 Mb of RAM. If we don't specify, they will run into all sorts of problems and think it's an application problem.

```
All will be equipped with monitors capable of VGA color
display and all will have hard disks with several megabytes
of disk space available. A mouse is required. Some Windows
functions may not be available without a mouse. Data backup
will be done according to standard internal MIS procedures
independent of System.

Printing will be directed to generic dot matrix and HP
LaserJet printers via parallel ports or network connections.

The equipment may be used for purposes other than running
System, but System will take precedence in terms of use,
access by Customer and Hentzenwerke personnel, and setup
parameters. In addition, Customer personnel will take
reasonable precautions that equipment is protected from
outside interference including, but not limited to, virus
infection and use or access by non-authorized personnel.

System will not perform environment checking such as looking
for the existence of fonts, non-FoxPro-specific system
files, or available memory and diskspace. Time spent on the
resolution of problems causes by the alteration of the
environment once the System has been installed is not
included as part of this proposal and will be billed on a
time and materials basis.
```

We also document additional requirements so should they run into network, hardware, viral, or data security problems, they won't expect us to fix the ramifications for free. We're happy to provide whatever support we can; we just make it clear that repairing their tables because a virus infected half of their workstations is not part of our fixed price proposal.

Throughput Analysis

It's not difficult to put together a system that suddenly snowballs into several hundred megabytes of data, or to have data entry loads explode from 100 records per day to several thousand in the same period. Because the demands on a system are different depending on the number of users and the data set size, we specify what type of load - original and additional - we can expect. While not a commitment, it helps us make sure we have scaled the application to the expectations of the user. In other words, we're not using this to price the application as much as to communicate with the user so they don't come back in a month claiming the system is awfully slow - and upon investigation, we discover that they've increased the daily load twenty-fold.

Table	Original Load	Weekly Load
CUST	50	1
PROJ	125	2
MOD	490	4
TASK	2900	30
ACT	7500	100
TIME	5000	50
INV	750	5

Implementation

The best system in the world isn't going to do the customer much good if it stays on your development network. However, a significant number of problems can occur during the installation of the application at the customer's site. This final section (yes, we're almost done!) describes the last leg of our journey.

Installation

Most companies now have somebody that is their PC person. We don't want to spend a lot of our time and talent doing things that their PC person could be doing a lot more economically

```
System will be installed on the office server and on one PC
that represents the standard configuration throughout the
office. Time spent configuring System to run on additional
configurations, if any, is not included as part of this
proposal and will be billed on a time and materials basis.
Customer will provide remote access through modem dial-in
software in order to facilitate long distance support.
```

We agree to install the application on the server and one work station that represents the general configuration use in their office. We will install additional ones if they would like,. Because it takes additional time, however, we charge them for it. We specify what we will do for the fixed price. If additional work is desired the price will be adjusted accordingly.

Deliverables

We describe what we are going to provide and what the customer will provide. If you are a one man shop, it is a good idea to describe what you and the customer will provide partly to satisfy the IRS so that it is documented that you are providing your own tools to do the work. It's nice for the customer to know what they should expect. Sometimes the developers forget to provide these things.

```
Customer will provide ...
•   All equipment and supplies necessary for the operation
    and maintenance of the System.
•   A test suite of data to use for development and testing.
    The test suite should include a variety of data sets
    that fairly represent data on the system and represent
    all possible cases of variance. Hentzenwerke will assist
    in the development of an acceptable set of data.
Hentzenwerke will provide ...
•   DOS and/or Windows executable software programs that
    perform the functions listed in this Functional
    Specification.
```

The complete contents of this box are in the Appendix.

Test Methodology and Plans

Most companies employ a testing plan that includes pushing most of the buttons at least once and then hoping the user doesn't find anything wrong late on Friday afternoon. While I'll be the first to admit that our testing methodology has room for improvement, we draw a baseline for what types of testing we will perform, so that it is clear to the customer that we're not expecting them to act as guinea pigs.

```
Hentzenwerke uses three distinct testing phases during
system development. The first phase consists of testing each
action in the system (menu choices and screen objects) to
verify that it operates without adverse effects. The second
phase consists of verifying that each function point in the
system (menu choices, screen actions, screen data fields,
and report objects) performs the function or contains the
data it is supposed to. The third phase consists of checking
that the business rules of the system (logic and branching,
algorithms, special cases) are carried out through the
operation of the system.
```

Section 2.2 Contents of a Functional Specification

```
Each phase of testing is planned prior to the testing by the
Software Developer. This is referred to as the Test Plan.
Upon completion of the Test Plan, the Application Tester
will perform the Test according to the plans and record the
results. This process will be followed for each Deliverable.
Hentzenwerke will perform all testing for each of these
phases before delivery of any working prototypes or final
programs.
```

Since we are just starting to be more rigorous with test plans, this section is not as detailed in our specifications as it will be in the future. The plan does two things; 1) let's customer know we will be checking our work and 2) acts as a check list our QA department. Just as we need a blueprint for the developer to write the code, we need to provide a blueprint or a description for the QA department on how we are going to test the application. We have been writing code for 15-16 years but have been writing test plans for less than a year so we have some catching up to do.

```
In order to test the system, Hentzenwerke's QA department
will perform the following functions:
♦   Enter a new customer into the system.
♦   Enter a new project and multiple modules for the new
    customer.
♦   Enter multiple tasks for more than one module.
♦   Enter time against several tasks in several modules.
♦   Run all reports and verify that new information has been
    recorded and categorized correctly.
```

What goes in a test plan? In the chapter on testing in the next section, we discuss test plans in more detail. The essential characteristic of the test plan description here in the spec is that we set expectations for the customer as to what work we will perform.

Modifications

There are three important pieces of information in this section of the specification.

First, we're telling the customer, by addressing the issue of modifications at all, that modifications are part of the game. All but the most trivial of applications require modifications. It's just a natural state of affairs. The key is that we expect modifications and we are set up to handle them - but we will not perform unlimited modifications to a fixed price system for free.

```
The menus, screens, reports, table structures and
functionality described in this Functional Specification are
final.

It is not uncommon for modifications to be requested after
such a point. Depending on the type of modification and the
stage of during development when that modification is
requested, the amount of work that the modification requires
may range from the trivial to the substantial.
Estimates for such modifications will be provided in writing
on a Hentzenwerke Corporation Change Order form and will
need to be signed off before they are incorporated into the
system.
```

The next important point is to specify that the customer can't modify the system while we are working on it. I've always been incredulous that a customer will start to modify code in an application that hasn't even been installed. That's like changing the carpeting or putting in new light fixtures while the construction company is still putting up floor joists or laying conduit. But it happens, so we want to make sure to explain to the customer that this is going to cost them extra.

```
Customer agrees not to modify the source code and/or design
surfaces during the development of the System.
```

The last big point, and this is one of my favorite clauses, is that we reserve the right to interpret functionality and performance issues that are not explicitly defined in this spec. This way, we don't get dragged on through the mud because a customer wants a screen to come up in a half-second rather than three quarters of a second. If they have specific performance requirements, then they should have noted this (and we should have asked, of course) at the particular stage in the spec where appropriate.

```
Hentzenwerke reserves the right to interpret interface and
performance issues that are not specifically described in
this Functional Specification as it sees fit.
```

Milestones and Delivery

According to the conversations we have had with the customer, we want to be able to deliver pieces of the application at separate times. We don't want to deliver an application in one swoop and say, "Here it is! Work on it. Let me know if you have any problems". We want to deliver an application in pieces so by the time they have seen the entire application, they understand how the whole thing works. They have bitten off a bit at a time, have had a chance to digest each piece, and by the time the entire system is installed, they're comfortable with all of it..

```
Delivery milestones will include the following:

Maintenance Screens

Customer Maintenance
•    Project Maintenance
•    Module/Tasks Maintenance

Data Entry Screens
•    Time Entry
•    To Do Entry
•    Reporting Module

Reporting Module
```

How do we break up the milestones? We simply ask the customer how they want it delivered. They have requirements within their organization - they may have people going on vacation or someone not familiar with working with computers who need more time to get acclimated. Asking the customer how they want application delivered is part of the design process. It is important not to schedule deliveries with hard coded dates unless you have absolute control over everything required to deliver .

All of you who have absolute control over the entire application environment - system and situation together - please raise your hands. Nobody has complete control. So why would you schedule a hard coded date that may get blown away because it's dependent on events outside of your control, or even possibly your knowledge.

You can state that you will deliver module X a certain number of weeks after each of the external events has happened because you do have some control over what you are doing.

Conclusion

That's the specification. Sure does seem like it would be a lot easier if you would do time and materials, doesn't it?. Well, at the outset, sure, but it is much easier to deliver high quality applications with a fully documented specification because you know what you are suppose to deliver. The customer knows what you are suppose to deliver. You have less arguments and disagreements and, frankly, it is also easier to write the code if you understand exactly what is supposed to happen.

Is this complete? Is this the be all and end all of all specifications and we will never make further modifications? Obviously not. There may be a time somewhere down the road when we want to ad something to it. In fact, I think it may happen next week. This specification is, despite years and years of work, still a work in progress.

You have other experiences, other situations and requirements and, therefore, you may decide to make changes to this and do things a different way. My hope is that I have provided you with some ideas you haven't seen before and some reasoning for doing some things that you already had put into place but didn't exactly know why.

I would love to hear from you about sections that you think belong in a specification. This is the way we do things, partly because of the way we write systems but also because of our set of experiences. You have different experiences and I would like to hear about those from you.

2.3 Pricing an Application

- **Function Point Analysis**
- **Time and Materials**
- **Fixed Price**
- **The Solution**
- **Finding Function Points**

    What's Wrong With FPA?

- **Our Alternative - Action Point Counting**

    How It Works
    What is a "Thing?"
    Forms
    Reports
    Processes
    What About Other "Things?"
    How Do You Arrive at the Weights?
    The Final Tally

- **Developing The Cost Per Action Point**

    Tracking Hours
    Charting Action Point by Developer
    Determining the Cost Per Action Point
    Handling Variances in Developer Productivity

- **Additional Benefits to Action Point Counting**
- **Don't Forget Overhead**
- **Where To Go From Here**
- **Let's Try One!**
- **The Cost Is Not The Price!**

Pricing an application is probably the single biggest mystery in the computing world, well, next to what's going to really happen on January 2, 2000.

How do most developers estimate the price of an application? Let's look at a few of the most common ways. The most immediate is the "SWAG" - Simple Wild-Ass Guess. Then there's the simple "eyeballing" technique, where the developer simply looks over the information provided and a few minutes later, after eyeballing the ceiling with a knowing gaze, announces a price. Wise developers (those who have been burned on estimates a number of times before) take this approach one step further by applying a mathematical formula to their estimates. They'll make their initial guess, double the numeric value they arrived at, then bump up the unit of measure to the next one. This way, an initial estimate of four hours becomes eight days.

If these methods are felt lacking, the developer may actually walk through the proposed application, taking notes, evaluating what needs to be done in each module or function, and try to estimate to a tight degree what amount of time is going to be required. The number of hours is multiplied by the developer's rate per hour, an extra amount is tacked on, due to any number of random factors, and the price is determined.

The ultimate step in sophistication is to attempt some sort of rational approach toward estimating. For example, the developer might count the number of screens, reports and other functions, multiply each count by a magic number, and arrive at a price. If a specification has been provided, an alternative to this is to count the number of pages in the spec and multiply that by a "magic number" to get to the final price.

Obviously, these all fall short of the goal since, bottom line, they're all just guesses. None of them use any methodical mechanism for determining the end result, and thus the end result is not reproducible. This means that the same application could end up with three different prices on three different days. Which one is correct? Is the developer at risk of losing money on one or more of these prices? The point is - no one knows!

The more you think about this, the more ridiculous it becomes to provide a fixed price on something if you don't know how much it's going to cost or not knowing what types of unexpected things might happen. Kind of like saying "I'll dig a hole in your backyard for $100." If you've never dug a hole before, or if you've just dug really tiny ones, you don't know how long it will take you to dig this one. And if you didn't do your research to make sure there isn't a LUST or a Really Big Rock or a subway tunnel down there, you could be in for a world of hurt...

We have developed a technique that we use for determining the cost of a custom database application, and have been using this method for a couple of years with extremely good results. By "good results" I mean that we haven't ever lost money on an application priced with this method.

Before I discuss our method, I should explain where it came from.

Function Point Analysis

There is a technique for determining the size (and thus, cost) of software projects called Function Point Analysis ("FPA"). Developed at IBM in the late 1970's in order to solve this problem - especially across languages, platforms and applications - it is a method of sizing software from the end-user (i.e. customer) perspective. It can be used to measure any type of software project, not just a specific subset.

I first learned about FPA from presentations made by Bob Kehoe and Ken Florian of RDI Software Technologies in Chicago. Following is a synopsis of what I've learned about FPA. If you ever get a chance to hear anyone from RDI talk about any topic related to software engineering, don't miss it!

By way of introduction to Function Point Analysis, let's look at two traditional methods of pricing software development.

Time and Materials

What's the problem with time and materials? The customer absorbs the risk. The unit of measure is an hour of the developer's time, and the customer becomes hostage to how competent the developer is. The developer will provide an estimate and try to stay within the estimate, but the customer is subject to the developer having to actually spend the time. The customer bears all the risk in terms of how competent the developer is and what they can produce and whether they actually produce it. We can have no end to the problems with this method. An experienced developer may just screw up the estimate, intentionally underestimate in order to win the job, or be unable to control a client gone wild with feature creep. An inexperienced developer may underestimate due to inexperience, or may also be unable to control a client's changes made during the project. A firm may create a good estimate, but then be unable to assign the intended or right people to the job. At any rate, the bottom line is that the customer bears all the risk.

Fixed Price

The other option is for the developer to quote a fixed price for a project. We've discussed the ways that developers estimate projects - if those estimates are fixed prices, the developer either then shoulders an unnecessary set of risks or subjects the client to an unreasonably large contingency fee within the estimate in order to obviate any possible risk.

What types of risks could the developer shoulder with a fixed price? The most obvious is that they guessed wrong - and that they're going to be forced to spend a significantly larger amount of time on the application than the price would warrant. While it doesn't appear that the customer loses from this aspect, they do indeed - two different ways. The first is the developer, facing an overwhelming loss on the project, may simply bail and leave the customer holding the bag. The second is that the developer will finish the job, but with such ill-will that the customer will be forced to find a new developer for any follow up work.

Another type of risk that the developer faces is that of "feature creep." No matter how good the specification is, the client will always find one more feature they "absolutely positively must" have, and will be reluctant to pay for it. Cagey clients will play this game to hilt, in order to maximize the amount of "stuff" they get for their dollar. Furthermore, as the size of the project grows, it's more and more difficult for a client to read, comprehend and remember the spec, so they're more and more liable to just assume "it's in there somewhere." Alternatively, they'll insist that, despite the feature or function not being written down, "don't you remember that we talked about that at our last meeting?" The developer may agree to provide additional functionality or provide things for free in hopes of winning additional business. Finally, the fixed price contract can initiate an antagonistic relationship, because the developer has an incentive to do as little as possible for the fixed price, while the customer will normally try to "get as much as possible" for the same amount.

The Solution

Obviously, these methods don't work. One puts the risk on the customers shoulder, one puts the risk on the developers shoulders. There's got to be a better way.

Despite what some other companies will have you believe, IBM is the largest software company in the world. In the late 70's they were having great difficulty, as was everyone else, trying to get a handle on how big software is. Their initial problem was that they were writing software for most every platform that man had ever conceived of, and it was getting rather difficult to continue to do so. In order to get a better handle on their software development efforts, they developed a methodology called "Function Point Analysis" which provided a method to size software across languages and applications.

It is a synthetic measurement, meaning it is not specific to a single language or family of languages. Thus, an application written in COBOL could be compared, using its function point count, to a completely different system written in C++. Much like the measure of "Square Feet" can be used to compare a doghouse, a beach front condo, and an office building, an accounting module written in RPG for use on a System/32 (yes, I'm showing my age, remembering a machine like that) could be compared to a process control system written in assembler for an injection molding machine. Unlike most attempts at measuring software, such as lines of code, function points gave an independent yardstick of size, and thus, cost and time requirements. So when we say one system is 500 function points, another is 800 function points, we don't have to know what language they are written in, what platform it's running on, we just know that the one is about 1.5 times the size of the other. Therefore, obviously should take about 1.5 times longer and cost 1.5 times as much to develop.

Finding Function Points

A function point is a unit of functionality delivered to the end user. How do we find function points? Well, the point of this chapter is not to go into great detail on function points, but simply some background on what function points are because we are going to take this concept and twist and bend it and mush it until it's barely recognizable. Essentially, in order to arrive at the number of function points in a system, one counts the number of inputs, the number of outputs, number of inquiries, the number of internal and external logical files as well as evaluating approximately a dozen general system characteristics to determine the overall system complexity. General system characteristics (GSC's) are things like data communications, distributed processing performance, heavy use configuration transaction rates, on-line data entry designed for end user efficiency, on-line updates, complex processing, installation ease, operational ease, and multiple sites.

After we have finished counting, we mash the counts through a formula, and end up with a final number of function points. How is that translated into dollars? Here's the "Oh no!" part of this explanation. Just as with anything else that you're going to project, you need some history first! In other words, a historical baseline of costs for projects is used to determine the costs for future projects. If a project in the past had 300 function points and cost $300,000, then the cost per function point is $1000. Of course, there are a number of factors that tie into the cost per function point. Just because an application has a certain number of function points doesn't mean that the application will cost the same to build regardless of the language and other factors.

You can think of this as similar to the square foot measurement. We can compare two structures with similar numbers of square feet, but if one is to be built over a hilly swamp with marble floors while the other is to built on level ground with pine floors, the costs per square foot are going to be different. Similarly, to be able to do some sort of screen design in a tool like C++ may take a fairly long time because it's a low level language - and it might actually take even longer to do it in something like assembler - whereas if you were using a language like Visual Basic, it would be very easy - and fast - to put that screen together. So you also have a multiplier based on the tool you are going to use. But, again, that is strictly to determine the cost. The number of function points in a system are the same regardless of what tool you are going to use to build it.

So now we have a number of function points, we have a cost per function point that depends on our history as well as the type of the tool we are going to use to build it, viola! we have a cost!

Now the "most excellent" thing about function point analysis is that this provides a mechanism to price the work according to what the end user sees - what they are buying - functionality! If they decide to add four more screens, we simply recount the function points, run it through the formula and this is the new price. Just as if you were going through the line at the grocery store and said "Hey, I need two dozen more eggs!" You put those in your basket, you count those along with whatever else you bought, and you have a new final price. The user has the determination of what they are going to buy. If the ultimate price is so much more than what they are prepared to spend, then let's take some stuff out of the grocery basket. Well, I guess we don't actually need this second box of Captain Crunch Crunchberries, do we? So the user has control over the price because they control how much stuff they are going to buy.

There is a published standard for Function Point counting, and there are a number of companies that do Function Point Analysis consulting and will provide an independent count of function points in an application. Thus, it isn't a matter of the client having to take the developer's word "Uh, yeah, there are 1156 function points in there somewhere, but you wouldn't understand the formula, so you'll just have to believe me."

The customer and the developer can hire separate organizations to do counts and measure and come up with numbers - if the final results vary (it's a science, but it's not an *exact* science!), generally the contract between the client and the developer has a mechanism for resolution.

What's Wrong with FPA?

So why don't we use Function Point Analysis at my shop? Because, in the immortal words of Andy Griebel, "That would be too hard." FPA is a complex methodology - RDI Software is a multi-million dollar development shop - and IBM is even larger. If you're writing $10,000, $25,000 and $50,000 applications, FPA is most likely to be overkill. If, on the other hand, you're involved in a 4 man-year project that's going to span 2,000 users and three continents, then our method is probably not going to be robust enough. (Of course, if you have no methodology in place, then our method is absolutely better than that!)

Section 2.3 Pricing an Application

Simply stated, Function Point Analysis isn't going to do you much good for a project that's going to take six weeks, but you need some sort of method to price it - because a six week application that ends up taking four months could put you under the table - forever. While FPA works well for a project of at least a certain size, we're not in that league (yet!)

Our Alternative: Action Point Counting

What I've done is taken the ideas out of Function Point Analysis and modified them to suit my company's needs as a smaller developer. What do I call this? I've jokingly called it "Function Point Lite" in the past but I don't actually want to call it that because I don't want the Function Point people or Miller Brewing to get mad at me. So I've been calling them Action Points because it's rooted in the same basic concept but the implementation and process differ.

How It Works

First, we assume that we have a rigorous specification - remember the trial and agony we went through in Chapter 2.2 to create one? The specification has to spell out exactly what the system is going to do, the rules that must be followed, and the components in each screen, process and report.

We go through the specification, and count the number of "things" on each screen, in each report, and in each process. I'll get to specific details on what constitutes a "thing" later, but for now, just take it on faith that a "thing" is one of those technical concepts that your spouse and kids wouldn't understand.

Let's look at an example. This form, written in the world's greatest development tool (sorry, couldn't resist), looks like it has five "things" on it - two labels, a command button, a check box, and a list box. Also, unbeknownst to us casual observers, but obvious to anyone who has taken the time to read the spec, there are two validation rules and one form-level rule attached to this form as well. The validation rules belong to the check box and the list box, and the form-level rule is fired when the My Button is pushed or when the form is closed.

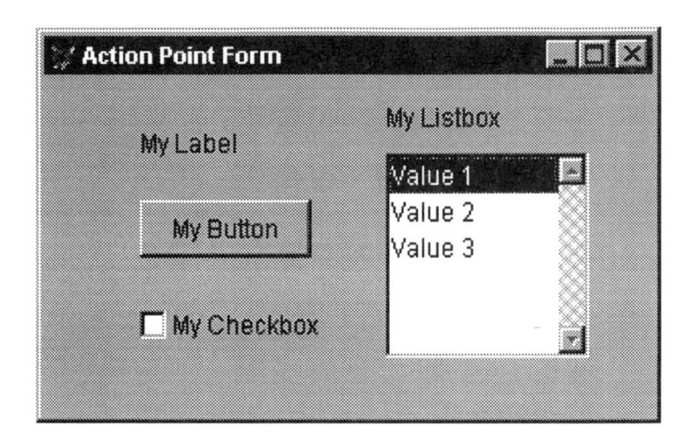

So we end up with a count of things like so:

Form Name	# Label	# Button	# Check Box	# List Box	# Valid Rule	# Form Rule
Form A	2	1	1	1	2	1

Form A has 2 labels, 1 button, 1 check box, 1 list box, 2 validation rules (you can't see them on the screen, but I know they're there - behind the check box and the list box), and one form level rule - which is attached to the button.

We also weight each type of "thing" to account for the level of complexity. So the above counts then get multiplied by factors, like so:

Form Name	# Label	# Button	# Check Box	# List Box	# Valid Rule	# Form Rule
Form A	2*1	1*2	1*2	1*4	2*6	1*10

A label has a weight of 1, buttons and check boxes both have a weight of 2, a list box has a weight of 4, a validation rule is weighted at 6, and a form level rule has a weight of 10. We multiple the number of objects by the weight of those objects to arrive at a total number of "Action Points."

The form also receives a weighting itself, according to the type of form it is. Types of forms may include simple maintenance forms, minor entity quick add forms, complex data entry forms, and picklists. Each of these has a different weight. In our example, we've assigned a weight of 0.1 because it's a pretty stupid form. We then multiply the counts times the factors and sum the results, multiply that subtotal by the form weight, and come up with a value for the form itself.

Form Name	# Lbl	# Btn	# ChkBox	# LstBox	# Valid Rule	# Form Rule	Form Type	Form Weight	Action Points
Form A	2*1	1*2	1*2	1*4	2*6	1*10	Simple	0.1	3.2

The number of Action Points is multiplied by the weight of the form, and we arrive at a total value for the form.

We run through this process, in more detail, of course, for every screen, report, and process in the application, resulting in a total number of action points for the application.

The next step is to multiply the number of action points in the system by the cost per action point, and arrive at a total cost.

What is a "Thing?"

Okay, you've been patient long enough. Let's get into more detail about these "things." Those of you with good memories or small children already know that a "Thing" is a little furry biped of indeterminate sex and age whose main function is to make even a bigger mess than The Cat in the Hat. But we can get more specific.

Forms

A form is any type of user interface that is displayed on the computer's monitor.

The types of "things" that can show up on a form vary according to the capabilities of the development tool you're using. We've already shown what a basic form looks like and how a few typical types of "things" would be counted and weighted. Let's get into a bit more detail about the types of things on a form and how they might be weighted.

The 'dumb' things, such as labels, images, and other 'view only' types of things have a minimal weight, because once they're placed on the form (and they're spelled right or their size is scaled correctly), there isn't much to do, and not much can go wrong. Note that if there is some odd requirement to have an action fired from clicking on a label or an image, or to have the text of the label or the image displayed change according to some other event, then those would be considered either validation or form level rules.

The next group of things that can be put on a form include text boxes, edit boxes, option groups (radio buttons to some of you), check boxes, and so on. The similarity between each of these is that there is probably a relationship to a field in a table, and so some work is going to have be done in order to make sure that relationship works and is sound, but this isn't usually difficult work.

The third group of things that can be put on a form include complex types of objects that list boxes, drop down combo boxes, grids, spinners, and so on. There may not be rules attached to things like these, but simply populating them requires more work than just a simple check box, for example.

Now that we've finished with the visual types of things that belong on a form, let's turn to the magic - the code underlying the objects that the user doesn't see, but feels the effects of anyway. This code generally takes one of two forms - a validation rule that is tied specifically to a single object, and a form level rule that spans multiple objects.

Once done with all of the things in and under the form, we then evaluate the form as a whole - how complex is it. We've generally broken down forms into five or six basic types, instead of trying to get too specific for every imaginable type of form, and then weighted each type. We also have an "adjustments" column that can be used to add or subtract action points from the form as a whole, in order to account for those situations where the counts, weights and form factors don't tell the whole story.

Finally, we have a multiplier column for the form as a whole. Multipliers that affect the entire screen - as opposed to simply adding a few action points to the form - are based on factors like the number of layers on the menu, the complexity of the user security required by the form, whether or not the user provides test data (or we have to create our own test data set for the form), the number of platforms the form will display on (a screen that has to run in DOS, in Windows 3.1, Windows95, and on a Mac will be considerably more of a pain than if it's a simple one platform screen), and, of course, in this day and age, the number of operating systems (which is slightly different than just platforms).

Reports

A report is any type of output requested by the user. The output may take the form a printed piece of paper, but may also be displayed to the screen, or result in a file created on disk or transmitted to another computer. As we go through the various "things" that can be put on a report, it may help you to visualize a printed report.

The first type of thing, like found on a form, is a dumb object, like a label or a box or a shaded background. Generally, these will be simple, but occasionally you'll find a rule that needs to be attached to one, like if the background should be shaded only if the percentage if over 10%.

The second type of thing is straightforward output - a field. This does not include calculated fields or rules that results in specific output (like the shaded background). The reason we differentiate like so is that for the most part, we create a cursor that contains a denormalized table with all of the data required, grouped and sorted as desired, on the report. Thus, placing each of these fields on a report is a simple matter. If the nature of the report is such that additional work needs to be done, like calculated fields or special rules, we count those separately.

The third type of thing is the aforementioned calculated field or rule.

The fourth type of thing is the actual number of groups required in the report. The reason this is counted is that not only do we normally have to place fields in special positions, but we also have to remember to mark calculated fields such as subtotals as grouped instead of simply totaled.

We use a third party reporting tool in our applications that requires a special type of set up, and so we also include a place to count the number of things we have to set up with this tool.

Processes

A process is an operation that runs without user intervention, and thus does not require an interface. Note that some processes may require a form in order for the user to provide parameters to control the direction of the process, but once initiated, the process generally needs no further interaction.

Processes are tricky - they kind of seem like one of those "none of the above" types of categories. We're still working on making the counting of the action points in a process more accurate, but at this point, we've got a stake in the ground.

So far, we've decided that processes can generally be broken down into the following operations:

- Match two records in different tables. For example, when importing a list of parts, match the incoming part record with the existing part, using part number as the key.
- Do a lookup. For example, when importing a hospital transaction, look for the diagnosis code in the diagnosis table.
- Make an assign. Assign the value of one variable to another for the purposes of stuffing the new value into a table (either overwriting an existing record or creating a new record.)
- Insert a new record. When doing an import or a posting, for example, adding a new record to an existing table.
- Create a new file. For example, creating a temporary file for intermediate processing.
- Delete a file. For example, deleting that temporary file that you just recently created.
- Write an exception. We typically write a record to an exception file when encountering an instance of data that shouldn't be there. For

example, when importing a file, we write an exception if a foreign key field is empty.

- Set a flag. In many processing routines, flags are set for a variety of reasons.

Does this cover the entire gamut of possibilities in processes? Probably not. But it hits a lot of the things that are routinely done, and so gets us a lot closer to sizing a processing module than simply saying, "Well, ya know, Ed, I think that's about a three day job."

You may also be wondering how to count each of these "things" without actually going in and writing the code itself. Well, in order to accurately describe the process in the functional specification so that there is no confusion about what will and will not be done, we need to be pretty detailed about the operations that will occur. For example, we need to describe if exceptions will be written, if a new record will be created and which fields will be put in that record, and so on. So, for the most part, these types of "things" have proven to be worthwhile and obtainable.

What About Other "Things"?

You're probably asking now, "How do you handle the myriad of things in an application that don't fall into the three categories listed above?" For example, what if an application had a toolbar? Are the buttons on a toolbar the same as a button on a form? What about rules that are embedded in a data dictionary? What about triggers? What if you have to be able to deploy across multiple platforms? How about if the application has to use multiple menus according to who is using the system?

And let's not forget about functionality that has to be included with every application, like data maintenance routines, help files, security, user preferences, and so on. Where are these included in the cost?

Well, first of all, we can't tell you everything in the first book, can we? Otherwise you'd never buy the sequel or see the movie, right?

Actually, there's a better answer. We have taken a concept - counting, weighting, factoring and summing the things in an application - and applied it to our way of developing custom software. We have a style and a philosophy of developing database applications that rely on our common libraries, the use of certain third party tools, and tailor our action point counting with those habits in mind. We also use specific tools with certain capabilities.

Since you may develop using different tools, and you're undoubtedly using a different application framework than ours, you'll need to modify the technique outlined here - add different types of things, include the capability to count depending on your style of application development, and so on - to suit your needs.

How Do You Arrive at the Weights?

Obviously, one of the key parts of this methodology is the weights used for each type of "thing." Okay, I'll admit it - we don't have a scientific algorithm for determining that a label has a weight of 1 while a check box has a weight of 2 and a list box has a weight of 5. Yes, we guess! Well, what I mean is that we don't have a dweeb in a white lab coat, Clark Kent glasses and a stopwatch timing each developer in order to see how long it takes to put a check box on a form versus a combo box. Let's be a bit realistic - where in the world would you find someone who is so desperate for a job that they'd actually agree to doing this?

Instead, we've just looked at the way we go about putting together forms, and kind of estimated the approximate differences between one type of object and another. Is it exact? No. Is it good enough for our purposes so far? Yes.

Can we have your weights? Nope. You will have to come up with your own set of weightings, based on your style of developing and your skill level with the language. An expert developer may have a smaller range of weights across multiple controls because they've got a number of automated tools that help build forms as well as understanding the tricks and traps of using specific controls, while a not-so-experienced developer may need a higher weight for controls that are more complex.

As a final analogy, if you were to learn to do the long jump, you could watch other long jumpers and pick up on their techniques, and you could emulate certain things they do, but it wouldn't do you any good to try to copy their steps, because each person is different, and their steps are suited for them - with their stride length, leg strength, speed, and tendon snap. Unless your physical attributes were identical, copying their steps enroute to the long jump pit would end in less than an optimal jump.

The Final Tally

Now that we've got all of these action point counts for the various forms, reports, processes, and other types of things, we need to look at what the Function Point Analysis people call "General System Characteristics."

If you're going to be putting this application on a simple four node Novell LAN, it's going to be a lot easier than if you need to span three continents, deploy on notebooks, and have a hookup to the EvilAlienOS that ran the intruder's spaceship in the movie Independence Day. (Don't laugh. It could happen...)

So there needs to be one final multiplier for the entire application, based on its relationship to the rest of the company's environment.

Determining The Cost Per Action Point

The next question - now that we know "how many things" (Action Points) are in the application - is how is much this going to cost? The answer is rather unpleasant for many people, because it requires a piece of information that they don't have - their history. Software developers, as an industry, are remarkably immature in this respect, in that we really don't have any idea of what our historical costs have been. I can think of a dozen good-sized MIS shops that do not collect any type of data on how long it took to develop applications in-house. These are the same companies that have an army of the green-eyeshade folk counting every penny that goes into the particular brand of widget or thingamabob that the company manufactures. And at the end of the year, the VP of MIS throws up his hands and wonders why all these software projects are over budget and late. Why? I'll tell you why - because their estimating techniques are all built on quicksand - the quicksand of having no historical records of what they did yesterday.

Tracking Hours

You must track your costs - the amount of time it took to develop projects in the past - if you are to have any hope of assigning a time value on an action point. We've been fortunate in that, before we had any inkling of what I would do with the data, we've kept detailed records on the time we spent on various components of each project we've done over the past three years or so.

As a result, when we came up with this idea of counting action points, we were able to get realistic values from the work we had done in the past. We took about a dozen applications, totaling about 4000 hours of work, and counted the action points in each one. We then correlated the actual amount of time spent (not the time we estimated or quoted at the time!) to the number of action points, and came out with some rough multipliers.

Charting Action Points by Developer

Note that the multipliers also related to the developer who worked on the project - and if more than one developer worked on the same project, we tracked the Action Points delivered by each developer separately.

We ended up with a chart that looked like this (numbers shown are totals for each developer across multiple applications):

Developer	Hours	Action Pts	AP/Hr	Rate/Hr
A	1000	2900	2.9	$17
B	1800	3000	1.6	$10

```
        C         2400               9100     3.4      $21
```

Given that Developer B is the least productive - whether that be due to experience or skill level - their rate per hour is pegged at an initial number that is used as the baseline for determining the hourly rates for the other developers. If their performance of 1.6 Action Points per hour corresponds to, say, $10 an hour (yes, I'm just making up numbers here), then the developer who can product 3.2 Action Points per hour should be charged out at $20 an hour. In practice, the disparity between production rates is higher, but you get the idea.

By the way, we also took these multipliers and went back to each individual project - the variance in most of the projects was within a close enough range, taking into account the skill level of the developer improving and so on, so that we felt the numbers were reasonable enough to use.

Determining the Cost per Action Point

From these numbers, we now know that an Action Point costs about $6.60 (another made up number.) We just took the base hourly rate and divided it by the number of Action Points that a base developer could produce. Since the hourly rates of the other developers are relative to the base hourly rate and their Action Point multiple, the cost per Action Point is the same regardless.

Handling Variances in Developer Productivity

You might be asking right about now "So, Whil, you're saying that if a screen has 50 Action Points, and you've got a multiplier of 1.5 hours per Action Point, it should take 75 hours? But doesn't this depend on the developer as well?"

Well, there's a bit of a jump in this question. Remember that each developer has a different productivity measure - a skilled developer should be able to do this screen in less time than a rookie developer because they can crank out more Action Points per hour. Note, however, that this skilled developer is also more expensive, right? So their cost - their compensation - would be higher per unit of time. So the cost of the screen is the same - whether you've got a highly skilled developer at $200/hour or a rookie developer who can only crank out a quarter of the Action Points of the skilled developer, but charges out at $50/hour. In fact, since the goal is to determine the cost for the action point, this works out perfectly.

Additional Benefits to Action Point Counting

There's more, though, so don't stop reading yet! As you are undoubtedly aware, a highly skilled developer can easily be ten times as productive as an ordinary developer, right? In fact, to say that an extremely skilled developer could be 20 times more productive than a hack isn't a stretch, isn't it? But even the most awful hack (and we have some of them in our business, don't we?) can get away with charging, oh, $40 or $50 an hour. How many highly skilled developers do you know who are charging 20 times $40 an hour - yes, $800/hour? Well, I can't count more than two or three dozen myself.

But using Action Point Counting, we can take advantage of the high productivity of a skilled developer and charge appropriately.

The second benefit is scheduling. Since we have the number of Action Points for an application and the productivity of a developer in terms of Action Points per hour, it's easy to determine how much time a given developer will need to complete that application.

Don't Forget Overhead

Through our historical records, we have determined how long it took a developer to write an application, and we know the cost of that developer - their wages.

We also know how much we spend on running the firm - rent, non-billable personnel, magazine subscriptions, goofy screensavers, and so on. The difference between the billable rate and the wages of the developer need to support that amount we spend on running the firm. If it doesn't - what do you do? You need to find extra revenues to pay those bills.

The first possibility is to raise the billable rates of the developers so that the numbers come into line. The other possibility is to raise revenues by charging more than the cost of the application represented by the direct labor (the developers.)

Manufacturers have been doing this for two hundred years - including the cost of running the firm - overhead (some firms refer to it as "burden") - as part of the price. Remember, we're producing a product - a widget - and good old cost accounting requires that you include both fixed and variable costs. As your firm gets bigger, you'll need to include things like brand new Pentium Pros (won't that reference seem dated in a year or so!), subscriptions to Dr. Dobbs, Software Development, and Object mag, a fancy phone system with voice mail instead of a $19 answering machine, administrative support and all that free pop.

Where To Go From Here

Is this all too much to do in one step? Probably. If it's all new to you, the first thing to do give this "Action Point Counting" a whirl on a few apps, just to determine the raw size of the systems. The numbers you come up with aren't that important - it doesn't matter if your app is 200 Action Points and someone else's is 380. What matters is that you can compare the relative sizes of the various projects you've done, look at the actual time you spent producing them, and then get an idea of the dollars involved.

From this, you can try to price an application - or even just a single screen or report - based on the hard data you've got, instead of yet another SWAG.

Worry about the sophisticated cost accounting once you've got the basics down first.

Let's Try One!

Okay, so this has been a great discussion in a theoretical sense. But what happens in real-life, when the customer has signed off on the app, and a developer starts working on it? The developer is compensated based on the amount of billable work they do, and the company is going to bring in a fixed amount of funds, regardless of how long it takes for the developer to do the work. How does this scenario play, depending on whether the developer is skilled or relatively new?

Suppose we charge $100 per action point. Thus, the screen with 50 action points is worth $5000. A highly skilled developer may only need 25 hours to do it, resulting in a rate per hour of $200, while a rookie developer may need 125 hours, resulting in a rate per hour of $40. As the rookie developer gains skill, they can produce more billable dollars per unit of time, and both generate more revenue for the firm and earn more compensation for themselves. The highly skilled developer also realizes a higher compensation, although it may not be exactly proportional to their hourly rate, due to having to factor in the company's fixed costs.

The customer pays the same for the specified functionality, regardless of who is doing the work. The highly skilled developer is able to earn significant income, because they are no longer tied to an artificial ceiling of "no one will pay more than $90/hour for a programmer in this market." And the company's costs are proportionally the same for producing the application - while the less experienced developer will take longer, they are compensated less as well. The total cost for that $5000 screen is the same whether the highly skilled or relatively new developer worked on it.

The Cost Is Not The Price!

I know I've said it before, but it is extremely important to stress that *this number is the cost, not the price!* We are determining how much it is going to cost us to build this project, not how much we are going to price it. There is a difference here. We want to make sure that our price to the customer is not lower than our cost. I know that I'm going against conventional wisdom but we can't make money on those kinds of projects - the kind where the cost to produce it is higher than the price paid by the customer - simply by doing a lot of them. We are not going to make it up in volume.

So how do you determine the value to the customer, and thus, how much you're going to price the application? Well, here is where the art comes in. You need to have a proper relationship with your customer so that you can determine, to the best extent possible, what the value is. If you've done your homework properly - found out what their pain is and what it's worth to them to ease that pain - you already know the answer.

Otherwise, it's the old "run this up the flagpole and see what happens..." avenue. Sorry, no magic formula or silver bullet here.

2.4 The Cover Letter

♦ The Cover Letter is a Separate Document

Format
Introduction
Project Components
Price
Price Escalation Terms
Delivery
Rules of the Road
Terms
Ask for the Order
Sign Off

The cover letter serves as the introduction to the functional specification. It is always a one page letter that summarizes "the deal." Why one page? Because there are only two things that the customer cares about when they're reading the cover letter - how much and when. They don't want to wade through twenty-three pages just to find out the price. Make it easy for them to get to the heart of the matter.

You, as the vendor, need to provide two more things - the terms and a place for them to agree to the deal. These fit on this same one page letter quite nicely.

Past this - shut the heck up! You have a big thick spec attached to the back of this letter to get into the details. Remember that this letter is a formality, not news, and so you want to make it simple for them to sign off and get going.

I feel pretty strongly about this, so let me say it here and then again later. They do not want to read through a big eighty page document to find out how much it's going to cost. Make it easy. They're going to find out anyway, and if they feel like you've hidden the price from them, they're going to be mad. They should already know because you've been working with them during the development of the spec, sounding them out about where their price points lie. Still, they're going to kind of like to make sure you didn't pull a fast one and add another $8,000 on it.

The Cover Letter is a Separate Document

The cover letter is always a separate document to which the functional spec (and anything, if need be) is attached. Why? Because the cover letter is the only place where actual money is described.

This way, you can keep the financial arrangements separate from the rest of the application. Virtually no one except the person cutting the check cares how much the app is going to cost (or, rather, no one needs to know). By keeping the cover letter apart from the rest of the spec, the recipient of the spec can send copies of everything except the dollars to others in the organization for their review, input, or reference.

Furthermore, your customer may end up sending copies of this spec to other developers for competitive bids. Again, the competition doesn't have to know, and shouldn't know, what your pricing is. Of course, you'd probably rather they do not shop the proposal around, but this way, you've made it easy for them to do so with a minimum of fuss. If you've got dollars buried in the middle of the spec somewhere, or, worse, scattered throughout the spec, it's going to be difficult or impossible for them to distribute copies of the spec to others without also showing your bid. If it's difficult, they'll end up making a mistake and your deepest, darkest secrets are laid wide open for the competition. Isn't that information you'd rather keep confidential?

Format

I'm old-fashioned, very conservative, and I want our image to reflect this bent. I want it to look like we've been around for 100 years. We do enough "far out" things (seen our web site yet?) that being solid and conservative is appropriate for the foundation. We need to give people a subtle level of comfort.

That's why we make all of our printed literature - business cards, brochures, flyers, and so on - look very conservative. The message we deliver may be radical, but the clues that the message is coming from a reliable, fundamentally solid firm also show. Some people may argue that that's a mixed metaphor and that we don't know what we're doing. Argue away. Marketing is not exact. I prefer to think of it along the lines of that we are providing somebody with a conservative business foundation yet, where it counts, we will be creative. The customer gets the best of both worlds.

```
April 1, 1997

Michael Austin-Thor
The Very Large Manufacturing Company
The Very Large Office Building
Milwaukee WI 53202-4104

Dear Mike,
```

Introduction

As soon as I got out of school, I worked for a company where the department I was in was to deliver proposals to customers for highly technical kinds of equipment configurations. The first line always read "We are pleased to present this proposal" and you are! What else are you going to say? You have to have some kind of lead in and this lead in is really kind of nice and classic and comfortable. You've also already given the thing a name in the first sentence so that you can refer to that from now on.

```
We are pleased to present this quote for the Time and
Billing Entry and Tracking (TABET) System.
```

Project Components

Next, we explain that we're providing an attachment to this letter. Normally, it's the specification, but if you need to vary the thing you're attaching, you can say that right here. Then we describe what the functional spec is. Again, what you're doing is repeating to the customer what they already know, but you're putting it down in writing and you're saying it formally. Someone else might be reading this cover letter and they may never have heard of a functional spec before.

```
Attached is the Functional Specification for TABET. This
includes (1) the TABET main application, including the
foundation directory structure, login and user and group
permission maintenance, and the TABET functionality and (2)
the TABET Reports. This Specification contains discrete
descriptions of the functionality of each piece but each
description references the other when applicable.
```

Price

The next thing is right away, tell them how much it costs. People want to know how much it's going to cost.

```
The total for the entire application is <$amount>. As
requested, I've broken out the price and delivery for each
piece separately. The Reports module can be viewed as an
"add-on" to the main system, but can't be provided
independently.

Main Application             $
Reports                      $
```

I learned this from one of the first jobs I worked on. I had delivered a 20 page specification and proposal and the only thing the customer did was rip through those pages, looking to see how much it cost.

This is also the place to tell them how the project is broken out as far as required and optional segments go. Tell them how the system is configured - a main application and a number of smaller pieces, or a shell and multiple plug-ins, or whatever.

Note that these segments are not the same as the modules that you are going to deliver. These segments are the various "things" that the customer could buy. It is still possible to have an application be comprised of a single purchasable segment but yet be broken down into many deliverables scheduled on several distinct dates.

Section 2.4 The Cover Letter

Price Escalation Terms

This next section is one that you may have never seen before. We give the customer a discount if they sign off on the application within a given period of time.

```
If this quote is accepted within 15 days, the price is
subject to a 6% <$amount> discount, resulting in an early
acceptance price of <$amount>. We reserve the right to
requote price and delivery after 60 days.
```

Before you get too upset at "giving something away" it's important to understand the positioning of this offer. We had considered providing a price and then adding a "penalty" if they don't sign off within that period of time, but felt that was giving the customer a bad message. Instead, we want them to perceive that they're getting a deal for acting fast. However, we take our original price - the one that they would pay if they bought the next day, and add the discount amount to it. This new price is the price they see, together with the discount if they sign off quickly.

The next question is - why bother at all? Here's our reasoning. We have just lived in this application for a while - designing, discussing, documenting, and so on. Right now, we know it pretty well. It is part of our being. We could recite functionality and validation rules by heart.

If they have to go through 15 rounds of approval and end up sitting on the proposal for two and a half months, we're going to forget everything we know. It's going to take additional time to get back up to speed - and, well, hey, that additional time is going to cost us money.

Furthermore, we don't make cans of tomato soup, where one comes off the line every second and a half. Our business consists of great big projects and we need to be able to schedule people for them. We can't just have people sitting around waiting for a project to be approved. Thus, it's in our best interest to get that project moving and signed off. A little financial incentive helps focus the customer's attention on getting this proposal approved.

Does this bother the customer? It shouldn't. It's the job of the developer to help them along during the development of the specification so that they are ready to sign off as soon as possible after they get the final document. The cardinal rule throughout this whole process is, as Steven Tyler put it so well, "No surprises." The customer doesn't like surprises, you don't like surprises. They should know what to expect and if they don't, the developer has made a mistake. The spec is to just remind them of what they already know.

Delivery

Tell them when you can start work, and when they can expect to get their stuff. Given the Price Escalation Terms just discussed, you may assume the customer will ask why they have to pay an additional amount if they don't approve the proposal quickly enough, but that you're telling them that you can't begin work for another period of time after that. The simple answer is that this time frame is already figured into the price - the discount is to encourage them to get things rolling just that much quicker.

```
We can begin work on this project within <TimeFrame> weeks
of acceptance. The final system can be delivered
approximately <TimeFrame> working weeks later.
```

Rules of the Road

We need to make clear to the customer - right up front - that this fixed price proposal is a fixed price for the spec attached. However, it is normal during the course of application development for new requirements to be discovered and additional functionality needs to be requested and modifications to be needed in the spec. We will go through our standard change order process whereby modifications to this spec are provided to the customer in writing and the customer will have the opportunity to either accept or refuse such modifications. Those changes become a part of the application just as if they had been a part of the original spec.

We also employ a bit of salesmanship here by explaining that we have a methodology for quoting prices - not some "pull a number out of the air" trick. By itself, the customer may not care, but if they're going to send this proposal out to other firms for competitive bids, we've now just raised the ante. The customer is now prodded to wonder how the other firms create their quotes, and those companies are put on the hot seat, having to come up with some sort of explanation for their "wild-ass guess" technique.

```
This is a fixed price quotation for the functionality
described. Please read carefully and confirm that the
functionality described meets your requirements. It is
extremely important that every function and operation you
are expecting is listed here; this document supersedes all
verbal discussions - any modifications or changes requested
after acceptance will alter price and/or delivery and will
require written confirmation by both parties via the change
order process described in the appendices to the
specification.
```

```
Note that this is not an estimate but has been determined
using our Action Point Counting system. Many software
development companies use unreliable or seat-of-the-pants
techniques to produce a rough approximation that is then
bumped up by some arbitrary factor of safety to produce a
price. Our methodology requires an accurate specification of
functional capabilities for the system in question and
relies on statistical analysis of historical performance to
determine actual costs for each component of the system.
```

Terms

Finally, we cover the terms of how we expect to be paid. This goes on the cover letter because it's the document the customer signs, and thus commits to. We've discussed the issues of getting paid earlier, so there's no need to do so again. Just make sure you state your terms on the document they're going to sign.

On a personal level, what we're saying in our own cover letter is that we are going to invoice the customer after we ship a module, and that we expect to do so on a reasonably regular basis. Our goal is to invoice every two weeks for the modules that we shipped those two weeks. This philosophy has two benefits. First, we need to keep paying attention to delivering things and that the customer see progress. We may not always make a shipment every two weeks, but we try. The benefit is that the customer sees regular progress and they can start working with the app quickly. We don't deliver the whole app in one fell swoop. But rather, in parts, so they can learn it incrementally.

The other benefit is that it gets cash in the door faster. And that's a pretty clear benefit to everyone.

```
Payment terms consist of invoices rendered every two weeks
for the work completed to that point, payable 10 days after
presentation subject to a 1.5% discount. Work will be
stopped in the event an invoice becomes past due. For
specific information on how the work completed is broken
into discrete deliverable components, see the section on
Milestones at the end of the specification.
```

Ask for the Order

We've been through this with the engagement letter, but it doesn't hurt to remind you. Don't just assume they know what to do - tell them what they'll have to do to start the process, and then ask them to do it!

```
In order to accept this proposal, please sign one copy of
this letter and return it to me. I'm looking forward to
working with you and the rest of the crew at your firm on
this system. If you have any questions, please call me at
your convenience.
```

Sign Off

And again, as with the engagement letter, give them a place to sign the letter and return it to you in order to commit to starting the project.

2.5 Getting Paid

♦ Handling a Retainer

Retainers on Fixed Price Contracts

♦ Invoicing

Progress Payments
Payment Terms for Invoices

Just as nothing happens until someone sells something, all the work in the world isn't going to mean squat if you don't get paid for it.

There will always be those few who are going to either try to get something for nothing, or don't want to pay for their own mistakes. You need to watch your backside.

Furthermore, you need to get the cash coming in on a regular basis. Unlike some businesses where they'll never see a sale for a three digit amount, it is not uncommon for developers to send out invoices for five (and six) digit figures. Get your invoices sent out regularly - and promptly - and keep a careful watch on your receivables.

Let's look at some details.

Handling a Retainer

A retainer is an account that the customer sets up with you. They supply an amount of funds, and then, as they use your services, those funds are drawn down. When the retainer (the account) is either exhausted or getting low, additional funds are requested.

Some companies will arrange a retainer basis with you; others will not. Generally, large public companies don't have a mechanism for this type of relationship, but, on the other hand, you may feel much more confident that you will (eventually) get paid.

If you are working with a small company where all the power is in the hands of one guy and he has the power to say, "I decided I didn't want to pay for that spec after all because my spouse wants a new car", it's a little tougher to go after them.

Bringing in the lawyers is never an option in my book. You should never get strung out so far that you're in significant danger. (Yes, we've all done it anyway, but, each time, we promise it's going to be the last.) If you are out more than $5,000-$10,000 then something is wrong. You should be billing often enough that you get paid on a regular basis. If there are going to be problems, you can see them quickly and you limit your exposure. This way, you keep your exposure to a minimal amount - but it's not worth it to go after someone for $4,000. You spend so much time and money - you're simply not going to get back the money.

The investment of your time and money toward recovering that bad debt doesn't produce an admirable ROI. Instead, you should be writing software to make up for it because that's what you do well. The reason why you charge $100/hour is because you have to set aside some for losses for the guys who don't pay.

Section 2.5 Getting Paid

Retainers on Fixed Price Contracts

You can set up a retainer for a fixed price job as well. Since you know the total price, as well as the price of each module, you can request a retainer for the pieces about to be delivered, and have the retainer refreshed as new modules become ready.

It's good to be cautious about companies whose procedures are either lax or nonexistent. The guy you were working with suddenly isn't working there any longer - and the company is too small to have a PO system. End result - your invoice never quite got into the system because your contact was playing fast and loose and hadn't ever quite mentioned to anyone that this project was even underway.

Invoicing

The alternative to a retainer is simply invoicing the customer for an amount of work done. This work could be a simple list of hours, or it could be a pre-defined set of modules that have been delivered and accepted according to the test plans in the spec.

We've discussed the reasons for the way we go about invoicing during the Customer Setup Form section in Chapter 1.7 (Engagement Letter) but there are some additional points that are worth covering here.

Progress Payments

Even for relatively small jobs, some sort of progress payments are a good idea. Suppose you're doing the design of the functional specification - do not wait until the delivery of the specification to invoice for work performed unless you can comfortably afford to wait for the entire amount.

Suppose you are a smaller shop and this spec is one of the only projects you're working on. You can't afford to get 2/3rds of the way through the spec and then have a set of unforeseen delays and interruptions cause the last bit of the project drag out interminably. It's a big danger.

Suppose you are working on this project for a healthy percent of your billable time. You start June 1 and suddenly you've got 70 hours into the spec. It's now July 1, and half of your billable work for the month is on this one project. But you haven't gotten paid yet because you haven't invoiced - you'll send an invoice as soon as you deliver the spec - it's almost done, after all. One more meeting, a few questions, and you're done!

Well, what comes after July 1st? The Fourth of July weekend. Now it's the 8th, the 9th, the 10th. You are finally able to touch base on the 11th, but your contact is going out of town for a couple of days - they'll call when they return. Now it's July 17th. They're busy from being gone - and then the other person involved is out of town for a week and a half on vacation. Now it's August and you have over 70 hours of work that you haven't been paid for.

Your meeting on August 5th gets postponed to the 9th, and goes well. Then your contact is on vacation - so the project is on hold again - until the 20th. One last meeting, wrap things up - but it's now after Labor Day - and you've been sitting on two solid weeks of billable time for more than two months. Sure, you'll get paid - but this type of scenario causes havoc with cash flow. Don't let it happen.

Payment Terms for Invoices

Don't assume they will pay invoices. You tell them when you submit invoices. We submit them every two weeks. Tell them what you submit invoices for; all billable work performed to that point in time. People will, once in a while, come up with the lamest of ideas: "Oh, no we never pay for the most immediate week of work." Make it clear that these are your terms and you expect them to be adhered to. If they choose not to, then you must pull back on your side of the contract as well.

There ought to be some sort of cookbook we can follow to figure out how to put a spec together so we can figure out how to write specs more efficiently and give a better price for them. Wouldn't it be nice to, say, have a set of questionnaires that you could just hand to the customer, say, "Fill these in!" and be done with it? Hey, maybe you could fax them to the customer, and then get the answers faxed back. And you wouldn't even have to talk to them.

I'm actually being half serious. If we could pull this off, we could get through a great deal of the mundane part of the design process, and then hook in with the customer at the time that a standardized questionnaire doesn't cover the ground in enough detail. I've fantasized about providing a more rigorous outline of "what to do" to my developers so that the firm wasn't as reliant on me to do all of the up-front design work. Eventually, we'll systematize this part of the application development cycle, and be able to do a better job from the very start.

Failing this, the best we can do is be prepared with what goes into a specification. This means having the necessary examples and groundwork laid out so we are prepared for each meeting with the customer. Be sure you've done what you said you were going to do, and have an agenda for the next meeting ready. You're the person guiding the design, and they're expecting to follow your lead.

Section 3: Manufacturing

Many people write applications like they drink beer - they drink one, and then they drink another. So when they write apps, they write some code, and then they write some more code.

There's more to the production of that final .EXE that gets sent out to the customer than simply typing text into an editor, dragging and dropping with a form designer, and then compiling the end result.

Why am I using the term "manufacturing" when referring to the process of creating software? I was brought up in an industrial type of world, and I'm comfortable with the lingo of the factory floor. It's comfortable and natural and I think it sounds cool. But enough of *my* idiosyncrasies.

The manufacturing paradigm also fits well with the way we've described the process up to this point. We started out on a sales call, we created a blueprint, we have a quote, and now we're going into production. We have a facility where we create our software, and during production, the folks working on the job will track their time and any other materials used in the creation of the widget so that we know what our actual costs have been.

Once the code has been produced, we'll test it in our QA department and then ship it. If at some point, the customer changes their mind (it *could* happen, you know), we'll write up a change order. After we install and the customer accepts the work, we'll invoice and, hopefully, get paid.

Well, enough chatting - let's put our work boots back on and start sweating!

3.1 - The Development Environment

- Where Do They Sit?
- Equipment
- Optimizing Your Developer's Environment
- Working On Site
- Administrative Duties
- Phone Free Zones
- Structuring the Firm to Make Money
- Communication
- Team Development Issues for a Small Shop

Much of the reason for the popularity of the Dilbert comic strip is because it's true. Yes, we see those things happening in companies all over. And while these events look absurd to us, they usually seem perfectly reasonable at the time to the people involved. People generally don't set out in the morning with the idea, "Hey, I'm gonna make a fool of myself today."

Nonetheless, a little common sense would go a long way at most companies - and development firms are no different. While I'm sure I've pulled my share of bone-headed stunts at the shop, I tend to spend an inordinate amount of time thinking about the environment that my people work in, and trying to make it better for them.

Before I go on, I must mention that many of my ideas have come from two sources.

RDI Software Technologies, based in Chicago, Illinois, is a custom software developer with approximately 75 people. Due to RDI's proximity and to the fact that I know a fair number of people there, I've been to their shop enough that I feel like I'm not getting an artificial view of what the shop is like. I've formed a lot of opinions about how a development environment should be organized by seeing how they do it. Doug Grimsted, Ken Florian and company do things right. I think most anybody would do well to emulate them.

The other source I have to acknowledge right away is a pair of books: *"Peopleware"* by Tom DeMarco and Tim Lister and *"Constantine on Peopleware"* by Larry Constantine. If you read only 10% of these two books, you'll be well ahead of most shops in the country.

The bottom line in software development can be summed up in one simple sentence. Treat people with respect and common sense and let them do their jobs. We'll talk more about that in the People chapter, but right now, part of this philosophy is relevant in how the environment that you and your developers work in. How is anyone going to do their best if their surroundings and tools are inadequate? We are trying to facilitate the developer's ability to do their work - develop software - and get all their roadblocks out of the way. What kinds of things could we do to the factory that would help them do their work better?

In this chapter, I examine a variety of ideas, in no particular order, that we've found helpful in improving the productivity of our "manufacturing personnel."

Where Do They Sit?

Just so you don't think this is a completely ridiculous question, I'll give you the short answer right away. They sit on chairs. In offices.

We let everybody choose their own desks and chairs. We give them a budget, but they can get what they want. One person wants a modular unit;

another wants a traditional desk and bookcase. Fine! People are different; why make them all conform to some impersonal standard - particularly when there isn't any specific reason to do so? The only rule we have is that they don't scrimp on chairs. They're typically going to be sitting there for 10 to 16 hours a day (OK, I'm just wishing here) I want to make sure they're comfortable. It's a no brainer to spend an extra $100 for a chair to make sure they're not walking around the office every day at 2:30 holding their back.

The other thing we do for every technical person is provide them with their own private office. These are software developers we're talking about - providing them peace and quiet so they can concentrate is an extremely good investment.

So now we've got a bunch of private offices with furniture that wasn't quite coordinated by the furniture police. Okay, maybe the office kind of looks like a bunch of college dorm rooms, but it becomes personalized. The office becomes home instead of their personal prison cell.

Each developer's office can be outfitted for between $500 and $1000 depending on the area of the country you're in. A remarkably small amount considering the money spent on computer hardware and software, compensation and other ancillary expenses.

Equipment

The technical infrastructure for the firm is critical - we're writing software, after all. It never ceases to amaze me to see how cheap some firms are. They have highly paid developers writing critical software applications and they try to scrimp and save a couple hundred bucks on a machine because the bean counters say so. The average investment for factory worker is well into six figures, but a firm will scrimp on the $3,000 or $4,000 machine that's all a software developer needs.

We have two practices that have served us well with respect to equipment. The first is that we always buy nearly as much machine as is possible at the time. Typically, this is one level below the current state of the art. When the best box available was a 486/66, we picked up 486/50s. When the best was a P100, we purchased P90s. We've found the performance difference between the very fastest and the next fastest isn't that significant compared to the premium being charged for the faster machine. Instead, we spend that money on supporting equipment such as additional memory, a bigger hard disk, or the newest version of MYST.

Some development shops argue that they don't want to get high-end machines for their programmers because their customers use tired, old machines and they have to make sure that their software will run on those machines. Well, in most development shops, old machines are not scarce - and this is why you should keep a couple of them around - for testing!

If you decide to keep your developer's hands tied by giving them low-end machines, an inadequate amount of RAM, and a poorly configured network, you're just costing yourself a ton of money. Every time a developer has to wait a minute and a half for a build instead of four seconds, it's going to cost you money. Since PC based software is done on an iterative basis -you may build a project 10, 20 or more times an hour. If each build takes 30 seconds instead of 5, that's five to ten minutes of dead time an hour.

But there's a second problem with pokey machines. Alan Schwartz said a long time ago that one of the keys in successful software development is to keep the span of the build cycle iteration shorter than your attention span. I'm sure you've made a change to a program, started the build, and by the time you were ready to test for the change, you'd forgotten what it was that you had changed.

If you invest in a reasonably high-end machine, your developers can iterate and not lose their train of thought. Given the natural state of offices, it's pretty easy for any kind of interruption to make their minds jump track - let's try to minimize those interruptions in any way possible.

Another good reason for investing in high-end boxes is that it shows that you care. Your typical software developer may not be that interested in Gucci loafers, Rolex watches, and flashy vacations - but they'll all crowd around in the office of the developer with the new dual Pentium Pro 280 with a 20 GB hard drive and a 27" monitor. High end machines are status symbols and provide tangible evidence that the boss cares about the staff. It emphasizes the importance of the staff by giving them the best tools available.

We try to outfit our machines with all the gizmos that a developer could reasonably use during the day. Lots of RAM - our current standard is 32 MB, and that's getting bumped to 64 MB sometime early in 1997. A 17" monitor goes without saying - developers have lots of things they need to see at the same time. They can still design their forms and run the application in a 640x480 window. Developers have better things to do than move windows around on the desktop.

The second habit of ours is the practice of, er, inheritance. The newest developer always gets the oldest machine. This way, the developers with the most seniority will receive an additional perk. This doesn't mean that the new developers are getting inadequate machines - when the situation comes up that the slowest machine in the office isn't sufficient for a developer, then additional machines will have to be purchased.

A network should be set up so they have as many resources on-line as possible. We have a knowledge base of CompuServe messages, TechNet and a number of other internally generated resources that are available to all developers. It's really not a big deal to set up a CD ROM caddy with several standard resources available all the time.

Optimizing The Developer's Environment

Depending on how network-savvy and how comfortable you are, you may decide to set up your network one of two ways. You may want to put everything on the server, set up a back-up server and pray. It takes more money, time and maintenance, but everything is centrally located.

We have opted for "Door Number 2." We give everybody large local hard disks and load them with all of the applications that they are going to use on a regular basis - the operating system, each development tool, a word processor, and so on. The server holds data - internal work as well as customer applications - and applications that are used on an occasional basis, such as Corel Draw, 400 Mb of clip art, a data repair utility, and an old (make that "ancient") version of a development tool that we need to keep around for one customer who calls once a year or so.

This gives us two advantages: 1) It is easy to configure and the applications can be customized per user and 2) If the server goes down, the developers aren't hung out to dry. A 2 Gb local drive is only a few hundred dollars, and by providing this tool, each developer still has access to the tools they use on a day-to-day basis. (Through the use of daily backups and incremental backups during the day, we always have a reasonably current copy of the work they're doing stored elsewhere.)

On the other hand, if everything is on the server and it goes down (and you haven't set up a backup server that is automatically kept current), the entire office has just been shut down.

The bottom line is to do whatever works for you - but you can't afford to be down - period. That's our philosophy.

When I got out of school, I worked for the largest robot manufacturer in the world. One of our hottest sellers was a spot welding robot - one of those big arms that hefts around a 300 pound spot-welding gun. The scene has been in every movie that has anything to do with Detroit - the steel gray automobile frames coming down the assembly line. A half-dozen of these robot arms on each side of the line would do their mechanical dance, the spot-weld pincers tacking pieces of steel together with yellow sparks flying around - you get the picture.

Spot welding is a really tough job - it's hot, the guns are very heavy and unwieldy, and it takes a certain amount of skill to do properly. Robots were an easy sell in this job. However, even robots go down - and, as Murphy's Law dictates, they usually fail when inside a car, holding onto the frame.

These robots are big, powerful machines - three to four tons, bolted the floor with anchors an inch thick - and so if the robot stops and the line keeps going, the robot is going to rip the car right off the line and cause quite a mess. As a result, when a robot fails, the line is automatically stopped at that instant.

That's a long introduction, but it was necessary to explain the next part.

One day, one of the robots goes down, and the line is stopped. If I hadn't made it clear before, as bad as ripping a car off the line is, it's only marginally worse than stopping the line itself. (If you're fuzzy on this "bad" thing, refer back to the first Ghostbusters movie.)

There are enough robots in this plant that the company that I worked for always had a technician on site in order to be able to quickly respond to machines that went down. The technician runs over there and within 45 seconds, he's got the robot computer control open, and is fiddling with the controls, trying to start the robot arm up so they can get the arm out of the car and get the line going again.

Suddenly the technician hears a "Whooosh!" sound behind him. He turns around and one of the maintenance men from the factory has just ignited a blow torch. "Get away from here. This is computer equipment. What are you doing here with that anyway?"

And the guy responds, "I'm going to cut the arm of that robot so we can get the line moving." The technician says, "What do you mean, you're not going to cut the arm off of this robot. This is a $100,000 machine! You can't do that!" He says, "We produce one car a minute and these cars are worth $10,000 each. If this line is stopped for ten minutes, we've lost $100,000 that we're never going to get back. So if you don't have that arm off of that robot in the next six minutes, I'm going to cut it off because it's going to be less expensive to cut that arm off than it would be to wait for you for another two minutes."

The moral of the story - think again about the cost of downtime.

Organizing the Server. We've found that organizing the server drive(s) according to customer works out quite well for us, and the reason I bring it up is that I'm continually amazed at the number of shops I see that have no rhyme or reason for their development project set up.

Each customer has their own root directory, and then each project for a customer resides under the customer's root directory. If we have information specific to the customer (documents or other non-project specific data), it is placed in a "OTHER" or "DOC" directory directly under the customer's root. In some cases, we've also set up a directory for customer-specific libraries that are used across multiple projects.

Under a specific project, we have a directory for project specific information, such as quotes, memos, documentation, and other non-technical data, called DOC. Sometimes we have another directory, called "OTHER", for "all that other stuff."

Each project also has directories for source, meta-data, and multiple data sets.

Organizing the Local Drives. On the local drive, we have separate directories for each operating system (usually we can get away with just one), as well as for each type of development tool. We do *not* accept the default choice of directory when installing new versions of our development tools. I feel pretty strongly about this, so let me explain why.

Suppose that we're developing in Visual Basic. We would have a directory called "VB" and under that, we'd have directories for each specific version - VB3, VB4, VB5, and so on. This hearkens back to the days when we were working with multiple versions of FoxPro so we'd have one for FoxPro 1.0, FoxPro 2.0, FoxPro 2.5 for DOS, FoxPro 2.5 for Windows, FoxPro 2.6 for DOS, and so on. We've seen cases where the directories were called "FOXPRO", "FOX", "FOXP", "FX", FOXPRO2", and it was pretty darn difficult to keep track of which version was installed where. We've even seen the situation where a program was installed several times with different parameters - and six months later, it was impossible to tell which one was which.

Furthermore, if you are involved with beta programs, it's a good idea to keep track of which build you're using. So when we install new builds of a beta program, we would install in directories like so: W50109 for Windows 5.0, build 109, W50226 for Windows 5.0, build 226, and so on.

Working On-Site

We don't work on-site - at the customer's location. We don't do it ever -period. End of sentence, end of story. This is in direct contrast from a lot of firms who will send people out on site to work all day, every day, for weeks, months or years. If it works for them, fine. It's not my philosophy, and here's why.

Simply stated, we can do a better job - and my people enjoy their work more - if we work at our place. We have better tools, we have better resources, we can control the environment, we have other developers around, we can control our hours, we are masters of our own destiny if we work at our place.

On the other hand, if we work on-site, we are completely powerless to do anything. We don't control our equipment, our resources, the environment - our productivity is going to plummet and that's going to make both the developer and the customer unhappy.

Let's paint the picture. You've already seen what a developer has at our shop. At the customer's site, they'll get an out-of-sync 14 inch monitor on a 486/66 machine without a cover or a CD-ROM drive that's been put on a table right next to the coffee machine. Their chair will be missing two screws on one leg and the phone won't be working.

They'll have to get to get to work at 8 a.m. and leave at 5 p.m. They'll have to wear a suit and won't be able to take work home (violation of company policy.) And listening to Nirvana or Belinda Carlisle is a no-no. Again, against company policy.

The person in the cubicle on the left won't stop talking to their spouse, their mom, or whoever. The person on the right comes over every ten minutes to ask about changing color sets in Windows and setting up a driver to play the newest version of DOOM while the boss isn't looking. And within a week, every weenie in the company is going to be coming over to say, "Oh, here's the new computer guy. Can you come over and take a look at my printer some time?"

OK, I've painted a pretty bad picture, but each of these events is from our own personal set of war stories. Sure, there are ways to deal with each of these situations, but *why?* I'm really serious - when you get to the next section, you'll see that one of the most important jobs you've got is to remove roadblocks that keep developers from actually developing. Why set up artificial roadblocks that will naturally occur at a customer's site when you don't have to?

Of course, let's look at it from the customer's point of view. There are several seemingly legitimate reasons for wanting a developer on-site.

The customer doesn't trust the developer to actually do work. In the case of fixed price, why should it matter? They're paying $50 for a hunk of software - it should be totally irrelevant how the developer gets it done. In the case of time and materials work, do you really want to work with a customer who has so little trust that "face time" is a better measuring stick than results produced?

The customer has to be able to meet with the developer on an ad-hoc basis. Again, given fixed price work - and thus a complete spec - this argument doesn't hold water. In fact, even for time and materials work, this argument tells me that the customer is poorly prepared and isn't planning their work out properly if they need to be able to drag the developer into a meeting at a moment's notice.

The customer's application, data, and/or systems are so specialized and/or confidential that they can't be taken off site. I'll accept this to some extent. However, it should be possible to create test data sets with dummy data that can be used for most development and testing. Shells or emulators that mimic the performance of the systems can be used for some parts of the system. In the rest of the cases, I still think that working on-site is so miserable that I'd turn down the work. But - that's my opinion. Some people *love* working on-site for the constant variety.

What if a customer insists that they will provide all that stuff? I'd love to see the customer that can. I've not had the experience where a customer says, "Yes, we'll supply you with a P200, a private office, 32 MEG of RAM, monster hard disk, you can shut the door, turn off the phone, come in when you want, wear jeans, and listen to Buddy Holly or Smashing Pumpkins." If that's the case, why are you on-site after all? You might as well be in your own office.

If the customer still gives you a hard time, simply explain that you have the tools you need to do your job correctly back at the shop and it's impossible to bring those tools in. You could use the comparison of someone asking an auto mechanic to come to their house to fix their car. The mechanic could only bring a hammer, a screwdriver, and something to gap the plugs. All the fancy diagnostic stuff would have to be left at the shop. How effective would that mechanic be? It's the same thing.

The bottom line for me is that we can be more productive if we develop at our shop. We've spent a lot of money and effort in making our factory efficient and good to work in - why not use it?

Administrative Duties

How about a few words about an Administrative Assistant? Many of you are individual developers who may be thinking about getting an office and working with somebody else.

Most developers do not want to spent a lot of money for an administrative assistant because they are a "non-billable" person. It's important to keep in mind that your assistant will free up a lot of your time, doing those time-consuming but non-billable tasks, thus allowing you to do more billing.

I've been faced with the decision of hiring an assistant three times in the past 20 years. Once, I did not and the other two times I did - and each of those two times, I repeatedly hit myself upside the head muttering, "Why didn't I do this sooner?"

It's somewhat difficult to hire an assistant if it's just you. Probably the optimal way is to bring in a second billable person, get them up to speed so that they can be billing full-time, and swap the phone answering duties so that one of you always has long blocks of quiet time. Once you have two billable people, you actually have enough administrative work to justify someone having on board at least part-time. Consider bringing somebody in from 9 a.m. to 1 p.m. Then, you and the other developer will have four hours of reasonable peace and quiet before you are interrupted by the phone.

The trick is getting somebody in as soon as you can. Having the right assistant is one of the most productive things you can do.

Phone Free Zones

I don't have to spend a lot of time on this because I can't explain it nearly as well as can the source - DeMarco and Lister's *Peopleware* describes the concept of having "phone-free zones" where the developer can turn their phone off for a span of time during the day.

I allow my developers to silence their phones (and shut their door and ignore me) for a two hour period in both the morning and the afternoon. They get two stretches of uninterrupted time for solid concentration. Upon completion of their phone-free zone, they return calls and otherwise get back to people. No one is left hanging for more than two hours at a stretch, and we've found that our regular customers have been most accommodating when we've explained what we're doing.

Of course, they can be interrupted for a true emergency - the idea is to give them some piece of quiet from those incessant calls about "Could you make the customer field another five characters longer?" and "We want to install this on another machine next week."

Structuring the Firm to Make Money

As you're building a firm, it's really easy to get caught up in a trap. The trap is to add a person, and assume that their billables will improve the financial position of the firm. Then another one, and another one, and suddenly you've got five, or ten, or twenty people. The only problem is that with each additional person, *your* billable time goes down. You need to add administrative support. Your technical infrastructure requirements increase. You spend money on marketing. Guess what? One day, you take a look at the books, and you're not making any more money with twenty people than you were when you were in your den. Okay, what's wrong with this picture?

Bluntly, it's kind of hard to explain this to an employee (and I'm sure my employees will get a real kick out of reading this themselves) but why do you bring more people into the firm? Well, one of three reasons.

Specialization. The first reason is so that you can concentrate on the things you do well and bring other people in to do things they do well. Maybe there are just certain things that go with the job that you don't want. For example, the books. A lot of people don't like working with the finances of a company. You'd rather be cutting code, so you hire a controller to crunch numbers. You don't like doing the nitty gritty hiring stuff. You want to talk to people, but not the whole process. So you hire a human resource person part-time. Testing, writing code, architecture, you can turn these things over to someone else too. However, you have to be careful that turning over these tasks enable you to make more money. (Philosophically, you may decide that "quality of life" is actually your ultimate goal, and that finding others to do certain tasks, even though it reduces your income, improves your quality of life enough that you're ahead of the game.)

Megalomania. The second reason for bringing someone into the firm is that you're a maniac and you want to build a 50,000 person company to take over the world. That's the topic of another book. Oh wait - someone's already written that one. Let's talk about the last reason.

Making more money. The third reason to add more people is to make more money. You must remember that there are costs associated with every person brought into the firm. Not just financial costs, but also the cost of your time and an emotional cost. Bringing people into the firm is not a simple logical act - you're dealing with people. When you bring an additional person in, you have additional emotional requirements. You have to make sure that the revenue that's being brought in and the synergy created by having another person on the team is greater than the costs that are involved as well. With careful attention to detail, and a little bit of luck, you can get good people, train them well and get the right customers.

On the other hand, we've all seen firms where the people are treated badly because the company owner feels like they have to make a buck at any cost - and people are just a disposable resource. Frankly, if you have to treat people poorly in order to make money, you're in the wrong business or you're the wrong person to be running a business. Part of the equation should be making your people's lives better. It's my personal opinion, but I think probably most of you would agree. It's easy to let the day to day pressures get kind of overwhelming and one day you wake up - all of a sudden you're acting like a slave driver. Plan in advance to watch out for the warning signs of becoming an ogre.

Communication

I thought about having one of those sappy cartoons where the punch line is "What we have here is the failure to communicate" like out of Cool Hand Luke. But then I figured that might be overcommunicating.

As my firm has grown, I've watched the difficulties in communication compound quickly. It was pretty easy when it was just me and one other person. We just talked to each other. With three, it was still pretty easy - I liked hearing myself talk enough that I was happy to repeat things. Once in a while, I planned ahead and said the same thing to both people at the same time. As more and more people came on board, this technique broke down. Different people had different jobs and different responsibilities, so not everyone had to hear the same thing - the QA folk didn't have to hear about this really cool way to refresh part of a form, and the developers didn't have to hear about my travel plans for next month.

On the other hand, some things do have to be heard by everyone. Hiring plans, for example, include a cardinal rule at our company: before we hire somebody, every employee at the shop has to meet them.

> Even this rule was broken once - by yours truly. I had been interviewing an individual for a couple of months, and finally made them an offer.
>
> Upon mentioning it the next day, someone else at the shop asked, "Oh, when am I going to meet her?" I just replied, "Ooops." Hopefully I'll never repeat *that* blunder.

The point is that it's difficult to remember who's heard what. Company e-mail is one answer, but I prefer "in-person" communication for a lot of things, rather than e-mail. Staff meetings are another option, I guess, but then you have to schedule them, and by the time everyone's schedule is open, the news is old - and the grapevine has probably taken care of most of it for you.

I don't have all of the answers as evidenced by the stupid action of mine in the last story I told you. As a result, I've decided that instead of trying to constantly achieve a state of perfect communication - one that we'll never reach - we'll accept the fact that communication will be imperfect, and adapt our systems to this assumption.

The purpose of communication is to transfer information from one entity to another. Since I'm assuming that this transfer of information will have interruptions, I've decided to use this book as a set of guidelines on how to do things. It would be impossible to have an answer for every situation that someone could run into. Instead, the intent here is to give a frame of reference so that someone would be able to make decisions despite the absence of enough information.

The idea is to keep people on the same course. You can't possibly dictate every single action that a person takes - and as the people you hire get smarter and smarter, it gets increasingly more difficult to dictate what they should do in specific situations. The best you can do is to make sure everybody's pulling in the same direction. You do this by providing a collective consciousness. (I would call this a corporate culture, but I'm afraid that I'll see my name in a future Dilbert cartoon.)

It's important to develop a set of shared experiences that serve as common ground for people so that they can, in the absence of a specific guideline, still have a direction to head. These guidelines, shared experiences, corporate culture - they all serve to direct people in a specific situation when there isn't a rule written down.

That's about the best I've come up with as far as providing a way to communicate successfully. In other words, if you can't communicate successfully, and I don't think you can - all of the time - things are going to get missed. Therefore, you have to provide a safety net for people when they (or you) fall off the wire.

Team Development Issues for a Small Shop

As a small shop, we don't have the same experiences that a 25 or 50 person shop may have. On the other hand, we're big enough that we've had to start dealing with some of these issues - and if you're still starting on this learning curve, perhaps a couple of ideas here will help.

The single most valuable technique we've implemented is to have a single lead person - a project manager who is also involved at a technical level. They collect the resources from other people in the company to supplement their ability if they can't do the project themselves. In this way, they treat the other developers as "subcontractors," retaining ultimate control, authority and responsibility for delivering the project to the customer.

The project manager takes responsibility for the code, for performance, and for delivery. We've found this helps focus the developer on code reviews and testing - when a developer takes responsibility for someone else's work, they sure do want to make sure it works right. We've also found out that since the project manager eventually has to take over somebody else's code, they make sure that it's commented right. We've also found that each of us makes sure that our own stuff looks better - the tables tend to turn quickly on many projects. Again this is a journey, not a destination. I'm sure we'll have more to add down the road.

3.2 - Tracking Time

- **Evolution: Custom Invoicing**
  - How TABET Came About
  - What TABET Does

- **Revolution: Capturing Metrics**
  - Tracking Time Against Tasks
  - Tracking Type of Time
  - Application Feedback
  - Metrics Are Not a Punishment Tool

When you're an independent developer, it's reasonably easy to track your time so that you can bill customers and determine how much time you are spending on other tasks as well. Many people just log time against a project, perhaps recording the start and end time, the billing rate if it varies from customer to customer, and a description of the work done. However, as you expand the uses of your time database, the manner in which you organize the data is increasingly important.

How TABET Came About

We go through a lot of effort to track our time, and, as you have seen, there is a good reason why. If we don't have metrics on our costs to do work, we can't determine costs for future work and for fixed price work, that would be deadly. We've developed an internal tool, TABET (time and billing entry/tracking), to do this. (I should mention - because some of you will ask - that TABET strictly an internal tool and we don't plan on making it available publicly.)

There is another benefit to strictly tracking our time. It's how we invoice customers! TABET is the tool around which most of our work is tracked: creating quotes for functional specifications, tracking daily to do lists, entering time against projects, tracking bugs and invoicing and recording payments. While the mechanism that a developer uses to track time is often as personal a decision as which editor to use, the things the mechanism should do are pretty generic.

The reason why we developed an internal tool, instead of using something commercially available for $99, was that we had a number of specific requirements that existing packages weren't going to meet. TABET started out a long time ago (yes, in that galaxy far, far away) as a simple time entry system so I could automate the billing of hourly work. I simply had two tables - one for customers and another for time entries. Since I was usually only working on one project at a time, it was a simple matter to enter the name of the project for each time entry. The invoice was simply a report grouped on project, ordered by date, and filtered by the lack of an invoice date.

Even at this point, I was able to go back and find out how many hours were actually required to do a project, and thus, was able to determine my cost per action point.

As I worked on more and more projects simultaneously, and had to go back to projects that were already shipped and do modifications or upgrades, keeping track of which project was which became more and more of a task. In turn I broke out projects into a separate table.

Several years ago, I landed two large projects that were going to require a great deal of ongoing work. Keeping track of tasks to do across literally dozens of pieces of these projects (in addition to the other smaller projects I was working on) became overwhelming. Thus, two more tables were added to the mix - Modules and Tasks.

At this point, it's probably going to get confusing, so I'll describe the relationship between each of these tables, and how we distinguish between each entity.

How TABET is Structured

Once you've accumulated a number of data points in your database, you can use this information to more accurately estimate future projects. You may also want to categorize the time as to what type of work was done. For big projects, you may need to break down time against specific modules. If your work load greatly increases, you may want to use this system to log actual time against estimates for specific activities.

Obviously, this becomes a data entry nightmare if you continue to use a single flat file. We've broken our time tracking system into five primary and three ancillary tables: Customers, Projects, Modules, Tasks and Activities, and Time, Invoices, and Bugs.

Customers

A Customer is an independent billing entity. Thus, if we work with four different divisions of Exxon and send invoices to four separate locations, we enter Exxon four times. Yes, we could probably normalize this as well, so that we could roll up data into primary organizations, but we've yet to have that need.

Projects

A Project is defined as work that needs a separate PO number or a new Functional Specification. A Customer can have one or more Projects. The customer's view of the work you are doing may also have some impact on what constitutes a Project. They may want us to break down various chunks of work into separate identifiable entities so that they can track costs against each of them. We have several customers for whom we maintain the systems they use to do work for each of their customers, thus we have created separate projects for each customer system of theirs. This way, even though they don't strictly require PO's, they can track the monies spent for each of their customers.

Modules

The third table is for Modules. One Project can have one or more Modules. The distinguishable attribute of a Module is that it is a deliverable. The Module is considered complete when it has been installed and signed off by the customer. The nature of the project determines what makes up a Module, but we typically break out a Project into at least five Modules: (1) The Specification; (2) The Data Structures and underlying foundation upon which all screens, processes and reports are going to be run; and then separate Modules for (3) Screens, (4) Processes, and (5) Reports.

Depending on the size of the system, each of these Modules is usually broken out further. For example, we may actually have two Modules for output - one for custom, standardized reports, and the other for an ad-hoc reporting system. Again, like Projects, we may also define Modules according to what the Customer wants delivered.

Tasks

The fourth table consists of Tasks that are attached to each Module. The need for this table grew out of the overwhelming amount of work and the difficulty in tracking (both for us internally as well as for reporting back to the customer) what we needed to do to before delivering a module. While a Module is a deliverable entity, it may consist of one or more separate programmable entities - such as a set of screens, a process, or a list of reports. Each of these entities - screens, reports and processes - can be priced out using our Action Point Counting method, and as such, has a specific dollar amount associated with it.

The specific Tasks depend on the type of Module - a Specification Module would have Tasks for Design Meetings, Review, Prototype Development, and Functional Specification development (the actual writeup). Modules that consist of application components have Tasks for Coding, Review, Integration, Test, Help and Documentation, Internal Bug Fixing, and Maintenance after Installation.

Activities

The last table consists of Activities - discrete action items that can be scheduled during a day, such as writing a process or creating a screen. A Task can be broken down into one or more Activities.

We also hook three other tables into this hierarchy: Time, Invoices, and Bugs.

Time

The first ancillary table is Time. As time is spent on a Task, we create a new Time record. You may be wondering why we don't track time against Activities. We use activities strictly to manage our personal To Do lists - but we don't have the need to break down the time we spend that granularly. We just care about how much time we've spent against a Task - a screen, a report, or a process. Eventually, we might want to bring that guy in the white lab coat and

Clark Kent horn-rimmed glasses in and have him measure the amount of time needed to put a list box on a form.

Invoices

The next table is Invoices. We attach Invoices to Customers, of course. In order to create an invoice, we display a pick list of available items that have been shipped - either Time records in the case of a Time and Materials project, or Module records in the case of a fixed price project. (The Module records that appear are only those that have been shipped.) The user then selects which records to include on the invoice, and those records are marked as having been invoiced.

Bugs

The last table is Bugs. Er, well, that should be "Application Feedback Incidents," which you will read about in an upcoming chapter. An Application Feedback Incident (AFI, for short) is attached to a Project, but we may also track which Module or Task that the AFI pertained to.

Revolution: Capturing Metrics

Eventually we wanted more than just a 'history' tool that allowed us to capture data for invoicing customers and perform a little To Do list management. We wanted to gather data that would allow us to plan for the future. We didn't know exactly what needs we would have, but we already had the guts of the information. It was simply a matter of organizing how that information needed to be presented. We found we had three immediate needs.

Tracking Time Against Tasks

As any manufacturer will tell you, if you don't know what the cost of your materials are, you won't be able to cost the product, and thus won't be able to price it. Since time is the single largest component of custom software, we needed to be able to track time against specific tasks. From this data, we are able to determine what our history is, and thus cost out future projects.

Tracking Type of Time

As we added people, more than one person began to work on a single project - for example, a developer would do coding, QA would do testing and tracking paperwork, and I would do some analysis and design. Other tasks that fell to various people included code reviews, installation and acceptance, and ongoing support.

We need to be able to determine what percentage of the time we spend on each type of time. All the books (the ones with 10 equations per page) say that design should take up 30% or 60% of a project's allocated time. And that testing should be at least another 30%. Is this true? We don't have enough data yet, but we're now tracking that information so that we'll be able, in the near future, to generate statistics that will tell us this.

We could have broken down the project into another category - within a Task, create sub-activities for Testing, Coding, Design, and so on, but felt this really made the hierarchy too complex. Instead, we decided to flag a time record as to the type of time being spent.

Application Feedback

One of the reasons we track bugs is to determine where we need to improve our development processes. If we find a certain developer has an inordinate number of bugs related to a specific technique or process, we can consider some sort of action to correct that. This action might be better training, it might be changing the architecture of that technique so that it's less prone to creating a bug, or it might simply be the assignment of the developer to a post in northern Greenland.

Accordingly, we track feedback on each application and attach the feedback data to the most granular level known. A request for an enhancement to the system, such as brand new functionality that doesn't relate to any of the existing modules, could only be attached to the project, while a bug report about a calculation being figured incorrectly would be attached to the screen or report it was found on.

Since we know who has done the work on a system, down to the task level, we can then count bugs, questions, and enhancement requests (ERs) per developer, and get an idea of the productivity and error-prone-ness of a developer as well. Eventually, we'll be able to put additional processes in place based on the defect count per developer.

Metrics Are Not a Punishment Tool

It is critical to ensure that, as you capture metrics on your development, you do not use that data to punish people. There are two areas where the system could easily be abused.

The first is the simple tracking of time. Some managers will insist that their developers track every minute of time, and then will rain holy hell on them if the time logs show any deviation from perfection. Well, funny enough, we kind of figure that people are human, and that their time records will not be perfect. People will come in late, leave early, have a two hour lunch, work till midnight one day, write off a morning because of something stupid they did - the whole ball of wax.

The same goes for bugs. We pretty much assume our developers will write code with bugs in it. What we want to do is sensitize everyone in the process to the idea that we're here to learn from our errors - not to use the discovery of those errors as a tool for punishment. Pro football players spend all day Tuesday watching game films from the weekend - and while the coach may occasionally berate a player, everyone knows that the purpose for these sessions is to discover mistakes and determine how to avoid them in the next game.

What I'm interested in is using the information in TABET as a means to correct behavior and activities that I don't want to see. If I see bugs, I work with the developer to determine how to reduce those bugs - I don't scream and yell and make a lot of threats. If I find someone billing an unacceptable amount, I'll find out why, and see what I can do to get them back on track.

I've found in my own experience that people will go the extra mile on their own a lot more readily if they know they have your support and your help.

3.3 - Code Reviews

- Definition
- Perfection: How Far Do You Go?
- Implementing a Review
- Sample Code Review Format

Section 3.3 Code Reviews

Code reviews are a lot like the weather - everyone talks about them but no one does anything useful after the discussion. Most references on software quality will tell you that code reviews are one of the more valuable practices that you can implement. Then these tomes spend pages and pages quoting statistics to prove their point. Once you've been sold on the idea, though, what's the next step? How do you implement code reviews?

A second problem arises once you've determined what your code review is going to look like, and how you're going to incorporate it into your day to day work. The best of intentions may win you plaudits in some places, but the hustle and bustle of customers hollering for their work somehow forces developers to cut corners and shorten delivery cycles. Since you can ship modules to customers without doing code reviews, these are often one of the first things to go.

Finally, since a code review is a process without a specific deliverable (to a customer), it often becomes a collaborative effort - without a leader, or an owner. And as Plato said, that which is owned by everyone is taken care of by no one. Again, another reason that they won't get done.

Here's how we have defined and implemented code reviews in our shop.

Definition

A code review can take one of two forms. The first is a one-on-one review, where a developer's code is reviewed by someone of equal or superior ability - preferably the latter. The second is a group review, where one developer shows their code to a group of several developers who then critique it in public. This group review is referred to in our shop as "Defending Your Life."

(By the way, while I'm referring to "code" reviews - this doesn't mean that I'm only referring to long listings of lines of commands. "Code" in this context means all of the work that makes up a system - projects, programs, forms, reports, libraries, classes, and so on.)

The purpose of a code review is not, as you might first assume, to find bugs. That's what QA does. A code review performs three other functions. The first is to provide a mechanism for sharing techniques between developers. As a reviewer sees the actual work of another, they are bound to pick up ideas, tips, tricks, and so on. You can read all the golf magazines you want, and play all the rounds you can stand, but until you also see others play, you're not going to reach your full potential. Of course, it's helpful to see others who are better than you.

The second function is to encourage proper coding practices. It's easy to, er, well, you know, get lazy. You know you should explain that magic formula, but you just couldn't. You did comment the code when you first wrote it, but then you kept finding bugs, and it took you all morning to get it right. By the time you were finished, you were just too tired to change the comments again.

Knowing, however, that this code might be the subject of the Defending Your Life meeting on Friday afternoon often provides an incentive to finish up the last 5% of the code - the comments, the indenting, the deleting of old versions of the program, and so on.

The third function is an offshoot of the second - it provides a mechanism that encourages developers to write maintainable code. Simply following the "rules" doesn't ensure maintainable code. It's easy to follow the letter of the law but break the spirit. One typical coding guideline is that a procedure or function shouldn't ever be longer than a single page - 25 to 50 lines long. It's easy to find a 20 line routine that is virtually impossible to understand, much less modify, while it would be equally easy to put together a function of 100 lines that is crystal clear and trivial to maintain. The 20 line routine keeps to the letter of the law but breaks the spirit, while the 100 line routine does the reverse.

By showing this function in a code review, the developer hears from others how good or bad their code is. If the rest of the room hoots and hollers, or starts cutting side deals about what they'll do in order to avoid getting stuck with this code, the developer knows they've written a maintenance nightmare.

This also forces the developer to be accountable to the group. If you see someone else's routine and say that you don't know how it works, it's more likely that the routine will get cleaned up.

Perfection: How Far Do You Go?

Have you ever written a piece of code that was perfect? I mean, one that was longer than four or five lines. Of course not - none of us have. There's always room for improvement - better comments, improved performance, more robust error trapping, whatever. However, when do you stop and say "Good enough?"

There is a point at which you will receive diminishing returns. Yes, you could implement every single idea that has ever been published, and turn a $20,000 application into a $200,000 application while improving the quality of the application by 4%. This does not sound like a good rate of return to me.

We have found that most of our bugs come from a few specific areas (see the chapter on Bugs for an explanation of how we know that), and that paying attention to those areas can generate an excellent return for a minimal amount of effort. As a result, instead of trying to investigate every line of code, we spend most of our time on those problem areas.

These areas are covered in a checklist that we've developed over time, based on our past history of creating bugs. However, it's not simply a matter of one developer reading down a checklist while the other one nervously awaits the final judgement, sweating profusely at each "Hmmm!" and "What the hell is this?"

Implementing a Review

You would think that there are three required items in a code review: A checklist of things to look for, code to review, and someone to review it. This assumes that the code review follows the rote mechanics described in the previous section.

We've taken a slightly different tack than many firms; we've determined there are actually two parts to a code review. The first part is a somewhat mechanical inspection that can be performed by a technical support level person, instead of a developer or analyst.

Our QA department has the responsibility of doing this first inspection. They use a checklist to inspect the code and then report back to the developer. It is ultimately up to the developer to make the changes, but the second part of the review process will catch the developer if they try to slide by.

Once QA has been through the code, it's time for a group review. Does every piece of code get sent through code review? Uh, yeah, sure it does. Of course! Why wouldn't it? Well, we're human. We make impossible schedules, commit to deadlines that are silly, and once in a while, people get sick or forget. But we do track which pieces of an application have been through a code review and which haven't. At some point in the future, we'll have enough data to do some meaningful analysis - I'm terribly curious about the effectiveness of code reviews - do the modules that have had code reviews reflect the effort in terms of quality? In other words, have our code reviews reduced bug counts?

Now it's time for a developer to Defend Their Life. While time consuming, the group review is a lot more valuable than a one-on-one. I've covered several of the reasons, but there's one more. Even the most senior developer (uh, I guess that would be me) is subject to a code review. Having the others in the shop ask me why I didn't delete a temp file at the end of a routine is good for their egos (hey, even he screws up sometimes!) and keeps me honest.

It is important to make sure that the code review is a building process, a process of constructive criticism. While I've joked about our group "Defending Your Life" reviews, it's still a positive experience - not an event where we're all going to rip on somebody, make fun of them and make their life miserable. If that's the type of attitude you have, then no one will participate in them.

Of course, we have certain expectations, and if someone came in unprepared and made a poor presentation, then they would get what they deserve.

The purpose of a code review is to make sure a developer follows the rules. This begs the question: What are the rules? Obviously, a worthwhile code review assumes a set of pre-defined guidelines that the developers should be following. It's pretty hard for a developer to write good code if there has been no definition of what "good" is.

Does this mean that you have spend hours, days, and months to put together a set of guidelines before you do your first code review? It depends. If you don't have any documented company standards, it probably means that you've got a number of cowboys who each do things their own separate way. You're going to have to spend some time to get them to agree on at least a minimal set of commonly accepted rules.

But you don't have to stop the presses for a year in order to do so. If your company guidelines consist of a half page of notes taken from a seminar someone attended three years ago, here's a trick that will get your guidelines up to industrial strength in a surprisingly short time.

You can gradually build a set of guidelines by having one person document "good ideas" as you go through your code reviews. (Yes, you still have to do your code reviews! You're not getting off *that* easily!) We started with a fairly detailed set of standards and guidelines, but we still add items to the list as we go through group reviews. This is an excellent way to build or enhance a code review checklist, because it achieves buy-in while it's being put together.

Your checklist does not have to be a 90 page manual, and, in fact, probably shouldn't be. If it is, no one will pay attention to it - who could remember all of it? And how in the world would you bring a new developer up to speed?

One more thing about the guidelines - the term is *guidelines*, not *absolute rules that must be followed or we'll cut off your hand.* There are always situations where a standard doesn't make sense. Forcing people to adhere to the standard mindlessly produces code no better than had there been no guidelines in the first place.

Sample Code Review Format

A lot of you are hankering for an example of a code review checklist, and here I fear I will disappoint. One of the goals of this book is to be language independent, but by its very nature, a code review is language specific. Nonetheless, there are some general practices that do not vary from language to language, or that can be adapted to handle the specific syntax and nuances of a tool. Let's look at an outline of a code review that you can use as a starting point.

Section 3.3 Code Reviews

The first part of the review is done by a technical support type of person. The first group of things to check don't even involve code, but I've seen each one of these violated in an application that someone has asked me to fix.

- Does the system compile without errors?
- Do all of the functions work (has anything been stubbed out)?
- Are all of the files (programs, screens, reports) and procedures used, or does the project contain things that aren't used anymore?

Getting into the code, here are some of the things that can be checked by a non-developer:

- Does each routine have a proper header?
- Are parameters described in the header?
- Are parameters checked immediately upon entering the routine?
- Are there comments in the code? Is the code formatted with indenting and white space?
- Does each logic structure check for the "in all other cases" structure? For example, does each IF have an ELSE, each DO CASE have an OTHERWISE?
- Are variables named consistently?
- Are any long or complex calculations commented?
- Are there complex nestings - many levels deep, or structures that look very elaborate?
- Are there comments that indicate code has been modified (this is good, by the way)?
- Are there chunks of code that have been commented out (but not explained why the code is still there)?

The next group of things to check can be checked by a highly skilled technical support level person, or by an entry level developer:

- Are string comparisons handled properly - both with respect to exactness and case? For example, which do you see:

  ```
  upper(m.cString) = "HERMAN"
      or
  m.cString = "Herman"
  ```
- Are file locations hard-coded or is the application portable?
- Are similar but not identical functions used as if they were interchangeable? (DTOS and DTOC, in FoxPro, for example.)

- Does arithmetic performed on dates handle turn of the millenium gracefully?
- Are divisors tested for zero?
- Are variables initialized?
- Does the code contain "magic numbers" or are they (1) explained, or (2) DEFINED as appropriate for the language?
- Are there blocks of repetitious code?

Finally, we get to the items that generally need the expertise of a developer to look at:

- Can custom code be replaced by common code or library functions?
- Is code in the proper place in the hierarchy of the call stack?
- Are variables scoped and released when appropriate?
- Are common cases tested first in logic structures?
- Do routines have one exit or does each exit call a single termination routine?
- Is the code contained within loops absolutely necessary?
- Are external device accesses trapped appropriately?
- Are files checked for existence (before creating, writing, or updating)?
- Is the environment returned to the same state at the end of the routine?
- Is there an implicit target environment (development language, operating system, machine/hardware)?

Obviously you'll be able to come up with additional items for your checklist that are a function of your chosen language and your particular development style.

3.4 - Bugs

- When To Start Tracking Bugs
- Categorizing Bugs
- What Information To Track
- Our Bug Tracking Process

Once someone other than the original developer sees the application, that person is going to find bugs. More accurately, that person is going to provide feedback. This feedback may be a bug, but it may also be a question, or an enhancement request. And it is possible that the user making the report can't necessarily make the distinction.

Ordinarily, a developer fixes the bugs, answers the questions, and offers to make the changes requested. And that's that. We decided that we need to track this feedback - and came face to face with four issues. First is - when do you start tracking application feedback? Second, how do you categorize it? Third, what mechanism to you use? And fourth - what information do you track about each feedback incident?

But first, let's talk about that initial assumption - that you want to formally track this feedback at all. Isn't it a lot easier to just deal with each communication from a user and be done with it? We've found two distinct benefits to formally tracking each application feedback incident.

First, we can provide better customer service. Feedback that the customer provides is tracked and thus, these reports are less likely to fall through the cracks. Also, one of the steps in our tracking process is to provide resolution to the customer.

Second, we categorize the bugs. One of the attributes we track for each bug is the type of bug and where it came from. From this, we can determine where our weak spots are, and, thus, determine where we need to improve our development processes. The bug reports are a tool from which the developer can learn.

Third, "feedback" might not be a bug. It may simply be a question, or it may be a request for a modification in disguise.

When To Start Tracking Bugs

We start tracking our bugs as soon as they go into internal testing. The reasons for this are twofold: The first is that we want to fix it, right? If we don't document each bug that our QA department finds, it's going to be really hard to keep track of them, and if we don't keep track of them, some will get lost - and they won't get fixed.

The second is that we want to track this defect and find out why it occurred. We want to find out who is putting bugs in the code, and why. Once we find this out, we can not only fix the bug, but also take corrective steps to fix the source of the problem. We can provide better training, better coding techniques to make a specific mechanism less fragile, or even learn to avoid certain types of interfaces, process or techniques that prove to be more fraught with peril than other types.

Categorizing Bugs

We're really critical about what is a bug and what isn't. Most people think that there are two kinds of bugs: those that the customer finds and those that they don't. We think about bugs a bit differently. We categorize bugs when we enter them into our bug tracking system. Here is how we categorize them:

Analysis. This means that we made a mistake in the analysis phase of the project. Examples of an analysis bug would be the situations where we misunderstood the way a customer process worked, or how they recorded data.

I've mentioned earlier about the application where we understood the term "part" to mean a component of the product that the customer was shipping, while they used the term to refer to a component of a machine that was used to make those products. We spent several weeks of iteration before realizing this - if we hadn't realized it at all, and had implemented a system based on our poor understanding of the term, we would have recorded it as a bug in analysis. True, it's pretty hard to document something like this, but we need to have a mechanism in place. It may not be that important to track when I'm the only one doing the analysis, because I never make mistakes, but once we have 38 analysts at the shop, we'll want to track these bugs just like any other.

Design. Two obvious examples of design bugs would be mistakes in data structure design and screw-ups in designing forms. A data structure design bug would be the incorrect normalization of a set of tables, the use of an overloaded table when it was inappropriate, or the use of data attributes as keys when the instances of that data weren't going to be unique. (Of course, if we didn't realize that the data wasn't going to be unique, that might be an analysis bug.)

An example of a bug in form design would be the creation of a form that required the user to hit four keys to save a record, and then three more keys to start the Add process for a new record - when the form in question is specifically a heads-down data entry tool. Again, if we heard this in analysis and didn't design the form to be able to do so, then it's a design bug. If we didn't catch on to the customer's requirements, then it would have been an analysis bug. If a customer calls and asks you the same question four times, it could be a design bug. If they have to ask you incessantly, then there was probably a better way to have designed the interface or process that the user is asking about. But it could also be an end-user training bug - that we need to do a better job explaining something to a user.

Coding. The third type of bug is a coding bug. We're all familiar with these. Syntax errors, mistakes in algorithms, incorrect usage of commands; a coding bug is defined as "We knew what to do (analysis and design were correct) but didn't do it right."

Environmental. We use this category to flag a situation when the application runs fine on our system, and runs fine on their system, but when they add another machine to the network the app comes crashing down. Turns out they didn't configure memory properly, or the network card is conflicting with something, or they installed an old set of DLLs, or whatever. In any case, the bug is resolved either by changes to the environment, or by adding features to the code that make checks for the environment problem at hand. The key is that we didn't have to change our code.

Installation. Installation issues are the fifth type of bug we track. These obviously only happen at one point during the cycle, but it's important to note them. This bug is flagged whenever we have an application that runs fine at our location but we fail to get it running at the customer's site. This could range from technical issues like bad drivers, lack of disk space, bad floppies to human problems like forgetting the diskettes or overwriting files by mistake.

Training. This next type of bug is a bit of a gray area, but we're paying attention to it nonetheless. If a customer has to ask a question about the application that they should have known after we were finished installing the system, then we mark it down as a training bug. For example, a question like "Why don't I see all of the transactions in the list box?" indicates that we didn't do a good enough job documenting or explaining how the list box is populated. The reason that it's a gray area is that we might have documented it and felt that we did a good enough job, but sometimes users need a bit more clarification than we need.

The important issue here is to make sure that we're taking care of the customer's learning curve - the best application in the world isn't going to do any good if they don't know how to use it.

Data. The next category is our most favorite and least favorite at the same time. We lump these issues under the heading "Data." Suppose the user imports a file and suddenly every list box in the system has garbage in it. They turn the system on and are getting intermittently screwy results and a lot of processing errors. The records in one table are missing most of their children. In each case, the error is not fixed by changing code, because there are problems associated with the actual data in the tables.

What happened? The import file was not in the correct format. The user went into the file manually and deleted all the fields with surrogate keys. A helpful administrator from another department restored a backup and overwrote the lookup table with an old lookup table without the most current values.

On the one hand, "it's not our fault" but on the other, these are issues that we should consider when enhancing the system and making it 'idiot proof.'

Irreproducible. Finally, the most famous category of them all: irreproducible. It's just one of those things. This could be traced to a flaky network card, an errant video driver, or just plain magic. I know of one installation where the notebook of a certain executive would flake out and just die every once in a while. It turned out that his office backed onto the freight elevator, and every time he had his modem on and the elevator went by, some sort of interference crashed the system.

What Information To Track

First of all, let me tip you off about a rather novel technique - we enter each bug into a database! Our table of bugs, however, is not just growing longer <sigh>, it's also growing wider. In other words, as we produce more bugs (and we do it all the time!), we learn more about the types of information we should track, and keep adding fields to the bug table.

Our bug table started out simply - the name of the customer and the system, the date the bug was found, a description of the bug, and when it was fixed. When I was one man shop, this worked out pretty well. But then I added more people, our systems got bigger, and we were more rigorous about tracking every feedback incident received.

We now also track who reported the bug (and this could be either an internal person or a customer), the specific module and task (screen, report or process) that the bug occurred in (if we can pinpoint it to that extent), and a number of dates and the initials of the person responsible for each of those events. For example, we track who investigated the bug report and when they did it, when we tried to fix the bug and who did the fixing, when we tested the fix and who did the testing, and when we agreed that the bug was taken care of. We also track when we got back to the customer about the bug - specifically informing them that the bug has been taken care of.

One note about attaching a bug to a specific screen or process - it's not always possible. The bug may be system wide. It might not be just a single combo box that's not working, but rather, when a toolbar button is pressed when opening a form that causes everything to come crashing down. Where is the bug? Which module or task do we assign the bug to? We don't know yet, so we just assign it to the project.

We also use our bug database to track enhancement requests and questions. Those will probably not be attached to a single task, they would just be attached to the project as well.

Our Bug Tracking Process

When someone encounters a bug, we make that person fill out an Application Feedback Incident form. Remember that our prime motivation is to avoid getting bug reports at all, and while some of you may think that the best way is to write flawless code, we've found that technique to be too hard. Instead, we just make the bug reporting process a real nuisance - and this starts with a long, intimidating name for the Bug Report.

Okay, enough jesting, at least until the next page. The reason for the long name is that oftentimes we get a form from a customer (or from an employee who is using one of our internal systems) and they are not sure what they are reporting. They think it's a bug when in actuality it's simply a question about a capability they are unsure of. Perhaps it's really a request for a new feature or a twist on some existing functionality. They will phrase the request in terms of a bug ("The Framboozle report doesn't break out the prior year and current year values") but when we review the "bug" report with them, we can show them that the Framboozle report was never designed to break out the yearly values like they want. Of course, we'd be happy to write up a Change Order and modify the report so that it does so!

Users don't tell you what is going on when their software breaks.

Thus, we let them enter all types of feedback onto one form, instead of blanketing them with a series of forms that they'd most likely lose. This form has spaces for bugs, for questions, and enhancement requests.

See Appendix for full text of the Application Feedback Report

Just like everything else in the world, we've borrowed liberally from other folk. In this case, we've adopted the format used by Microsoft in their public beta testing.

First, we ask if the bug is reproducible. Many times we'll find a user finds out that the problem they are having is not a bug, but that they forgot step five in a seven step process.

Next, if it is reproducible, we ask them to describe the steps to reproduce the bug. This is the hardest part for the customer to fill out.

An ideal response to this question is along the lines of :

1. Select File, Parts to bring the Parts form forward.
2. Press the Add button.
3. Enter a name with some digits in it, like "herman444"
4. Press the tab key twice

But very often we get "steps to reproduce" like so:

"Add some data with a number in it"

The third part of our form is "What happened?" It's amazing the number of times that the user will fill out the steps to reproduce and the last line will say "And see what happens?" or "Then the system died."

What do they mean by "died" - did the current form disappear and return them to the main menu, did the system lock up, did they get the blue screen of death, did the power go out or what? When they say "See what happens when you press Tab twice?", they are assuming that the same thing happens on our system - and it might not!

The fourth part to this form is "What did you expect to happen?" Occasionally, they will indicate that they expected something to happen which reveals that it is not a bug, but a misunderstanding of the way the system actually works. For instance, we received this bug report once:

"Add a record without pressing 'Add.' Record not added."

We were not surprised. The problem was that the user was in "live edit" mode, but thought that simply entering new data would add a new record instead of changing the current record. So while we still charted this as a bug, we marked it down as attributable to training.

Of course, when we received four more bug reports from this same user over the next month about this same issue, we realized that it wasn't a training error after all <g>.

My friend Eldor Gemst has a routine that he calls from his applications when certain types of events happen. The user will perform some function, and suddenly see the message:

PEBCAK Error 101
Please inform your supervisor.

"PEBCAK" is an acronym for "Problem Exists Between Chair And Keyboard." When a supervisor hears of a PEBCAK error, they know to take appropriate action - which usually doesn't include notifying the developer.

The user should also fill out the name of the system, put down today's date, and note the personnel involved. Once we receive the application feedback form, our QA department enters it into the database, and the internal process is started.

The developer is notified of the receipt of an AFI form, investigates, produces a fix if necessary, and sends the fix off to QA. Once the fix passes, the fix is given to the customer, and the bug is closed. If the AFI is actually an enhancement request, the developer writes up a change order, and that process is started. (See the last chapter in this section.)

Whether the AFI is a bug or not, we report back to the customer as to the proper resolution. Each week, QA produces reports for all bugs, questions and enhancement requests that haven't been closed, and follows up with the developer as to their resolution.

3.5 - Testing

- Testing Personnel
- Testing Process
- Techniques to Make Testing Easier
- Regression Testing

Testing? Isn't that what the user is for? I guess I can see the reasoning of some developers here - but again, our philosophy is that we are manufacturing a product. How would you like to buy a car and find out that the right turn signal didn't work because the manufacturer's mentality was such, "Testing? QA? That's what the customer is for!"

We feel it's part of our job to ship the software to the customer without bugs - they're paying a fixed price and they should have a complete, finished product.

Testing Personnel

Who is the worst person to do testing? Your mom. Who's the next worst person to do testing? You. I realized this early on, and figured out a very valuable solution to the problem.

High School and College Kids. One of the smartest things I ever did, next to proposing to my wife, was to hire part-time high school and college kids to do testing for me. At the time, I was working out of my house but was still delivering applications that were big enough that I needed to have them tested.

I lived in a suburban kind of environment, so it was easy to find kids in my community to come over to my house and help. I went to the local high school and explained to the calculus teacher that I was looking for some kids that were pretty bright, had a good work ethic, and wanted to do some part-time work would be more stimulating than cutting lawns, flipping burgers or baby-sitting.

This was something the calculus teacher had never heard before, and got pretty excited about it. She gave me a list of four or five names and I ended up with some extremely bright kids who were able to come in afternoons, evenings or weekends during the school year. In summer, they could work during the days as well.

These were very bright high school kids who had been accepted to a very good college and were motivated to do a good job because their job was a lot cooler than what they're friends were doing. I also tried to provide a good work environment - flexible hours, casual dress code, and so on - and treated them with respect instead of as if they were 12 years old. In retrospect, I think what I did was just spoil them. Now they are going to have to find real jobs, and they'll eventually realize that they will be living in Dilbertland.

Another benefit to them was the fact that they were actually doing something important - that the results of their work were going to impact the people at another company - my customers. Some of their friends were sweeping the floor at Pizza Heaven - if they died, another kid would be plugged into the job in about five minutes. With me, they could actually see the effect they were having.

On the other hand, these *were* high school students. They may or may not have had experience with computers, and they definitely didn't have experience with FoxPro, relational database structures, or custom database applications.

They needed training. The first thing I did was make sure they were comfortable with DOS, Windows, and all the usual things with a computer that you and I can take for granted. I always had some type of 'grunt work' around, and so I'd have each new kid just crank out some of that for a couple of weeks, getting familiar with everything. There was a second reason for this work as well.

You know how when you're performing some task and suddenly you get this feeling that "something's not right?" You can't quite put your finger on it, but you just have this gut feeling that something wrong has happened. This simply comes from experience. When you're testing, you need to have some sense of a gut feel that something doesn't feel right. I wanted the kids to get comfortable enough that they would develop some sense of how FoxPro operated.

Full-time Testing Staff. Eventually, I moved out of the house and into the office. It was not nearly as easy for some of these kids to get downtown, and when they could, it was on a much more limited basis. So for about a year or so, we struggled with getting things tested, and looking back, we can see that the quality of stuff that we shipped was not as good. We found that the students could come in once or twice a week, we could give them something to do at home, or they could come in on weekends, but this lag time caused a lot of problems. We didn't always have the luxury of finishing code Monday night and have somebody coming in the next day to test. The customer wanted it right away, so we shipped without independent testing.

As this book was being compiled, I brought in our first full-time testing person. Let me reword that - she is full-time and one of her primary responsibilities is testing. You can actually think of her as our QA department - in large part, testing, but she has other responsibilities as well.

These other responsibilities all involve the monitoring and handling of our processes. As you have already seen, we have a number of forms and mechanisms that we are starting to fill out. It's starting to feel like "paperwork city" but every manufacturing facility runs on paperwork - potential orders, specifications, requisitions, change orders, QA results, and so on. If this paperwork (or the electronic equivalent) is missing, you can't get things through the system. Verbal communication simply does not work. Our QA person makes sure that this process is running smoothly. However, since this chapter is on testing, let's get back to that.

Testing Process

Okay, so we've got somebody ready to hammer away at testing. We've also got somebody who is ready to deliver something to the testing person so they can test it. Of course, this is the developer. The application is running on our LAN, and the developer lets QA know that something is ready for testing - either through an e-mail or by entering an activity for QA in TABET. The testing person has got a clean desk and the application is ready to be beat up. What, precisely, does QA do?

Step One - Push All the Buttons

Yes, this sounds really stupid, but how many times have you gone into a customer and said, "Oh and by the way, if you push this, oh no! I thought that was working!" We've all done it. This is QA's first responsibility - is to make sure that every one of those buttons does something. Sometimes we even forget to put a button in on one screen but it's on all the other screens. So they push all the buttons and make sure everything is functioning.

QA creates a sheet that lists every object on a screen, and then checks off each object as it's tested. All the buttons are pushed, all the checkboxes are checked, all the fields have data entered. Tab order is another item that is checked in this phase - when you tab through the screen, does the focus shift appropriately - and, do all the keyboard shortcuts work?

Step Two - Test The Functionality

When you hit add, enter data into every field, and press Save, is the record actually added? Does all the data get added? Did the entire entry in the field get saved, or did we chop off the last five characters in the invoice number? This is why QA has to be comfortable with FoxPro - they need be able to verify what is happening in the application down to the raw table level.

Step Three - Test The Rules

There are three general types of rules in an application - those attached to a field, those attached to a form, and application-wide rules. In all three cases, these rules have to be identified and then we have to test for them. The description of how we are going to do so is our test plan, and it's contained in the functional spec (or the change order.)

What is the role of the testing person? Most people say, "To make sure it works." No. The role of the testing person is to break the application. This distinction is really important.

The next step for QA is to execute the test plan. It is up to the developer to make sure that the test plan is robust, but it is also up to the QA person to figure out ways around it and figure out ways to break it.

The developer should be able to put together a case chart to handle all of the possible options within a program and provide test data or require a test plan to handle these cases. As QA tests each option, they should be able to check off which options were tested and what the result was.

Step Four - Break It!

As developers, we know our application works. Right? We don't need anybody to prove to us that it works - we've run the application after writing the code and we've seen that it works. Of course, we've only seen that it works one time - why would we waste our time trying it more than once?

The mission of QA is not to prove that the application will work - their mission is to break the application. And note that testing is a different type of activity than any other part of the software development process - because the testing is never done. A thousand hours of testing can go into an application, and the only thing that you can be sure of is that you haven't found a bug - yet.

So the final step in the testing process is to pull out all the stops and to be devious, conniving, downright evil in trying to find ways to break the applications. The greatest fear of a testing person is that there's a bug in the system that they didn't find.

Techniques to Make Testing Easier

Two very frustrating situations that occur during the testing process are (1) testing something that just worked a minute ago but doesn't any longer, and (2) having to restore the environment because the application blew up and took every special setting and switch with it.

Original Data

One of the most common reasons that a routine works at 11:46 but not at 11:47 is that the data that was entered in the last test is causing problems. Either it was bad, it got corrupted, it was incomplete, or it wiped out something else that shouldn't have been wiped out.

One of the two fundamental rules we've had was to create a clean set of original test data so that you have an accurate and measured baseline from which to start. Each time you are ready to run a test, you can copy all the data from the original test data directory into the current test data directory and run off that new set of test data.

If you are testing a long process, you may want to create several data sets that represent different points in the process. The cardinal rule for original test data: Make it clean, robust and keep it in a location that can be accessed easily so that the test data directory can be replenished with this clean data on demand.

Original Environment

The second thing you have to be able to do is restore the environment back to its original state. Even if you try your best to clean up the environment and keep things orderly during the execution of your application, a failure of the system will take the environment with it. For example, suppose your application always runs with the flag for exact comparisons set OFF. However, during one specific point in a routine, you need to have the flag set to ON, so at the beginning of the routine, you do so. At the conclusion of the routine, you set the flag back OFF.

But, somewhere in the middle of that routine, the system crashes. If you don't reset the flag, and simply run the application again, any comparison that was relying on the exact comparison to be off will now fail - and send you down a blind alley for hours until you realize what happened.

Create a quick general purpose tool that will automatically reset your development environment back to where it came from so that you're always starting with the same baseline, just as you did with a clean set of test data.

Testing Tools

There are a number of other techniques that can come in very handy during testing in order to track down problems. Here are some of the tools we use frequently.

Track Users. Even if you are creating a single user system, track the user who is on the system. Often times, there will be more than one person using the system, and providing them each with their separate login allows you to determine who was using the system when problems occurred.

Track Activities. We have a function at the start of every routine that logs the name of the user and the date and time that they called the routine. The table that this information is placed in is relatively small compared to the rest of the application, and we can clean it out at any time. (The file is created on the fly if it's missing, so we can simply delete the file if we desire.)

Knowing who was in a routine (and when) provides valuable information when trying to track down particularly thorny or infrequent bugs. We've also found it useful when a customer claims they've been using a certain module or routine, and that it "suddenly" broke. This log tells us how precise their claim is.

Track Errors. It's still amazing to me that people write applications that don't log errors to a file that can be picked up and investigated later, but I see it all the time. We keep a very detailed error log that captures everything we can think of. We log to a file the error message, the line of code that causes the error, the call stack of programs that led to the error, any parameters that were passed, the name of the user and the time stamp, and a host of environment information, including files open, libraries loaded, all memory variables, the current state of the environment, and so on. It's a very rare error that doesn't just jump out at us given this information.

Some developers grab a screen shot at the time an error occurs. They take a snap shot of the screen at a particular instance and store it to a file, and so can see what the user is seeing at the time of the error. The only difficulty is that these screen shots are pretty big - several hundred Kb - and an error that occurred numerous times could chew up disk space quickly.

Audit Trail. Track the user and the date/time that a record was last changed, and, if you have the space, log this same information for when the record was added. Yes, this information takes another 30-40 bytes per record, but it is invaluable to being able to save to do detective work on what is happening later on.

A second part of an audit trail feature tracks every change to any field. While this log can get awfully large awfully quick, it can be useful to be able to turn this on and off on demand, in order to isolate a specific problem.

Error Log Access. Another tool we use a lot is a one step tool to access the error log because, unfortunately, we're looking at it an awful lot. We have this available on our Developer menu so that we can access it at a customer site if we've logged into the application.

We don't call this file an "Error Log" because it tends to unnecessarily worry some users. "What? You've got errors?" We call it an "Activity Log" and explain to the customer that this file is used to store any kind of activity that we're not expecting. These could be errors, unexplained problems, data problems that shouldn't have happened - just anything we didn't figure on happening. They are free to send the activity log to us at any time. We also allow the user to delete it completely - the next time an error occurs, the file is created if it didn't already exist.

Debugging Tools. If you haven't already, set up a series of developer tools on a menu pad that is only available to the developer. These tools should allow you to suspend program execution, or cancel the program outright so that you can halt and investigate the environment at any time. Make sure all of your debugging facilities are available and ready to be enabled whenever you need them. These will differ according to what development tool you're using, but take full advantage of those as you can.

Regression Testing

Regression testing refers to the practice of testing an application after a change was made to the application to make sure that the change (or fix) didn't break anything else.

There is no magic formula, no silver bullet, for performing regression testing for the type of applications this book is covering. There are some automated test tools that perform some of the mundane testing - and they can prove very handy precisely in this situation. However, as we've already discussed, there are limits to these tools, and so the burden is still on the QA department to ensure that nothing has been broken.

Adherence to a couple of techniques can help to some extent. Modularizing your code so that there are distinct boundaries between functions is one useful procedure; using common routines and libraries as often as possible is another.

Doug Hennig uses a detailed change log that documents every change made to an application in order to aid in hunting down the problems causes by changes to code. While this doesn't solve the problem up front, it makes a great deal of difference in tracking the problem down and determining where else the bug might manifest itself.

3.6 - Change Orders

- The Need for Change Orders
- The Change Order Process
- Pieces Of A Change Order
- Tracking Change Orders
- Delivering the Application
- Skipping the Process

We have gone to great lengths to document in laboring detail how an application is going to function. We need to do this for a number of reasons:

1. To determine the cost.
2. To determine how to test it.
3. So we can put this in help.
4. So we can document whether we have bugs later. How can we define bugs if we don't know what the expected operation is?

This process is relatively useless if the documentation process stops here. Once the functional specification has been accepted, we must have a mechanism to handle further changes to the system - whether those changes come from the discovery of additional requirements or simply from the user being wishy-washy.

The mechanism we use has been stolen (surprise!) from the manufacturing world. It's not uncommon for a part, a component or an assembly to need modifications after it's been designed, prototyped or even cast. The manufacturer will create a document that describes the change, the cost and the ramifications. This document, a change order, is just as useful in our world, and, in fact, might be more useful. The ethereal nature of software development lends itself to misunderstandings between the user and the developer - seemingly simple changes that are verbally communicated can cause huge problems later on. A formal method to document even the most trivial of changes will pay dividends by the end of the project.

The Need for Change Orders

We have gone through great pains to convince the user of the need for a formal specification - but, due to Murphy's Law - the user will call you up the day after the specs were signed off, and ask for "just one simple change."

There are several things that could happen. Most often, all of them happen.

The first scenario that could unfold is that the change is simple, you agree to add it in, and do so. Months later, someone else asks why the system doesn't meet the specification - this one specific thing is different - and could you please change it so it meets the spec? This could cause a problem because the change was needed and the person requesting that the system be brought into conformance doesn't understand it. On the other hand, if it wasn't needed and you made the change and then un-make it, you've just performed the equivalent of moving the couch from one side of the room to the other and then back because the homeowner can't make up their mind. Both of these situations will cost you money (and aggravation.)

The second thing that could happen is, now that the user has seen how nice you were, they ask for a second "very tiny change." And then a third, and a fourth. Where do you draw the line? It's a rare developer who doesn't get caught in this trap occasionally.

The third thing that could happen is that the change turns out not to be "that simple" after all. However, since you've agreed to "just throw it in" for free, you're committed to more work than you're comfortable with. Either you'll do it right, spending a lot of time, or you'll try to compromise with a quick fix, and end up shortchanging either the customer or yourself.

You can respond two ways to this state of affairs. Either you can get bugged about it, or accept that changes from the user are a part of nature. We prefer to do the latter. So now that we're going to figure that they're going to ask for changes after the spec has been signed off on, but that our process is predicated on having things written down and documented, we're going to document the requests for changes in just as much detail.

We need to write out a change order for two reasons:

- Inevitably this is going to have a cost.
- We need documentation on what the system is doing so that when we look at the system a year later we can say, "Oh, yeah, we did say that it would do such and such." And then help can be updated and all that sort of thing.

The Change Order Process

First, the customer contacts the developer, requesting a change. They typically do this verbally, but occasionally something will arrive in writing. We don't accept their written change orders any more than we accept their written specs. We'll use their information as a starting point to create our formal change order.

See Appendix for full text of the Change Order

Second, we'll write up a change order, including description, test plan, ramifications, and cost. The change order is also entered in TABET as a new module, but with the flag "Accepted" set to false and the "Date Accepted" field left blank.

The change order is sent to the customer, who then has to either accept or reject the change order, much as they would accept or reject the proposed functional specification.

If the change order is accepted, the "Accepted" flag in TABET is set to true. In either case, the "Date Accepted" field is filled in. (If the Accepted flag is set to false and the Date Accepted field is filled in, we know the change order was rejected.)

We make it clear that we will not begin work on a change order without a signed change order form. We don't accept verbal approvals. Generally, we don't have a problem with this, but in the event that a developer is getting pressure from a customer to start work before the paperwork has begun, the developer has the right to paint me as the bad guy: "Gee, I'd love to, but my boss won't let me." It gets the developer out of a potentially sticky situation but if the the situation escalates, I'm more than happy to step in and take a firmer line with the customer. This helps the developer to allow the customer to potentially save face.

We do charge for the design of the change order. Hopefully, they have asked for several changes at the same time so that we can do them all together; it's more efficient for us and thus less expensive for them. But we always charge - they are asking us to do analysis and design, and just like the creation of the specification, we charge for it.

If you have a Czar (or Czarina) of change orders, it makes life a lot easier. Initially, I intended on having my administrative assistant help out with monitoring some of those processes. Unfortunately, she was so good at doing so many other things that monitoring the processes items tended to fall through the cracks.

I eventually decided that we would merge the monitoring of our processes in with our QA group and have them handle all of the tracking processes. You could argue that this is somewhat like having the Fox watch the Chicken coup, because they are also responsible for testing and checking things in and out. Well, remember that we're a FoxPro shop. We see nothing wrong in having the Fox do this. <Sorry, bad pun.>

Yes, it is possible for things to slip through the cracks. We're not terribly concerned with this - one of the processes we've put in place is a set of "exception" reports that will call to our attention anything that is out of the ordinary. Furthermore, even if something does slip through - it's a lot less likely to do so now than it was before. Maybe our process is only 95% fail safe but considering the previous method was 0% fail safe, I think it is a tremendous improvement.

Pieces of a Change Order

The first part of the change order is a description of the change as the user sees it. The user doesn't really care what we're going to do inside, but they are interested in the change in functionality - much like we did in the specification. They are going to see an extra button on the screen, a new screen, a report that prints five times faster, or that the subtotals calculate differently. Not only do we want to document what they will see, but how their life is going to be different. In other words, they are probably requesting this because their life isn't as good as it could be and they want to make a change so that their life is better.

The second part of the change order is a description, somewhat technical, of what the developer has to do. Since the developer has already spent time investigating the requirements of the change, they probably have done some brainwork in terms of what they will have to do if the customer accepts the change order. Do I have the add a field to a table? Do I have to change the indexes? Do I have to add this to a screen? Do I have to change these rules? We might as well document the work that the developer has already done so we don't lose that knowledge. We've also found that, in many cases, the customer can review this part and offer input. They may not be able to create this section, but often they can spot missing pieces.

The third part of the change order is ramifications. "This is going to require an additional 4 Gb of storage space." The customer needs to understand what impact the change is going to have on their existing system.

The fourth part of the change order is the test plan. This is a To Do list for the QA folk, just like we have in the functional specification. And the final part of the change order is the cost - how much, and how it's going to be determined - either time and materials or via fixed price. In some cases, we have to use time and materials because the changes are widespread and varied. But we can often use the same Action Point Counting methodology that we used for the original specification. The end of the change order also includes a place for the customer to sign off so that we can be sure that that the customer has okayed the work. If the customer doesn't okay it, then there is a place for them to decline.

We follow up on all open change orders on a weekly basis to ensure that the customer has received it. Often times, a customer will not return a change order that they are not going to accept, figuring that it will automatically end up in the bit bucket. Developers are usually in close contact with the customer to find out if it was accepted or not we want to make sure we don't let anything fall through the cracks. This is about as high-pressure as we get in our business trying to track down people for additional work.

If a change order requires a change to existing code as opposed to a new function or module, we mark the code with the date and time of the change as well as the change order number, so that we can go back and find out more about the reason for the change. A two line comment in the code doesn't always jog the developer's memory sufficiently.

Tracking Change Orders

We track a change order as a module because it is a specific object that we can ship. It is important to realize that this is what we are doing - tracking widgets that we can ship, and therefore we need to enter them into TABET. Thus, a change order has a number and the module screen has a place to record the change order number and thus track whether the change order has een accepted or rejected, when it's been tested, approved, and shipped to the customer. We can also, amazingly enough, track bugs against change orders.

Delivering the Application

Upon delivery of a module, the developer takes one final form with them - the On-Site Activity Report. This form lists all of the "widgets" that the developer is going to deliver, together with a sign off by the QA department and a space for the customer to accept (or reject) the delivery as well.

See Appendix for full text of the On-Site Activity Report

The first column acts as a To Do list for the developer - both when assembling materials to take to a customer, and while at the customer's site. The second column serves two purposes - an audit for us to make sure that the specific deliverable was OK'd by QA, and to reassure the customer that our quality control procedures were followed.

We also use this form to document what action items come out of the meeting - if there are any remaining tasks, and who is responsible for those tasks. With some customers, we end up with more to do when we leave than we had when we arrived (even taking into account our deliverables.)

We also have a space for recording how satisfied the customer was with the visit. We've found it a good idea to document customer dissatisfaction immediately. Customers often delay this type of bad news until the invoice comes due, and by then it's too late. If they're forced to measure their level of satisfaction immediately, you can find out quickly, instead of having to wait. An added benefit is that you're less likely to have an invoice thrown back in your face with the excuse that "All the work you've done is unacceptable" if they've had to sign off at each meeting. It's not impossible - just less likely.

Skipping the Process

This whole book has been about process - but nowhere is it easier to get sidetracked than during the actual manufacturing process. Customers are always in a hurry - during the sales call, they want to get moving into design; once the design has been started, they're anxious to see some code being cut, and as soon as screens are being tested, they want to start entering data.

Given that impatience is the norm, often it's worse - the customer is in a near panic - some deadline is always around the corner, and the developer is under the gun to deliver something, anything as soon as possible - in 30 minutes, if that isn't asking too much.

As a result, it's tempting to forsake the procedures we've just described - because, "just this once," it's different.

It's an *emergency*, this time.

Well, I've got some bad news - and some more bad news.

The bad news is that this time isn't different. Every customer is in a hurry. Every customer has a drop dead delivery date. Every customer is a special case. You can't simply suspend procedures once, for a special case, because you'll end up suspending procedures again and again, until you've done it for every case.

I spent a winter in a foundry, where the primary work was supplying castings for other divisions of the company. Since the foundry was a captive facility, they weren't treated terribly nicely - each division was extremely demanding, as if they were the only division of the company whose products and customers were important. One result was that each division always expected their jobs to be expedited.

Once in a while, someone from one of the divisions was successful in badgering a foundry supervisor into bumping their product up in priority. (More often, the salesman from the division complained or sweet-talked a corporate vice-president into calling the general manager of the foundry and getting their job moved up in the queue.)

Since the scheduling process was automated, the job tickets that determined which castings would be processed on any day were printed first thing in the morning, and that's how the shop workers knew what to do. Expediting a job became a problem, because the tickets for the entire day couldn't simply be re-run when the order came down from on high to move a specific job through the shop faster.

Finally, management came up with the idea of putting a red ticket on the casting to indicate that it was to be handled out of order. Human nature being what it is, eventually 90% of the castings on the floor were carrying red tickets.

One day, a salesman touring the foundry realized that the red ticket that his job was carrying looked just like the 270 others on the floor. There was no way his job was going to make the promised delivery date if the casting had to vie with the 270 others also carrying the "high priority" tag.

When the salesman left the foundry that morning, one job was carrying two red tickets - obviously indicating that it was much more important than those jobs carrying only one red ticket!

The second bit of bad news is that the more special the situation is, the more important it is to maintain the use of your procedures. Let's use the analogy of a hospital. One important procedure is to track what drugs have been given to a patient, along with when and at what dosage.

Now let's move out to the field - a MASH unit where the wounded are coming in faster than the door can be opened and the physicians and support staff rotate in and out of the unit nearly as fast. Given the breakneck pace, it would be easy to suspend some procedures because there simply isn't the time.

However, it's precisely due to the special situation that the procedure of tracking the administration of drugs must be followed - and, in fact, is even more important. In a normal hospital setting, it's conceivable (if, well, not particularly comforting) that the drug history could be reconstructed at some later date if it hadn't been maintained contemporaneously. The physicians and support staff could be interviewed, drug inventories could be checked, and the relative calm of the hospital (well, relative to a battle front) makes the process somewhat more stable.

It could likely be impossible to reconstruct that same history for a casualty at the MASH unit. As a result - keeping contemporaneous records would be critical in that setting.

I'll argue that this applies equally well to the special, rush-rush job when a customer puts you under the gun. You have to write down the work you're doing, you have to track change order requests, chart bugs, and keep the documentation in front of the customer. You can always find another 30 minutes in a day to do the paperwork - and if you can't find the time, you'd better make the time. Else, you're going to have to find the time at 8 P.M. or this coming weekend. I know - I've done it myself <sigh>.

Section 4: People

Many companies say your most important asset rides up and down in the elevators every day. Actually, every company says this. But there are a couple of things wrong with this claim. First of all, what if you don't have elevators? What's your most important asset then, huh? Second, this is a classic lip service statement - along the lines of "Quality is Job 1" (or, as they say at certain large software manufacturers, "Quality is Job 1.1.")

People are your capital equipment. Without people, you can't do anything. This is in direct contrast to a factory where you can get rid of a person, plug another one in, train them for three minutes, and you're off and running. If a person leaves the knowledge factory, you're hosed. There is no way to capture all of the knowledge that an individual has in their head. When they leave, you have lost part of the asset base of your company forever. As a result, the hiring and keeping people process is incredibly critical, yet we've been conditioned to treat people as interchangeable parts that can be replaced without consequence.

Let's look at the right way to do the people thing.

4.1 Finding People

- **The Recruitment Mentality**

  Want Ads
  Customers - Yes and No
  Community College Classes
  Elsewhere
  Part Time People

- **The Sales Packet**

- **How To Get Rid of People Who Call and Don't Have a Chance**

- **The Headhunter**

- **Conclusion**

Finding employees is just like marketing. And if you've already read the chapter on marketing, you may be tempted to throw your hands in the air again. Yes, that's the bad news - no matter what you do, nothing works. Truly talented people are rare and must be sought after regularly. Software development is an intellectual activity. Despite the strides made in automated tools, it requires the unique talents of an individual's mind.

Recruitment must be an on-going process. You must always be thinking about hiring, even if you don't have a current need.

The Recruitment Mentality

An independent developer quickly finds out that they must keep marketing throughout the year. If they land a job and then stop selling, they'll find out that when the job is over, they'll be up the proverbial creek if they haven't continued to market during the job. The same goes for finding employees. Most firms treat employee recruitment as a one-time activity, to be performed when a person quits or when the firm lands a job and needs additional people.

The first trick to successfully bringing people on board is to have your "people finder" radar turned on and running full strength all the time. I remember walking through a trade show one time, passing by a booth exhibiting equipment that was of absolutely no interest to me, but being drawn by the woman doing the demonstrations. Even after politely declining her sales pitch, she continued to pursue me, and in a few minutes, it dawned on me that she might be a good candidate for future work at my shop. I turned the tables on her, suggesting she give me a call sometime if she wanted a new position, and six months later she was my star instructor.

So what avenues do you have when wandering around with your "people finder" radar? Let's examine some of the typical places, and then wander a bit further afield.

Want Ads

As the type of position you are trying to fill becomes more and more sophisticated, or as the number of openings increases to outnumber qualified candidates, the want ads become less and less a viable option. Typically, you place an ad, get a few responses and then fend off headhunters for a year. Nonetheless, it's an avenue that should be investigated, if only to turn it down later.

Don't forget that you have many types of want ads available - not just in the big metropolitan paper but smaller papers as well - suburban weeklies, specialized publications and so on. The trick to successful recruiting in want ads is to look at what your competition is doing, and beat them. You're not just trying to cast a net, but you're trying to make sure that the net you cast is appropriately assembled for the candidates you want to attract. As the pool of available candidates becomes smaller, they'll become more selective, and you'll need to do a better job of selling them on your firm.

Just like marketing, you want to set yourself apart from the others. Technical people are hard to find, therefore, you have to be smart about finding them. You can't just say, "Programmer wanted; competitive wages offered" and be done with it. There are gazillions of those ads. Why should the superstar programmer out there answer your ad instead of someone else's? See what the other firms are saying and then tailor your ad differently.

The first mistake they make is that ***they all sound the same.*** Read through a dozen and you won't remember the first one you saw - and if you can't, how can you expect the candidate pool to?

What can you do to differentiate your shop from the others in print? I've already gone over a couple of reasons why you do business differently (remember that chapter on Positioning?) Tailor your ad so that your company sounds different, exciting and attractive. Some questions you can ask yourself:

- Do you have a distinctive environment?
- Do you specialize in some particularly cool area of technology?
- Is there some other attribute of your firm that makes you stand out?

As you see in our ad, I stress a few unusual attributes that are particularly attractive to the software developer type.

```
Nationally recognized software development firm keeps
on growing.  In dire need of entry level and
experienced programmers.  Full time or part time
available.  Downtown location.  Flexible hours.
Casual dress.  Must be non-smoker with sense of
humor.  All the Diet Coke you can drink.  Send resume
and code samples to...
```

Programmer Want Ad

You can do yourself a world of good by going outside conventional wisdom. Here's an example: one of the great hidden resources in this country is the huge population of parents that are now at home but would still like to continue working. They'd like to keep their hand in what they do so that once the kids are at school or out of the nest, they don't feel like they've lost touch. However, many of these parents can't or won't go back to work full time. (Note that I say "parents" not "moms" because it is very possible that mom is working full-time and dad is staying home - or, in their ideal situation, that's what they'd like to do.)

Most employers see this as a problem. They think the employee will leave work early to go to soccer games, or have to skip work because the kids are sick, or that the insurance premiums will be too high, or that the employees will be distracted with the multitude of kid problems, and so on.

Software development is one of those areas where part-time, flexible types of situations are a great match for the employee and the firm. This is the type of thing you can stress to candidates in your ad.

Let's take this one step further. There may be a weekly or monthly suburban publication in your area that caters to working parents. In Milwaukee, there is a monthly rag called *Metro Parent* that is chock full of ads for diaper services, reused toys, obstetricians and all that kind of stuff. Obviously, the readership is precisely your target. I placed one ad in this paper looking for a part-time marketing professional and was quite pleased with the response. It is important in that ad to stress three things: 1) family friendly, 2) part-time, and 3) professional position. This isn't a $7 per hour spot licking envelopes at home.

Customers - Yes and No

It's pretty common to have an employee of a customer and have one of their employees approach you for work. This sword cuts both ways.

I did some consulting at a firm a few years ago and years later, one of their employees saw that I was running an ad. This person called me up and since I had already spent twenty-some hours of consulting time with them, I knew quickly where that person fit, how they interacted with others, and their technical skill level. Once I was able to determine what would happen at my customer's firm if they left and joined my firm (and that no bad feelings would occur), it was a pretty easy decision to bring them on board.

Of course, this begs the question - what would happen if an employee of a customer left and joined you? The first thing to consider is who approached who. In the case above, since they approached me, and they had already told their boss that they were looking around, there were no hard feelings. One doesn't always get that lucky.

A long time ago, I met someone at a customer site who was extremely sharp and personable. We hit it off quickly and I, being somewhat less experienced then, asked this person if they'd consider coming on board with me. They were pretty interested, but wanted to think about it. While they were thinking, I called my prime contact at the customer to see if there would be any problem, and he consented as he didn't see any direct problem. What I didn't quite catch on to was the fact that the candidate I was pursuing wasn't a direct report of my contact.

Well, as you can imagine, word of this informal "OK" got back to the candidate's boss, and tensions between our contact and the boss were rather high for a while: "What do you mean by telling someone they can go hire my people out from underneath me?" Yes, in retrospect, it was a stupid thing to do - one of those "What was I thinking?" kind of moments, but it sure seemed logical at the time.

Before you go after a customer's employees, or let them come after you, take a couple of steps back and reconsider the long-term ramifications.

Community College Classes

If you have the opportunity to teach classes at a local community college, such as a once a week night class, you've got a potential source of hot prospects. There are two advantages to this avenue. First, you are now in contact with people who are motivated and interested in learning more than what their daytime job will teach them. They're making an extra effort to attend a three hour class once or twice a week while still holding down a full-time job. The other advantage is that you can evaluate them for potential - without them knowing that you're doing so! It's expensive in terms of your time, but you may get really lucky.

I taught a Visual FoxPro class at a technical college and I spotted one person in the class who had a great attitude and incredible desire. She was working a full-time job and taking three night classes at the same time. I was able to watch and evaluate her for several weeks without her knowing I was doing so. I was able to see that she was the quickest in the class and had the technical knack of picking up things logically. This is normally a difficult attribute to evaluate because it requires a greater amount of time than just a one hour interview. It is also difficult if the candidate knows you are watching.

At some point, you need to approach them. They are generally flattered, yet they also realize you know what they are really like. You hear them curse, you hear them complain about work and their spouse and see them in a bad mood. In general, you get to know what they are like in a way that you generally don't during the formal interview process. We'll discuss how important this is in the next chapter, but for now, we'll leave it at that. You can get a better evaluation of them if they are unaware of your interest for a while.

Elsewhere

Keep your eyes open everywhere - everybody you meet - everyone you see. You know how life insurance sales reps look at every person they meet as a potential sale? Well, that "I've always got my marketing hat on" attitude isn't quite as applicable for our business - lots of people buy life insurance; not quite as many spend $5,000 to $100,000 for a piece of custom software. However, there is always someone you will know who knows a programmer or has someone in mind. A lot of people are turned off by the omnipresent salesperson, but not many are offended by a potential job offer. So they are generally not threatened if you say, "Well, what do you do for a living? Do you like what you are doing?" You are actually curious - and, hey, who isn't looking for a better job? (Well, the folks at my shop aren't, but you'll find out why shortly…)

You should also investigate user groups and individuals in the same industry who aren't direct competitors. You may have a Visual Basic shop and your friend may run a Powerbuilder firm or do AS/400 work. You can both be on the lookout for each other. There are so many niches in our business that it's easy to keep in touch with other technically savvy people. Hook up with people who have the same types of needs but for a specific technical requirement that is not applicable to your business. It doesn't hurt to keep a network of people out looking for you.

Part-Time People

I mentioned the possibility of part-time before, and I'll mention it again. If you're a business owner, you probably think of your employees who work five day weeks as part timers, anyway! So what's the big deal if your part time people work three days a week or five?

The Sales Packet

Remember that you're trying to accomplish two things. The first is to evaluate them. The second is to sell them on your firm. One thing we're beginning to put into place is a more aggressive response to people who have approached us.

We screen them by sending them a packet of information about the job, the company, a job application form and a list of other things they'll have to return. They are instructed to go through this information and return the job application (and the other stuff) before we'll consider them.

The first advantage to this additional step is that you get to weed out those who are not interested. A lot of applicants don't care and won't bother to return the info. You probably don't want them. Those that are truly interested will answer correctly.

The second advantage is that you make sure you have the same info from everyone. Some people send in a resume that doesn't have all the facts you need, other people send in a cover letter, still others just leave a phone number. You can make sure you're treating them all as fairly as possible, and make sure you're getting the basic info from everyone.

How To Get Rid of People Who Call and Don't Have a Chance

If you have developed any type of visibility at all, eventually you will get calls from other programmers asking for work. This is good - it's the reason you've got your "people finder" radar turned on 24 hours a day. However, you can't afford to talk to every person who calls - you don't have the time. That is why you have recruiting procedures for handling such inquiries. The solution, of course, is to get them on the right track and have them send a resume and some sample code in. You can then evaluate them in the normal course of operations.

However, there will always be those who believe that they have such personality and smarts that your recruiting procedures don't apply to them. Instead they will call and want to talk to you - to "get to know you," to "do lunch," to "talk about some opportunities" or to "do some networking." There are a dozen job-hunting manuals and a few placement firms who actively encourage this activity. This is a problem.

The problem is that they want to waste your time. I don't mean that they woke up one morning and said, "Hey, I'm going to call this guy up and waste his time," but in effect that's what they are doing. Let's take a real life example of someone who called me, oh, an indeterminate time ago. He called and wanted to talk about Internet, blah, blah, blah, FoxPro, blah, blah, blah Visual Basic blah, blah, blah application design, blah, blah, blah, their cool home page with Java, blah, blah, blah. While he may have been smart and clever, he would have gone on forever if I had let him.

I have a quick solution to get those people off my back and at the same time not offend them. It provides them with the ability to save face and does not burn bridges in the future. That guy may be a lousy Access programmer but he may know a thing or two about OLE (and OLE might actually work some day!) So don't lose the possibility of getting together with them at some later time.

See Appendix for full text of The 17 Questions

A number of years ago I developed a set of "17 Questions" that were designed to give me a quick overview of the person's technical abilities with the language that we were using. They are wide ranging and yet, at the same time, very specific to the kinds of things that we do. We didn't do event-driven programming at the time, so we didn't ask about DEACTIVE WINDOW. We didn't write our own DLL's so we didn't ask questions about C. We do employ a rather sophisticated set of interrelated function libraries, so we ask about functions and procedures. When I get one of these guys on the phone, I pull out the list and start talking tech. "Can I ask you a couple language specific questions?" and he thinks he's already got the job.

Then I roll down the list of questions, each of which has a very clear cut answer. At the end of the 17 questions, which has taken about one and a half minutes to ask, he's said, "I don't know" eight times, has given six wrong answers and hit the other three on the head. Usually he's not aware of how he's done at this point. I tell him he has gotten three out of 17 correct, and then, as gently as possible, explain that "he may be highly skilled in some areas of the language but doesn't have the knowledge needed in order to be successful here."

Then I continue, "This means that I would have to bring you in as an entry level developer and since you consider yourself experienced, you are probably expecting to be compensated as an expert, so bringing you in as a rookie will not make you comfortable. It doesn't make sense for us to try to train you because we're not going to be able to make any money if you're being trained for six months and being paid an advanced developer's salary." This is a pretty humbling experience, and gets the guy off of the phone quickly and at the same time is able to help him save face. Instead of being told that he's a loser, the simple fact is that their skill set doesn't match our needs. It also doesn't wound our reputation by criticizing or bad mouthing somebody about their abilities.

Furthermore, he now gets the idea that, "Wow, I thought I was good but there is an awful lot that I don't know." And by having this set of questions ready to ask, he is also surprised that I am prepared. He is now left with three good impressions of our firm: 1) We are highly skilled, 2) We are highly organized, 3) We don't dump on people if they are not a match.

The Headhunter

Remember that I told you that I'm opinionated? Well...

The other nuisance call is the head hunter. These guys are terrible. I have yet to meet a single head hunter that knew enough to get out of the rain. I'm not saying that they are all like this - it's just that I haven't met one yet. As one of the perks of running a user group, I get a lot of calls from headhunters with a "once in a lifetime" opportunity - this programmer just became available but is liable to be snatched up at any moment. I offer a free one paragraph ad for their position in the user group newsletter and that's it.

If he asks if I am interested in hiring this person - after all, "this guy is probably just perfect for your firm" - I translate this into meaning that the person put the word "FoxPro" on his resume and he spelled it correctly.

I indicate that in the X number of years I have been in the business, I have yet to find a head hunter who can find a person who has a clue, and I'm rather curious why he thinks this person is any different than the last 30 calls I have gotten over the last three months. This usually shuts them up nice and quickly.

If the head hunter really pushes, I'll fax him the list of 17 questions and ask that the developer fill it out and return it to me. That gets most head hunters off your back. They can make the next phone call and hopefully land some chump who will believe the headhunter. Once in a great while, the guy will send the questions to his developer and once in a greater while a developer will send it back and we're back to square one where the guy gets 14 wrong. What's even more telling is that this guy didn't have to come up with the answers on the spot. He could research them and still gets them wrong.

Conclusion

Many projects go astray not because of technical incompetence, but because of people issues. A large number of developers either try to do too many things or simply don't learn the language well enough. As a result, they struggle to 'make things work' as opposed to 'making it work right.' The time you spend in finding the right people is the best investment you can make.

4.2 Hiring People

♦ Getting Resumes

Set Up Criteria For the Job
Evaluating Resumes
Cover Letter
The Resume
Code Samples
Due Diligence

♦ The Phone Call

Set the Stage
About the Company and the Job
Basic Data
How to Terminate a Conversation
Get Them Talking

♦ The In-Person Interviews

First Interview
Second Interview
Twenty Really Weird Interview Questions (and the reasons for asking)
Subsequent Interviews

♦ The Offer

If you've done your homework right, you will soon be inundated by people looking to work for you.

Getting Resumes

The first step in hiring people is to get names, not resumes. You will get people who call you up on the phone and leave a phone number. You will get people who E-mail you with a two sentence statement, "I'm an experienced programmer and can add a lot to your team!" You'll get scraps of paper shoved under your office door. The end result is a stack of names with various stuff attached to it, which some may refer to as resumes.

The first thing you do is to look for some way to weed out the, er, the rubbish. That's the one thing that most people looking for jobs have never figured out - that the guy on the other side of the desk is looking for a reason to get rid of a resume. He has too many pieces of paper and can't deal with all of them, so they are looking for any excuse to get rid of some of them.

However, you can't use "any excuse" - both morally and legally. It ain't right and it ain't legal. So how do you perform this 'weeding out' process correctly?

You want to start on as level a playing ground as possible, and that means getting resumes from every applicant. Everyone who has contacted you should be sent a "Sales Packet" as described in the previous chapter so that they're at least starting out at the same place. It's then up to them to do the best they can in the contest once the whistle blows.

Set Up Criteria for the Job

The trick to organizing this race properly is to write out your evaluation criteria before you start looking at resumes. Actually, you might even consider doing this before you run the ad, but that really smacks of being too prepared, doesn't it?

Think about the person that would ideally fill this position, and what attributes they must have in order to be successful in this position. Then consider what attributes would be helpful but are not required. And finally, which attributes are 'extra credit' but won't matter if the first two groups are lacking - these can be used as tie-breakers. Take this list of criteria, write it down, and date it. Dating it is important so that when someone you interviewed three years ago comes back and tries to slap a lawsuit on you, claiming that you wouldn't hire them because they were X, Y, or Z, you can pull this list out as evidence of how you went about hiring.

"Actually, the reason why I didn't bring you in is because your resume stated that you wanted an entry level analyst position with no programming required. At the time, our requirements included about 25% programming."

You've got to do this. It's kind of hard because it's not black and white. There is a lot of gray in this process. But you have got to protect yourself. If you have shown that you have a methodical process for looking at and evaluating people and that those criteria are not biased, your life will be a lot easier.

The second advantage to writing out your criteria is it helps you to make a decision. We are all influenced by irrelevant factors. If somebody comes in with great qualifications but they look like the guy who stole your girl just before Senior Prom, well, they're going to have a really hard time finding work at your shop, aren't they? You want to provide an environment where the effect of those irrelevant attributes is minimized or eliminated.

Let's take a look at some possible criteria.

- What is this person going to be doing on a day to day, hour by hour basis? What actual skills do they need to possess?
- What experience does this person have to have? Is it something that they can learn, or do they need to be able to hit the ground running?
- What background must they have? Why MUST they have it? A lot of jobs "require a four year degree" when, in fact, the work that they are going to do makes schooling irrelevant.
- Will other non-technical skills be required or helpful - customer management, writing, speaking abilities, etc.
- What other factors are relevant? Do the need to be able to travel? Do they need their own transportation? Will they be working in specific environments that are dangerous or hostile? Is there a security clearance required?

Evaluating Resumes

You'll also want to establish a base set of rules about the resumes you're going to go through. Supposing you've got a stack of 50 resumes you want to have an objective set of measures that will help you divide the pile into the contenders and the pretenders. These criteria might include:

- Is the package they sent you tailored to the position advertised? Or did they just mail out yet another stack of after circling every remote possibility in the Sunday paper?
- Is the package they sent you complete? Did they include a cover letter? Did they include code samples if they were requested? Did they send a complete resume or was it thrown together at the last minute?

- Is the package presentable? They are trying to sell themselves to you, and the manner in which they present themselves to you can be indicative of the way they would present themselves to customers as your employee. This means original versions of a cover letter, a nicely printed resume, no typographical errors, reasonably organized and easy to read.
- Does the cover letter indicate what they're looking for? Did they mention the job they're applying for or is it obvious that they're just using a shotgun approach?
- Did they do something, anything, to indicate that they have a real passion for the job? Did they possibly do a little research on your company, on the industry, on the business?

Given these types of criteria (please feel free to add your own!), you can quickly create three piles - the contenders, the "Well, maybe..." and the "Yeah, as if..."

Now that you've got a list of requirements for the job, you're ready to start pawing through the stacks of hopefuls.

As noted, you will get resumes from a wide range of folk. Some of these folk have been through the job hunt before; others are brand new (or it will appear that way.) So let's be really, really picky about what we see on a resume.

Cover Letter

These are professional positions - somewhere above the level of assistant fry cook at Burger Boy. They should have a cover letter that explains what they're looking for, why you should be interested in them, and contain a call to action. They should also spell everything correctly.

In the olden days, when I had more time on my hands, I would occasionally take a particularly horrible resume, pull out my red pen, and grade the thing like it was a homework assignment. Yes, I'd circle spelling errors, correct their grammar, ask pointed questions like "How can you claim that you're an expert in C++ if you've only been using the language for three months?" and so on. Then I'd mail it back to them. I *never* received a follow-up to one, which kind of saddened me. I'm sure most people were either very angry or simply horrified that they got caught with their pants down - but I sure would have liked to seen the individual with enough chutzpah to make the corrections and try a second time.

Next, I look for something compelling! They're are trying to sell you on how great they would be for this position. "They're dedicated and hard working and they stand for quality," and so on, that's all standard stuff. So when you have 50 people beating their chest, each proclaiming that they're king of the programmer hill, what is going to set one apart from the others? If someone figures out the answer to this and communicates it to me, this tells me maybe there is something worth investigating further. What I want to hear is **Passion!**

In his book "*Dynamics of Software Development,*" published by Microsoft Press, Jim McCarthy has this wonderful line.

"The role of passion in software development can't be overstated. To some people, the computer represents the ultimate in self-expression and self-discovery. As the pen is to the poet, the palette to the painter, is a compiler to a software developer. When the passion burns out, the compulsive interest in pouring oneself into an invisible yet coherent and dynamic stream of bits goes with it."

Frankly, I have no place for people who are applying for a software development job but are treating it as if they were selling furniture in the evenings.

Have they looked up to see what your company does? Do they have any motivation, ambition about finding out what it is you do and how they might fit in? Have they talked around town to see how your company is regarded? Have they checked on the kinds of projects you have worked on or talked to your employees? Do they have really more of an interest than, "Oh, here's another company, I'll send them a resume."

If any of this comes through the cover letter, then they've risen to the top.

The Resume

Basic information. Their resume should have a name, address, phone number (day and night). Extra credit for the person who has an unusually spelled name and provides either a nickname or a phonetic interpretation of their name. Either they've been through difficulties before or they have a bit of empathy for the reader - a sharp quality to have.

Objective. What are they looking for? Do they have an *objective* on their resume? When someone sends me a resume and goes into a list of jobs they've had and what school they've been to, but assumes I know what they're looking for, I get quite distressed. I can't read their mind, and I think it's an unreasonable assumption for them to think that I can. I want to know what they want to do. Some people don't put down an objective because they are afraid they will be eliminated from some position. They're just throwing resumes into the mix and hope something will find a match.

Furthermore, it is rather common for a person to have access to a word processor, so the expectation that they could tailor a resume is not terribly onerous.

School Experience. If they have been out of school a long time, they will probably list their work experience first, while if they've only been out for a year or two, they may well place their school first. Let's tackle school first.

I don't care where they went to high school, and am not all that concerned with where they went to college unless it was a really high-end college or if they did spectacularly well. A 4.0 at most any school means they paid attention in class a little bit. If they went some place like Carnegie or Stanford, I would like to know that. Frankly, a 2.6 at "any old school" - I'm not really sure how relevant that's going to be to me. I guess I'd like to know what degree they have, whether or not it took them nine years to get through school, and so on, just to get a feeling for who they are and what types of life experience they have.

Work Experience. Do they list their work experience in chronological order? As an engineer and programmer I like to see this in black and white. I like to see work experience listed from most recent to most outdated, and after ten years or so, I don't really care. However, if a person has a, shall we say, checkered job history, the "resume books" advise that work history should be organized in functional order, showing a progression of increasing responsibility and expanding skill set. Of course, for anyone who has looked through a dozen resumes, this treatment is a red flag saying "I hopped from job to job and I'm trying to hide it." There isn't anything inherently bad with a number of jobs in a short period of time, but I want to know about it.

First, there *could be* something bad hiding in the wings, and it's up to you to find it. Somebody who says "13 years in a variety of positions in the food service industry" and lists a few of the companies they've worked for but doesn't list the dates could be hiding something. It could be something perfectly reasonable, like they went travelling with their spouse through Europe for a year, and the candidate is simply being shy about admitting it. But I want to know.

On the other hand the person might have just run across a streak of bad luck - it does happen. This is a mobile, transient economy and having a period of unemployment or having a period in which you switch from job to job is normal. I can understand that.

Second, I don't particularly like being lied to, and this type of misdirection feels a lot like subterfuge. If you're trying to hide this from me, what else might you be trying to hide? Software development requires an incredible amount of trust, and you have to be really confident that you're getting the whole story from one of your developers.

This issue of honesty is another reason I like to see dates attached to all schooling and work history. Dates are very specific facts that can be checked, and if someone has a propensity for stretching the truth, this is an area that can be validated quickly. I have a responsibility to my customers, my other employees, and myself to practice due diligence during the hiring process.

The key point is that they have to be able to perform, they have to be dependable and I have to be able to trust them. People with outside influences that make them incompetent, unreliable or dishonest are not qualified for the position.

Professional societies. Many people list professional societies they belong to. While I'm sure it's valuable, and in some occasions actually means something, most people are just looking for another line item to add to their resume. I really don't care about most of that stuff. When they describe these activities, you should be looking for action verbs and that they actually got something done as opposed to "was a part of a team and all I did was watch" or even worse - "all I did was to get in the middle and screw things up until I was moved somewhere else."

Hobbies. I like to see hobbies listed. It tells me that they have outside interests, that they are looking to expand themselves past sitting at home and watching TV, and that there might be some commonalties. It's nice to find someone else who is into body-surfing - particularly if you live in Kansas. It's also an opportunity to break the ice with them in a non-threatening way.

You can also use their hobbies to get a better feel for their level of passion and commitment to life. Looking for someone who has a drive for excellence in another field is a good idea - these people are devoted to excellence in all aspects of their life, and that will generally carry through in whatever they do, be it raising kids, making furniture or writing custom database applications.

What to do if they are involved in an activity you don't really care for? Well, frankly, blowing off a resume just because they belong to a religious or ethnic or political group not of your choosing is illegal. Period. End of story.

What if something on the resume that makes you think they might not fit in with your crew? If their other qualifications look sound, keep your mouth shut. Trust in the team you've already assembled and let them pick up on the "team chemistry" issue during the interview stage.

Code Samples

I like to ask potential developers for code samples because most of them will not do it. When I put an ad in the paper, I expect people to follow instructions. If they are going to be belligerent and bad about following instructions when they are starting to look for a job, I don't have a lot of confidence that they are going to be good employees later.

Why would someone not provide code samples when it was requested? Well, some of them don't have a clue what you are talking about. Others will think that they are above the ordinary candidate and that they don't have to comply with this requirement. Some will want to, but won't have the confidence. And some might cite seemingly reasonable excuses such as confidentiality issues.

Yet some will send in a listing, or maybe even a diskette. And once in a while - yes, this actually has happened to us! - someone will send you code that works. The superior candidate will find something to send - if confidentiality worries them, they'll "change the names to protect the innocent."

One final note. Be sure to respond to every resume you receive, even if to simply state that "Your qualifications don't match our needs at the present time."

```
April 1, 1997

Dear Mr. Joe Schmoe,

Thank you for your interest in the position of
Programmer at Hentzenwerke Corporation.  However,
your skill set does not match our needs at this time.

Sincerely,
Hentzenwerke Corporation
```

Kiss Off Letter

Due Diligence

Before we go on, let me offer a few words of caution. Hiring is a tricky process. Once you start communicating with applicants you must document your contacts carefully. By practicing due diligence, you are more liable to avoid frivolous lawsuits and other problems. There are two fundamental rules to follow. First: see a lawyer to make sure you're doing things right. Second: document, document, document. Document everything. This started with the written criteria you used to weed out resumes, and it continues with your first phone call to potential candidates.

Practicing due diligence can help defend you from three angles: customer liability, against charges of discrimination or unfair hiring/firing practices, and from being defrauded.

Customer liability. You are liable for the actions of your employees. You will be sending them out to meet clients, giving them access to your client's confidential information and charging clients for your employees abilities. You must make sure that your employees can be trusted and are capable of doing the work.

Charges of discrimination. Remember all your documentation of resumes and phone calls? By being able to show that you had consistent criteria to apply, you reduce your exposure in this area.

Fraud. Just like thieves, people who are out to defraud will look for an easy target. I recently read a story of a person who started work at a company, and then filed for workman's compensation as well as a civil suit using Carpal Tunnel Syndrome as the reason. This was after only four days of work. The company settled rather than litigate, despite the fact that the person had retained a lawyer to handle this claim *before* they started work. But the company couldn't risk litigation, and ended up paying out just to get the case off their backs. If you make getting a job with you a bit more rigorous, they'll look for someone else.

The Phone Call

Set the Stage

Identify yourself. The first step - identify yourself and explain why you are calling. You know who you are and what you are doing. You've probably just made 12 phone calls and so you're "in tune" with this process. However, they're probably not prepared. They may not quite understand what you are saying right away. Give them a few minutes to get their bearings.

Do they have time to talk? Next, ask if this is a good time to talk for 15-20 minutes. They might be in the middle of something and you will want their undivided attention. Also, you want to give them a shot a making their best impression. Make it easy for them to tell you they can't talk right now.

Party Manners. The whole key behind our interviewing process is to get people off of those interview manners. We sometimes call them "Party manners." You know, saying "Thank you" and "Please," opening the car door and so on. When people are on Party manners, they don't get too comfortable or let their hair down. They're thinking, "what if they find out what the real "me" is like and they don't like that person?"

Same idea goes for interviewing. People will be reticent to show their true colors too early - or at all. My point of view is that I'm going to find out what this person is like sooner or later. I want it to be sooner. Furthermore, they need to find out what I'm like and what the company is like - and again, I want to show them sooner rather than later so we don't waste each others time.

Hiring, to me, is a long, in-depth commitment second only to marriage. In a lot of companies, people spend more time at their jobs than with their spouse. Yet they will spend years dating someone before getting married, but take a job on the basis of two 40 minute interviews. What are they thinking?

We want to find out what this person is really like because we will be living with them for a long time. If both parties are not compatible, we need to know as soon as possible. It does take a long time to really convey that attitude to somebody, and you have to be very good at it. As the advice to the budding actor goes, "The key to successful acting is sincerity. Once you can fake that, you've got it made."

Why 15 minutes? So now, in the first 30 seconds, we've told them who we are and asked if they have time to chat for a while. Let's assume they said yes and we're now at the point where we're going to talk for 15-20 minutes. Why 15-20 minutes? Well, 15-20 minutes is still a short enough time that if after the first few minutes, you can tell that the chemistry isn't there, that something is not clicking, you won't make them feel uncomfortable if you cut the conversation short. Yet, it's long enough that you can actually get some decent information - if you plan it out in advance.

Get a pen and some paper. The second thing to say after confirming that they can talk is, "You may want to get a pencil and paper and take a couple notes." It also allows them to write down questions during the course of the conversation. One thing I get rather annoyted at hearing is "I had a question but I forgot what it was." Well, if they had a pencil and a paper right there, they could have written that question down and wouldn't have forgotten it! Seems like common sense, but you'd be amazed how many people decline your offer.

Intelligence and common sense we are looking for. If someone says, "I wrote down a couple of questions earlier - can I ask them now?"this impresses me. This tells me that they are a little more organized than the average bear. And we want people more organized than the average bear, don't we?

What to expect during this interview process. Now that we're actually talking (I know, it's taken 20 minutes just to read about the first 30 seconds of this phone conversation), I explain the ground rules of the interview process with our company and what they can expect. They should understand that we don't hire on the first or second interview, and that we expect them to meet everyone else in the shop. We want them to have enough opportunities to gather as much information about our company and the job as they need. If they're in such desperate straits that they need a job by Thursday, then they're not going to like our interview process. I tell them that they could have four or five interviews, and that if we get that far, it's not because we're flakes or indecisive, but rather, it is good news, because they've made it that far through the gauntlet.

The Responsibility Speech. Most companies treat employees like 12 year olds. And while I can think of a few 12 year olds who I'm very impressed with, I'm not sure I'd turn over a $25,000 custom software development project to any of them.

We treat people like (gasp!) adults. This means that they are expected to be responsible, contributing members of the company and that we don't look over their shoulder every five minutes, micro-managing how they do every little task. At the same time, we don't cotton much to excuses. They have the responsibility to get the work done, and that's that. If they get stuck, it's up to them to get help - I'm not going to come around and check to see that they've done every problem on their arithmetic homework.

At the same time, I tell them, to the best of my ability, what they can expect from me and the firm. But I remind them that since I'm human and fallible - I forget things, I make mistakes - I'll also have them talk to others in the shop so they get a better, more rounded picture of the firm. It's their ultimate responsibility to gather the information they need.

Now, I've laid down the fundamental law in our company, and *I will hold them to it*. If they think they can get away with irresponsibility at some point, I'll remind them and if push comes to shove, I can shove harder. At the same time, while this is a powerful stick, it's a more lucrative carrot, wouldn't you say? Which company do you want to work for - the one that assumes you're a 12 year old or the one that actually treats you like a grown-up? Tough choice, eh?

This little spiel has taken about a minute of the conversation.

About the Company and the Job

About Hentzenwerke. Next on the list of things to cover is a bit about the company - what we do, company history, something about the glamorous founder, that sort of thing. I'd suggest having a checklist of things to mention - if you don't, you'll yak for hours during the first interview or two, but then you'll get tired. By the time you're talking to the tenth candidate, you'll barely say two sentences about the company.

About the job. Next you'll want to discuss the job itself - what the position entails, the general environment, what they would be doing, and so on. Again, a checklist is a good idea here.

Well? Are you interested? This now should have taken between five and ten minutes - depending on how yakky you are and how many questions they ask. At this point you may have already determined that you're not too interested in them, so you'll need to go to the next step to determine how to let them down gently. But it's usually too soon to find out. So all we're trying to find out is if, given this additional level of detail, they are happy they contacted you.

Basic Data

Confirm the ad. Now we get to the nitty gritty. I go through the ad that they answered, and confirm every requirement listed in it, as well as a few more that aren't appropriate for the ad.There are weasels out there who will answer an ad that they're not qualified for. Just because they answered the ad doesn't mean they have each of the attributes listed.

Note: when you're doing this, be careful. Be very careful. Consult a lawyer. There are a lot of rules about what you can and can't ask. Here's what we can:

Full or part time? Are they looking for part or full-time work? Our ads often indicate an interest in both, but the candidate does not always identify which.

Do they smoke? We ask them this flat out. If you, the reader, are a smoker, you might be offended, and I don't mean to be offensive, but this is an important point for us.

Location, location, location. Are they interested in working downtown? Some people, incredibly enough, do not care that downtown is where the lights are bright, and they want to stay out in The 'Burbs.

Hours? What kind of hours are they available? Will overtime pose a problem?

Are you working now? A surprising number of people answering ads in the paper aren't working. If they say, "No, I'm not," there could be a lot of good reasons for that, and that doesn't particularly bother me. However, if they try to dance around the question, I start to get nervous. If they really hedge around, do all sorts of fancy talking and refuse to tell me, then I won't talk to them anymore. If they are going to be that evasive when trying to make a good impression, I can presume what kind of employee they are going to be. There are many good reasons that someone is not working. It's how they give you the answer rather than what the answer is that's important.

Why are they leaving? Again, it's not really the answer that is important unless they say, "Well, I knifed my old boss and had to leave before they found out who did it." That may be an answer that would disqualify them. It's how they deliver the answer. Are they comfortable and do their answers sound reasonable, or do they sound defensive, hostile and wary? *Do they bad mouth their current boss or employer?* People generally don't leave because they are thrilled with their job. They leave because they want something better, different, they're unhappy, whatever. I want to find out how they react in that kind of position. When things go wrong, when things go bad, can they keep their cool? Are they smooth with a customer during a difficult situation? There are always two sides to every story. I'd like to know what both sides of the story are.

How much are they making now? This tells me expectations, and whether I can afford them. People generally don't take jobs with a significant pay cut. I once had a situation where the candidate called up and seemed pretty sharp, I thought I would like to speak with him some more. Then, I found out he was making well over twice what I was making. While he may have been very well worth it, I simply couldn't afford that type of cash flow hit at the time. It would be unfair for me to have talked to him for a long period of time, only to find out that he would have had to sell for three months prior to his employment here in order for me to cover his first paycheck.

The reverse is also true, of course. Suppose the position you are offering is for $25,000 and a person is making $6.50 right now. They are going to see $25,000 and fall over themselves, promising the moon to you because it's more money than they could ever conceive of in their life.

If someone refuses to tell you, end the conversation. That's all there is to it. You have to know and if they are not going to tell you, then how are you going to work with them? Some people think by telling you they will loose their negotiating strength. If they are going in this with that kind of attitude then they should talk to someone else. It's not as if we are going to magically find a way to bump up their salary 40% if they play some fancy negotiating game. What we can pay is what we pay. If they are not going to believe that we will treat them fairly along those lines, then the relationship won't work.

How much do you want to make? At the same time, people get put into situations where they are truly underemployed. They get down-sized out of a job, they need to bring some bucks into the family, they take a job that is less than optimal and as a result, they're underpaid. If this happens it's perfectly understandable. Suddenly, you see a programmer that's making $30,000 and you're thinking, this person has an awful lot of skills and states they are expecting to make $48,000 and I can appreciate that. They took this interim job just to put bread on the table, but they really should expect compensation at that kind of level. Frankly, if you try to save a buck by figuring they were making $30,000 and so you will give them $34,000, they may come on board, but they'll still be looking and they'll jump ship at the next best offer.

Very few people will be nasty and aggressive about that, so it really isn't that big of an issue. But it is something we need to know because compensation is very important and if the expectations are out of line on either side then one of us or both of us are wasting our time.

What do they want to do with the rest of their life? I ask them if they won the lottery which would guarantee them approximately their current salary for the rest of their life, what would they do with their life? The money means that they could support themselves comfortably enough but, that they just don't have to work.

The first thing most people would do is drive their spouse crazy, but after that - what comes next? Most of the time they just fumble around with an answer. That means they will give me a pretty truthful answer because they will say the first thing that comes to their mind. What I want to hear is something along the lines of, "I'd write computer programs, I love writing computer programs. I would do it without getting paid at all!" That's the *passion.* That's the person I am interested in. The person who thinks computers are so cool that by the time the sun starts setting, they realize they forgot to eat lunch again today.

There are so many people that go to work and just can't wait to get out of work at 5 p.m. so they can do something they really like. If you go to any office park or downtown office building, you'll see them blast through the doors at 5 p.m. You can see in their eyes that they are finally free to do something else.

I want to find the person who comes to work saying, "I do something really cool! I like my kids and I like knocking around on the bike, but I also really, really like computers." As the ad goes, "Life is short, play hard." It is far too short to waste time on doing things you don't like. I want to find the people who have a passion for writing software. Not only are they going to have a better quality of life, but they will make life for everyone around them easier as well. Not only are they getting compensated dollar-wise, benefit wise, and so on, but they also have a job they love. Someone else will come along and offer them another 10%, but if they think this stuff is cool, we will probably hang on to them.

Other important questions. We also ask very important questions like, "Do you drink Diet Coke?" (We do occasionally hire people who don't drink Diet Coke, but we don't treat them as nicely.) This is one of those goofy things that lightens up the conversation a little bit and gets them comfortable and relaxed and a little off of their interview manners.

A turning point. These are the topics we hit in the first 15-20 minutes. At this point we are going to have an idea if we want to continue talking to them, or let it go. We can continue to evaluate passion. Are they interested? (Of course, if they have any brains at all, they will act interested.) Have they been asking questions all along, or just listening to you yak?

It's important, while you're talking about how great you are and how smart you are, to be really jazzed about it. First of all, that shouldn't be hard because you really should be excited about it. You don't want to sound as if you are reading off of a check list in a monotonous tone. While you're talking about the firm, you should also be listening - do they start asking questions or do they just listen and say, "Uh-huh, uh-huh, that sounds interesting." It's one of those subjective things. Do they sound like they want to hear more or are they really bored?

How to Terminate a Conversation

OK, you've done your best sales job, tried to draw them out, but they're simply not interested. Or perhaps, unfortunately, they are interested - really interested - but the door isn't swinging both ways. The golden rule is to let them save face.

You want to give them a good reason that this relationship isn't going to work. You want them to understand that they're not a bad person but that "What they are looking for and what I am looking for are different things."

On the other hand you could explain that "You just don't sound that interested, so let's not waste our time any further." This is a bit more of an "in your face" approach, but, if it's really true, then go for it. If they protest, explain what led you to that conclusion - that in 20 minutes, they haven't asked a single question about the job or the company. Either this will shake them up into getting more involved, or you can save yourself the rest of a one-way conversation.

Get Them Talking

On the other hand, let's suppose that the first 15 or 20 minutes are successful. We've told them a little bit about the firm and about the position and we've confirmed some basic information about them. During this phone interview we now want to evaluate them. If you're going to continue talking ask them if they can still talk. Remember, when you first called - you said this would just take about 15-20 minutes. Make sure they can still give you their undivided attention.

Tell me about you. Now it's their turn. How do we get them to talk? Easy. Say, "So tell me about yourself." Then, shut up and listen.

> This reminds me of an episode of *Cheers*. Sam is talking to his date, and delivers the line, "Well, enough about me, let's talk about you. What do you think of me?"

Ask open ended questions. What do you like about your current job? What do you hate about it? What do you do in your spare time? What kind of hobbies do you have? Tell me about what you've done at work? What have you actually accomplished?

We want them to start conversations and find out what's on their minds. Can they initiate and hold a conversation? Now remember, we're talking to nerds, so they may not be all that extroverted.

However, even the most introverted, geekiest, nerdliest programmer in the world will have a hot button. What might this be? Ask them about the last hunk of code they wrote. Ask them about the last cool thing they did. Ask them about the last great project they worked on. Even the most introverted of them will get all fired up about this topic and you won't be able to shut them up for hours.

If you don't get a response to this, it either means, 1) You're talking to someone who simply can't communicate regardless, 2) You're talking to somebody who isn't very interested in you or your firm, or 3) You're talking to someone who hasn't actually done anything and therefore they can't talk about it. There is the final case of someone who's under-employed or mis-employed right now. In this last situation, ask them what is their ideal project.

The key is details. Some people may be, at first, a little reticent to talk because they're shy, because they're on party manners, or because they're nervous. This is only 20-30 minutes into a phone call. But by now you should have been able to draw them out to some extent.

Other topics and questions. There are a couple of other standard questions you can use to get the conversation jump started if it starts to die. You can find many of these in any standard text about interviewing, of course. A few of my favorites include:

- Which development tools have you used, describe a project you did with the tool, and how would you rate your level of proficiency at each one?
- Describe three things you really like about your current job.
- List three things that you really abhor about your current job.
- Describe the ideal job - including the environment - for you.
- Where do you want to be in five years?

If you don't bring them in for an interview. We've already discussed how to tell them that you've decided not to continue - you explain a factual reason that you don't feel there is a match so that you can help them save face. Most of the time, the candidate will feel pretty much the same way, and will accept this as is. However, there are times when they won't. Remember, they're programmers, just like us, and social skills are not always an abundant attribute.

If, after hearing the news, they start whining and begging for a second chance, you may need to be, at some point, simply firm. No easy way around this one. You're the boss. At some point you just have to say, "Sorry, but this is my decision that's that. Thank you for your time."

One other possibility is that they turn your opinion around in that last 30 seconds - the half-court shot, the Hail Mary pass from mid-field. I'm always open to a zinger like that - it impresses me that they have the tenacity not to give up, and to do it in an elegant way.

Finishing up the phone interview. Over the last 15 to 30 minutes, you should have formed an opinion on whether you want the person to come in for a face to face meeting. At this point, it's not only important to set a date and time, but also to set expectations - an agenda - for that first meeting. "Well, I'm pretty happy with our conversation and would like to have you in for an interview.

You'd get to see the shop, meet a couple of the people, and we can talk more in depth about what this position entails and get to know each other better. How does that sound?"

Post Mortuum. As soon as you hang up the phone, stop and jot down some notes about the conversation. What's your overall impression of the person, their potential with your firm, their interest? This is especially important if you are on a phone interview marathon. Write it all down while the individual is still fresh in your head.

The In-Person Interviews

There are two significant attributes to every employee. We've covered one already - passion. The other is brains. Languages change so quickly that specific knowledge sometimes is irrelevant, or, at least, not as important. We need to find if they have the brains to learn on an ongoing basis. During our numerous face-to-face interviews we will find out.

The face to face interviews, while they take a fair amount of time, are really expanded versions of the phone conversation. What you do during them is pretty much up to you in relation to the job requirements. As we go through the multiple interview process, the actual things we do each time change. I've already discussed in great length my philosophy about employees and how to treat people; the interviews are merely a chance to gather additional information on things that you can only pick up face to face.

First Interview

So the door opens at 5:45 p.m. and a somewhat timid fellow (or gal) with tape holding their glasses together peers into the office. The very first thing to do is make them feel comfortable. Remember, they're still on interview manners, and just possibly they're playing games, so you want them to let down their guard and get to know them as soon as possible.

The tour. Offer them a Diet Coke and some Doritos (you want to verify that they're really a developer), and walk them around the office. Show them your fancy file server upon which you sweated blood when installing a new 9 GB RAID drive, show them the refrigerator and microwave and the box of candy on top of the tape backup unit.

Poke your head in each developer's office, make some wise cracks about the decorations (or lack thereof), ignoring the fact that there might actually be a person in the office, and finally, take a gander out the windows. The idea is to get them used to the "look and feel" of the environment.

Then pop back into your office, offer them a comfortable chair, and start yakking. A couple of rules here - I always try to keep my desk completely clean, so that there aren't any distractions, and I always try to be available at precisely the scheduled time. Nothing bothers me more than having to wait for an appointment (you should see me at a doctor's office!). I don't feel it's fair for someone coming to see me to have to wait.

Small talk. What do we talk about in our interview? A little small talk, of course, perhaps bringing up something that happened in the industry recently, or an event around town - whatever comes to mind. If it's not natural to make this type of small talk, then you shouldn't. Subjecting a candidate to artificially induced banter is worse than having to listen to it on the 10 p.m. news.

As soon as you can, review the agenda for the interview that you set out over the phone, and then proceed to check off each item.

Demonstration of some applications. It's usually a good idea to demonstrate the types of things your firm does, so fire up a machine and go through a few applications, explaining what makes your development style particularly unique, interesting or special.

While you're doing this, be sure to note their reactions. (You *are* taking notes yourself, aren't you?) Are they paying attention? Do they understand what you're talking about? Do they ask questions? Are they good questions, or are they simply being polite?

The company. I usually spend some time during the first interview to bore them with more information about the company - how it got started, a few war stories, a lecture about the company values and philosophy, that sort of thing.

Their experiences. Now that they've been put to sleep, it's time to get them talking. Ask them again about the applications they've worked on, how they develop software, what their coding style is like, and things they like to do.

Get them to tell you some war stories of their own, engage them in technical discussions about specific applications or implementations, and go over some stuff that didn't work out all that well.

This last topic is particularly interesting, and if you can draw them into it without them realizing what you've done, so much the better. You're trying to get them to feel at home, so that you can get a better idea of what they're like, and if they can feel comfortable enough to share some failures as well as successes, then you've started to make some inroads.

The job application. You may or may not have a job application that you have them fill out; if you don't, it's probably about time to make one up or pick up of those $49 Your Personal Lawyer pieces of software. I've found it handy, if you are getting bad vibes from someone, to have them fill out the job application twice at two different times. I simply explain that, "Silly me, I must have misplaced the first one - would you mind filling it out again?" Then, check the information they enter on both forms. If there are any significant discrepancies, it's time to verify all of the information on the form to see if your gut feeling was accurate.

The 17 Questions revisited. If, after the phone interview and one face to face meeting, your gut still suspects that they're just talking a good game, now is a good time to bring out the 17 Questions.

The minutes of the meeting. The last thing I do at the close of each of these interviews is rather unusual. I ask them to write out the minutes of the meeting - of the interview. To a person, they look at me like I'm from Mars. It's truly a wonderful experience to see this response, though. When they realize that I'm serious, they usually buckle down. I give them a few pieces of paper, a pen, and then leave the room. If they've taken notes during the interview, that's good, but it's also a rarity.

Why do I do this? First, I get to see them freak out to one extent or another. I've seen people totally lose their cool on this one, and that's been valuable information. One person actually refused to do it - and I promptly showed them the door. This may be an unusual request, but it's not illegal or kinky, and when this person showed such reticence, I found out that this was not the person I wanted to deal with as an employee.

The second benefit is that I get to see how they do brain work - how do they organize their thoughts, how do they communicate, and what do they do in a potentially stressful situation that requires them to think on their feet.

Third, I find out what they remember. This is a new job we're talking about - their career - and if all they remembered is touring the office, looking at some apps and having a Coke, then perhaps they weren't that interested after all.

Finally, I get to see how badly they write. Yes, that's an assumption made in advance, but it's right on the mark - most people write badly, and the rest write even worse. And while there are a lot of sharp programmers, not too many of them can communicate in writing. If this person has particularly abysmal (or, conversely, unusually good) writing skills, I want to know.

Closing. The goal of this first interview is to get a face to face "are the vibes good" as well as to learn more in detail about their technical experience and how they do their work.

When they leave this interview, I want them to know what, in detail, we do for a living, what their daily job would generally be like, and what the environment is like. If you can get them to feel that their first day at work would be like coming back home, instead of the first day of a strange new experience, you might have a match.

They should have a clearly defined set of expectations and you should be comfortable with their level of intelligence and passion. If things look good, you can invite them back or you may defer until you've had a chance to interview with some other candidates as well.

Second Interview

At some point before the second interview, your candidate should have answered the 17 questions. These are good for providing you with a snapshot of their technical skills and general thinking abilities.

The second interview is used for a longer technical exam (67 Questions) that determines, in detail, what skill level this person possesses. This test requires them to know their way around quite well.

See Appendix for full text of The 67 Questions

The test includes a number of trick questions, a few without any answers, a few with multiple answers, and so on. We even make them (the horror!) write some code and defend it.

We also discuss the rules of the road - what it's like in terms of daily routine, what the sales call process is like, how we go about designing, coding, testing and all of that magic. Yes, we've discussed this before, but most people are so nervous in an interview that they really don't pick up on most of it the first time around. By this time they've heard a fair amount of it a third time, and we are starting to expect them to remember it.

Twenty Really Weird Interview Questions (and the reasons for asking)

Give them a program in their chosen language without any comments and ask them what it does. First of all, they get to find out just how awful it is to work with a program that has no comments in it. Second, you get to see their thought process at work - how do they go about this - from scratch? And third, seeing as this is a reasonably pressurized situation, how do they react? If they freak out, what might they do in front of a customer who asks something *really* unrealistic?

If I had to fire you, what would it most likely be for? The correct answer is "personality conflict." Most people have trouble on the job not because they are technically incompetent, but because they don't play well with the other boys and girls. Most people don't know this, and it's quite telling to see them squirm, trying to answer this question "correctly." You can almost see their mind churning, thinking out loud, "How do I answer this? Do I tell them the truth - that I'm completely useless before noon - or do I fabricate some sort of story, like "I work so hard that the other people in my department try to sabotage my work?"

What do you do when you get mad? I love this question, because it's not a common question, yet it's a very useful one. People tend to do one of two things - either they go ballistic, or they pout. In other words, they're either demonstrative or they withdraw. I don't really care which they are, but I want to know which it is, so I can deal with a mood appropriately. If they come into work one day and they're totally withdrawn, is it that they're mad at something, hung over, or just concentrating on some really ugly problem? And I'm also interested in their level of self-awareness - do they even know the answer to this one?

Name three things about work that you really truly passionately hate right now. What are their hot buttons? Do they even have any? Or are they really basically level-headed folk?

What would lure you away from your job here at the company? Right away, I find out what's really important. Is it money? Maybe their spouse gets transferred. Is their family out of town? Do they really want to be an aerobics instructor, and computer programming is just a way to pay the bills?

What's the one thing I can do that would keep you here? OK, this one doesn't require a lot of explanation. But it's good to hear them give you the answer.

What were the last three books you read? The really smart ones will name my VFP 3.0 book as one of them. I'll give them extra credit if any of the Calvin and Hobbes collections show up in their list, but they get docked big time if Judith Kranz or any Star Trek book shows up in the list.

Describe a situation where you really screwed something up. It's interesting to hear the situation they choose, as well as how 'honest' they are in admitting it. The stupider the situation, the more believable it is. And I also enjoy finding out how they admit to weakness and mistakes - or if they can even do it!

Describe a good performance review format/method. People often have some very good ideas about things but most companies aren't in a position to take advantage of those ideas. How much thought have they put into this? I'm always on the lookout for new ideas.

28 people out of 147 did something or other. What percent is that? You would be shocked at the number of people who can't calculate a simple percentage on paper, much less in their head. It should take any developer about a second to come up with the rough answer (20%) in their head. If they can't, should they really be in front of a computer?

Give them a page of poor grammar and ask them to correct it. Again, another pressure filled situation, but this time with a slight twist - most programmers try to avoid writing a sentence if they can at all help it.

Tell me your favorite joke. I'm always on the lookout for good jokes, for one. Second, a sense of humor is really required at our shop. Can they think on their feet? Most "How to prep for a job interview" books leave this question off.

Here's the number of a friend in mine in Germany. Call him. It seems like a trivial task, but one that most people don't know how to do. How do they go about figuring this one out?

What were your New Year's Resolutions? OK, this one is a little whimsical, but it's fun to see what the answers are. Again, we're trying to see if they're on interview manners or if they have begun to feel comfortable.

Name the only band that declined an invitation to play at Woodstock. Next to a sense of humor, the ability to win rock trivia contests is the most important asset at our company. And no one knows the answer to this question. What I want to know is, once they admit they don't know, do they let you go on to the next question without giving them the answer? Some people just go, "I dunno" and look at you. I'm looking for the person who goes, "Well? Who was it?"

How many people live in Wisconsin? (You could substitute the name of your state here, or you could find out if they've even heard of Wisconsin.) Here's a bit of factual knowledge - but should also be easy to sort of figure out, or at least make some sort of ball park guess. If they give some ridiculous answer, it tells me that they may not be the most logical thinker in the world. How are they going to debug programs? Just random, wild guesses?

What is your favorite band, movie, TV show? Just trying to get to know them and provide some possible topics for small talk.

Where are Zip Codes 01010, 30011, and 98052? If they've been doing anything with databases, they've had to have worked with Zip Codes enough to have an idea of how Zips Codes are distributed. And the last one is a gimme, isn't it?

Subsequent Interviews

These next interviews all serve two purposes. As our shop is pretty small, I want each new employee to have met and spent at least a half hour or hour with everyone else in the company. Yes, it's actually quite time consuming, but it does two things. First, you have a better buy-in from each employee in that they've all had a chance to evaluate this new person and provide their feedback. You don't have to follow their advice, but at least they've had the opportunity to provide feedback.

Second, the candidate feels more comfortable with your company, and more a part of the team (gag, I used that T word!). They've made it through the gauntlet - the initiation rite - the hazing rituals. They've been subjected to the torture test and if they're offered the job, they know they've passed. No, it's not actually all that bad, but this long process shows them that you actually mean what all the other companies just say - that employees are important and you invest a lot of time and effort in making sure you have the right ones on board.

Each of the other employees has been briefed on the topics already covered with the candidate, and gets an opportunity to quiz them, subtly, on some part of that information. If we've discussed Functional Specifications with the candidate three times but if when asked, they go "I'm not sure what you mean by specification," then we can assume that this person is either really, really, really nervous, really stupid, or just doesn't care a whole lot.

Finally, it gives the candidate a chance to ask your employees questions - to verify some of the conclusions they've arrived at.

Preparing them for an offer. At each of these interviews (there may be two or three), we cover topics such as compensation, benefits, holidays, billing expectations and the corresponding work load, and other general topics that would be covered in an interview situation, and that would be included in the offer.

At some time during the interview process, I make it clear that should we extend an offer, they will be expected to accept or reject it on the spot. This sounds pretty rough - shouldn't we give them the opportunity to at least go home and discuss the opportunity with their spouse or significant other or a friend or their current boss? Again, I liken this to the process of marriage. If you dated a person for several years, and got ready to propose to them, you'd expect that, given your relationship and the conversations that you've had with that person, they would say yes on the spot. If you propose marriage and the person has to say, "I'd like to think about it for a while" then perhaps it wasn't a very good idea to propose in the first place.

Same thing here - this is a significant commitment of time and energy, you've discussed all the details, and have pretty much agreed to agree. The offer is setting it down in black and white. If they can't agree on the spot, then something is wrong. Either you've done a bad job in making sure expectations were in line, or they're pulling the wool over your eyes and they're still playing games.

I've had the situation where a candidate has told me that they needed to take an offer back to their current employer. At this point, I terminate the relationship. Any number of studies show that a counter-offer is ineffective and simply a means to hold on to someone for a short term while they line up alternatives. And if the candidate would truly stay in their current job because they were offered another $1500 or promised a promotion in six months, then it's clear that they don't want to write custom software with us.

The Offer

If all goes well, you'll eventually want to give them an offer. If they're still alive by the time you've gotten through this marathon of meetings, they might want to accept.

See Appendix for full text of the Job Offer

We've already covered what an offer would look like in previous interviews. The offer itself is a mere formality to confirm what we've discussed over the past half-dozen meetings. It is my opinion that by this time, there shouldn't be any doubt.

The written offer should include: their salary, a description of their benefits package, and a complete job description. We also specify their work environment - office & equipment. Put this in a format that shows them its total value. Salary is not the bottom line.

We make a written offer, as much for our records as for anything else, but I've found that if putting it in writing makes them that 1% more comfortable, and I'm happy to do it.

4.3 Keeping People

- **Why Do People Leave?**

- **Fundamental Principles**
  - The View of a Coach
  - Upward Delegation
  - Keeping Your Cool

- **Compensation**
  - What If Someone Bills More Than Their Target?
  - What If Someone Bills Less Than Their Target?
  - How Do You Set Your Hourly Rates?
  - What Benefit is There To Staying Around and Gaining Seniority?
  - Additional Ideas
  - Unusual Situations
  - Encouraging Teamwork
  - Conclusion

- **Training**
  - Technical Training
  - Rituals

- **Reviews**
  - New Employees
  - All Employees
  - Why Quarterly?

- **Not Keeping (Firing)**
  - Laying the Groundwork

The staff is the single most important piece of the puzzle. Great developers with mediocre tools will outperform mediocre developers with great tools every time. So why do people ignore the staff? We've just spent pages on finding and hiring people. Why spend so much time on recruiting if you're going to let them wither once they're on board? It makes a great deal more sense spend a little effort to keep hold of them once you've got them.

Why Do People Leave?

What can you do to keep an employee once they've joined you? Take a look at what makes them leave! First of all, generally, people do not leave just to make an extra buck or two. If the financial difference is large enough, sure, most people will perk their ears up at a new opportunity. But unless their current situation has significantly changed, people tend not to look around just for a slightly larger paycheck.

Instead, they tend to get pushed out the door, either by work conditions or a job that makes them unhappy. If you can make them say, "Life is good" four times a week, you'll likely never lose that person. You should focus on treating them correctly so that the grass will never be greener.

Here are five major questions that you should ask about your people on a regular basis:

- Are they being paid fairly for the work they do? Are their wages, benefits, and bonuses at the very least competitive with other similar type positions in the area?
- Are they doing work that they love? Do they get to do their job or do other things get in the way?
- Is the work environment comfortable? Is the atmosphere friendly? Do they enjoy walking into work in the morning?
- Is there an opportunity for future growth, either in terms of new types of work, or actual promotions within the company? Can they foresee doing the same thing five and ten years from now?
- Do you listen to them? Are their contributions valued, or are they treated like machinery?

These areas tend to be the five things that most people leave their jobs over. If you can make sure to pay attention to them, the rest will take care of itself.

Fundamental Principles

The fundamental principles of keeping people once you have snared them are basically to do everything opposite from Dilbert. If there is something they are making fun of in Dilbert, it's because it's really happening in management and it's really stupid.

The View of a Coach

What are some of the fundamental principals people tend to lose site of? There are two big ones in this book: treating people with respect, the way you want to be treated - and recognize that as the "boss," your role is to help people do their jobs. I view myself as a coach, not as a dictator. I'm trying to leverage myself, and I can do that best by helping them do their jobs better.

Most companies throw so many road blocks in front of their people that it's a wonder that anything gets done. Most people would like to do a good job but they are hamstrung by rules and regulations and policies and all that kind of stuff. We try to keep as much of that junk out of the way of the developer as possible.

For example, it makes their lives so much easier if you have a contact person that can handle administrative tasks and managing the day to day tasks that gets in the way of their real jobs. Yes, these days, it's quite fashionable to "downsize." What this means is that you end up with a lot of highly paid, highly trained people doing things like making copies for a half-day instead of writing code. Does it make sense to have a skilled software developer spend an hour every morning for a week trying to track down the right insurance claim form? I don't think so! In the book "*Peopleware,*" the authors relate the story of a memo being passed around to a group of software developers, scolding them for having their phones forwarded to the receptionist. "We know that you would like to have peace and quiet to do your work, but if continue this practice, she won't be able to get her work done!"

It makes a ton of sense to have one person - even a part-time person - handle a lot of these things. If they are a software developer, they should spend their time developing software. Your job is to help them do that.

Upward Delegation

What else could you possibly do for your people? The idea is to enable them, which means training, coaching. The one thing you don't want to do is their work. And a lot of folk, either deliberately or unintentionally, will delegate back up the food chain. "I ran into this bug and I don't know how to do it. Could you look at it for me?" People will do that - it's human nature. When this happens, deflect the request by suggesting "Okay, let's do it together." Instead of giving them a fish, I teach them how to fish. In the case of a bug, I'll ask "What is the behavior that is being exhibited?" and they say, "I guess I really don't know," I tell them to figure out what is happening and then come back.

Sometimes people will try to get you to do their thinking for them. Instead, you are to help them learn to think properly or how to guide their problem solving approach. So they come back to you and have figured out what was happening. Then I ask them, "What was supposed to happen." And they say, "Well, I think...." And I say, "What do you mean you think? You don't know? Come back when you know."

To my way of thinking, there is no excuse for somebody saying "I'm not sure" when they have the tools to find out the answer. Why go off on a wild goose chase based on a wild hypothesis? Go back and find out what should be happening and come back and they say, "This is what should be happening and this is what is happening, I don't know what to do." Then we take the next step. "Well you can start at the very end or the very beginning to hunt down where the paths diverged." Alternately, you can start at the end and see where the actual results diverged from the expected answer.

For example, let's say you are running some sort of posting process but only every other value is being posted, and the rest are zeros. There are a bunch of temp files and a bunch of things being written here and there and all of that other stuff. Have them start at the beginning. Is the original file full of the proper data? Is the data being flagged properly according to transaction type? Is the proper data being put into a temp file? Have you scanned the contents of a temp file? You guide them, having them work through one step at a time. The key is that you're coaching, not taking the keyboard in your own hands.

If you have to do this for three years, maybe your developer should be in another business. Many developers will go manic when faced with a nasty bug. They will try this and that and then a third thing. They will try a bunch of random fixes. Finally, they will get one that seems to work, be happy and put it away. This is the way I would panel my basement - but it's not the way to develop software. The key is you have to help them do the work themselves. Yes, I know - it's a pressure situation and the bug has to be fixed right now, but, as you've found out, there **is** time to do it right - because you don't want to spend the time to do it over.

Keeping Your Cool

Sooner or later, you'll run into an employee whose primary mission in life is to make your life miserable. The worst part is that they never seem to be bad enough to just outright fire - they delight in taking you to the edge, and then keeping you there. When you finally figure this out, you've already won the battle, but the trick is recognizing the situation.

I had an employee once who exhibited this precise behavior. Fortunately, she does not read books, so I'm not too worried about her seeing this. It turns out that I looked just like her father (yes, handsome hairline and all), and that she hated her father. Why she joined the company, other than to taunt me, I've never figured out.

Anyway, she'd misbehave just to the point where I was ready to knock her block off, and then she'd back off. Time and time again, until finally, I had enough. Remembering a rule from up above, I had documented her various difficulties. We sat down one afternoon, and I read her the riot act, indicating that her behavior had better improve. Yes, this was a formal warning.

Before I knew it, she was in tears. Evidently an uncle of hers had died over the weekend and she was still pretty broken up about it, and having this discussion with her at this time was just too much for her to bear. Well, naturally I backed off, her behavior improved a bit, and things were tolerable.

About six months later, things had deteriorated again. Yes, you guessed it. She again started yanking my chain, and we finally had to have a talk. I brought out the documentation, and had even prepared a written warning. I called her into my office, and again, the tears flowed. The airplane crash that had happened over the weekend? Well, naturally, she had known the pilot, and she was just beside herself with grief. This was a bit much, but again, I relented and things got better.

The written warning straightened her out for a number of months, and we were getting along quite well. Eventually, since her lifelong mission was to make me unhappy, she resorted to her old tricks. I guess I had kind of accepted that, in return for her outstanding performance in the classroom (the students simply loved her, and the other employees for the most part liked her as well), I was going to have to lock horns with her on a regular basis. So I started to get ready for another one of these meetings, and as I was doing so, my wife asked me, "Which one of her friends or family do you think you're going to kill this time?"

It was never a problem to confront her from that moment on. Finding absurdity in adversity makes any difficult situation much easier to bear.

Compensation

People want security, generally, or else they would go out on their own. So you need to give them a salary and set realistic billing goals - but not scare them if they don't hit them. Your job is to make sure they can reach them. And to help them reach them.

We're going to talk about compensating employees who are billable. There are other issues with folk who are on straight salary, but those aren't really unique to the software development biz.

First, let's presume that a billable employee can be billing both hourly and on fixed price work. I know, I've been arguing that fixed price work is the way to go, but, in a pragmatic sense, most billable employees will need to bill some hourly work - either from folk who refuse to work with fixed price jobs, or during work that can only be done on an hourly basis, such as the design of functional specifications and change orders, and some types of maintenance.

In general, a billing professional should be compensated at 40-45% of their billings. This may vary somewhat - in a big law firm, the grunt associates get a smaller percentage and the partners - what a surprise! - get more. But as a general rule, it's a pretty good target.

As the person's hourly billing rate varies, so does their paycheck. The person thus has a high incentive to increase their skills or do whatever else they can in order to raise their rate and the corresponding take-home. You can use this as a rule to pay your people, or you can use it as a starting point to create a more worthwhile pay structure. I don't view pay as a nuisance that must be handled in order to get something done, but rather as a tool that can be manipulated to get a better deal for both you and your employees.

Since the wages of the billable employees are a significant factor in the cost of developing an application, I have taken those percentages into account, and have gone much further. Here's how we work the compensation plan - and, please note that in all of this discussion, I'm referring to compensation as the total dollars earned by the employee. How it is split up into pre-tax benefits, gross wages, after tax benefits, and take home pay is another discussion that is actually not specific to our industry.

A new employee generally comes into the firm with an expectation of earning a certain amount of money. This amount corresponds to a certain amount of billable work. For example, if a person wants to earn, say, $4250 a month, they'd need to bill $10,000 per month. Their compensation expectation and the matching billable requirements have been discussed during interviews. Through the long recruitment process, we've determined that they do have the skills necessary to produce the amount of work that corresponds to that billing level. Of course, we're quite conservative - we make sure that it is very likely that a developer meets their monthly billable target.

As you can see, it's a simple matter to change a person's compensation based on their performance. As soon as they regularly bill more, they can be eligible for a raise. Now it's time for a few questions.

What If Someone Bills More Than Their Monthly Target?

We pay quarterly bonuses based on the amount by which they exceed their monthly targets. We use a quarterly period for several reasons. First, they fit in with our general philosophy of bonuses.

A bonus is additional compensation that is earned according to performance of an individual or the team to which that individual belongs. A few observations about effective bonuses. First, a bonus should be paid often enough to be seen and felt immediately, but not so often as to be thought of as just a part of their check. (GM workers who eventually came to regard overtime as standard pay, and made financial commitments based on that overtime pay got burned when their hours were cut back.) Second, a bonus should also be based on factors that the developer has control over. A bonus given because Herman over in the Lab invented a new polymer is never refused, but is regarded as 'a gift' - not as a bonus that can be affected by their own performance.

Three months is also long enough for variations in billable time to even out. Billing on software projects can become somewhat cyclical, and this time period allows the developer to ship enough work to make their targets.

What If Someone Bills Less Than Their Monthly Target?

We monitor the amount a developer bills on a weekly basis, so we're aware of divergence from the monthly goal right away - we don't get a "end of month surprise." This means we can take mid-course corrections quickly, resulting in minor adjustments instead of panic swings to starboard (or was that port? I don't know! Eeek! Panic!) at the last second. Second, given the potentially cyclical nature of billable work, we also watch the cumulative amount billed, to make sure we're on track and stay on track.

However, it is still possible that at the end of a quarter, a developer's total billings are less than their target. It depends on the reason that they missed their target. If they came in under the target because there wasn't enough work, it's not their problem. Selling is management's responsibility, not the developer's. (Of course, if the developer is responsible for losing accounts, then that must be handled, but that's a different issue) If, on the other hand, everyone else is backlogged and one developer is still way under, it's up to me to determine why, and take action. However, I should have been doing this all along.

What reasons could there be for a developer not to make their target? The first one is that they're going over budget on a particular project - they're having technical trouble, the estimates were bad or there's a problem with the front end of the work, not necessarily the work that the developer has done.

The next reason is that the developer has a problem customer. If difficulties with the customer are causing the developer to miss their target, then it's time for me to step in and help out - by getting the customer back on track.

It is also possible that the developer is simply goofing around, and if so, then it's also my responsibility to straighten them out. If this becomes a trend, then I need to do one of two things - either adjust the compensation of the developer (which actually may be a reasonable alternative for the developer - as opposed to losing their job), or adjust the responsibilities of the developer, which may include termination. After all, for X amount of compensation, the developer is expected to produce Y results. If they're not able to or willing to, then the other side of the equation has to be changed to keep in sync.

How Do You Set Your Hourly Rates?

Remember that our developers can do significantly better on fixed price work than on hourly work. As a result, we revise hourly rates based on their Entry level employees rates are set around the third quartile of the generally accepted billing range for the geographical region. For example, if the general rate is $40 - $80 in your area, entry level programmers would bill $50 - $60.

What Benefit Is There To Staying Around and Gaining Seniority?

Monetary compensation is only one piece of a total compensation package. The newest people get the hand-me-down equipment while the most senior developers get the newest equipment, the best offices, and other related perks. They also get the first chance to go to conferences, and are often the best compensated. Due to their experience, they get the better, more interesting, and higher margin projects.

Additional Ideas

There are a number of additional twists to the compensation scheme outlined above. First, note that the total compensation for the developer depends on the billable dollars they bring in. As the developer's skill level increases, the number of dollars they bring in through fixed price work increases, and their variable compensation goes up.

Second, should a developer gain a certification of some sort - one that is marketable on the behalf of the company - we provide a one-time bonus. And, of course, ideally that certification also translates into a higher skill level, which makes its way back to the previous paragraph.

Third, remember that the developer's compensation is a percentage of the amount billed over the quarter. This percentage can be changed for selected circumstances. Once we have a more sophisticated bug-tracking system in place, we're going to implement a mechanism whereby the percentage varies by the bug count. This has a double benefit in that the lower the bug count and the higher the amount billed over quarter, the better end result for the developer (as well as for the company and customer.)

Unusual Situations

Compensating people fairly is a difficult situation, and that's why we're so particular about hiring people in the first place. Most companies use completely ridiculous schemes to pay their employees. For example, you can bet that a secretary that's been with the firm for 12 years earns more, on average, than the one who has been there 6 years, and even more than the one who has been there 3 years. There is no taking into account the abilities or the actual amount of work done by any of these three people - their primary criteria for pay is the amount of time they've been with the firm.

Correspondingly, this means that it's easy to run across a developer with such a minimal skill level that I can only justify paying them at a rate that corresponds to an entry level monthly target. However, this person has already been out in the working world for a few years, and thus is making significantly more money than what their skill level maps to. A common example of this situation is the corporate MIS programmer who hails from the mainframe days, but in these days of "right-sizing" finds himself pushed into PC based systems. With 15 years at his previous employer, he had a healthy salary. To me, his skills with the PC based languages place him in the Entry-level area. But, perhaps I feel that his project management skills and customer management skills are worth adding to our repertory.

There is not an easy answer to this solution. One possible way to handle it is to bring the developer in at the level of compensation they are expecting, and eat the difference for a while, planning to make it up once the developer is up to speed. However, this method is fraught with peril, as it is a distinct possibility that such an individual may leave the firm as soon as their skills have grown to the extent that they are more marketable and attractive somewhere else.

The second way to handle this situation is through fixed price work, and effectively splitting the difference with the developer. Since there is often a significant margin built into a fixed price project, this room can be used to pay for the developer's training time. While another developer may be able to do the work considerably more efficiently, the firm is still not losing money by assigning such a project to a developer still in training.

On a related note, one other thing we do is make it explicitly clear that doing work on the side without written permission is grounds for immediate termination and basis for lawsuit for recovery of wages that is equal to the time spent moonlighting. All side work must be okayed in writing. This is a direct conflict of interest and we won't tolerate it.

Encouraging Teamwork

Suppose Herman and Olga both get individual bonuses. It can be hypothesized that Herman will not be inclined to help Olga if Herman perceives that by doing so, they will lose time on their own project and thus their billable work will suffer. This could happen if Herman is more experienced than Olga and thus, the tables will never turn - Herman will never have cause to turn to Olga for help.

There are two possible solutions to this. First, depending on the makeup of the developers in the firm, it is possible that Herman won't ever ask Olga for help, but Herman may need tons of help from Inga on another language. The second possibility to consider is set up a company-wide bonus as well as individual bonuses in order to encourage teamwork. This may or may not work because (1) now management has to spend more time figuring out how to do this new, more complex formula, and (2) it is difficult to weight the components of a multi-piece bonus. For example, in an ideal situation, the company bonus will be $100 and the individual bonus will be $100. But what happens if it's possible that the company bonus will be $10 and the individual will be $200? A developer will still be less likely to help out because the perceived benefit is much less appealing.

Here, I feel you have to rely on your people to do what's right! If you treat your people fairly, they will be more likely to respond in kind.

Conclusion

The beauty of this compensation system is that the developer has a steady income, measurable results by which they can receive bonuses, and firm benefits if the developer is more productive.

Training

Training is yet another topic that is paid far more lip service than true attention. Throw a couple of books and the tutorial in front of a new employee, spend an hour with them twice during the first week and - viola! - a new project has sold, better get Biff or Muffy cranking on it and - well, don't you worry, you can go back to the tutorial as soon as you finish the project, OK?

Yup, we've all seen it, haven't we?

Technical Training

This is one of those areas in the book where I don't have a lot of magic answers or sophisticated schemes. Part of the reason is that, after hiring five or six people, I've found that I'm simply not that good at this aspect of the business. I don't mean that I'm not good at training, necessarily, but I lack the discipline to regularly sit down with my people and get them up to speed. I have the best intentions, but, well, you know. (In case you're wondering, yes, this comes out in the interview now.)

We've tried to institutionalize training - for instance, we spent this summer trying to do some informal sessions between 1 and 2:30 PM on Fridays (we close the office early on Friday, so this seemed like a good time), but it only worked about half the time. You could argue that half the time is better than no time at all, but there's got to be a better answer.

We're currently involved in getting everyone in the shop certified with the Microsoft Certified Solution Developer designation, and our study group (formed with several other companies) is meeting on Monday nights. This has worked out well, except for those times that the Packers played a Monday night game. It's just terrible having a sports team that actually wins games. (And who would have guessed it would happen in Wisconsin?)

Rituals

The one thing we've done reasonably well is form a corporate culture. I know that we have a strong, consistent philosophy about doing things a certain way. It may not always be the best way, or even the right way, but we generally do it the same way, time and time again.

Part of the reason that this is happening is the use of rituals. A ritual is an act that is performed over and over in the belief that it will cause or perpetuate the occurrence of an event. In our case, we use the telling of stories to preserve the communal knowledge. As you've already seen from the rest of this book, I tend to tell a lot of stories, and, without realizing it at first, these stories are our version of folktales. The stories get told over and over, and become ingrained in our company's history and our company's attitude.

Here's my favorite story, and how we use it to illustrate my point about rituals.

> A high ranking admiral was visiting a battleship a few years ago that had been outfitted with a new set of very powerful guns. The ship's commander had the gun crew demonstrate the firing of the weapon, and the admiral was suitably impressed. However, he had one question - five of the six members of the crew were furiously busy, but the sixth simply stood at attention during the whole exercise. What was the purpose of this sixth man, the admiral wondered. The ship's commander wondered as well, and promised to find out. A week later, he called the admiral. "The sixth guy? Well, his job is to hold the reigns of the horses so they don't get spooked when the gun is fired."

We tell this story to every customer when we are evaluating a process of theirs for potential automation. It tells them, in a nice way, to think carefully about the assumptions that they make about what is required and why. We use this story on a regular basis. It's become part of our culture to be able to explain the situation to a customer without being potentially threatening or condescending.

Of course, we have dozens (OK, *hundreds*) of stories. For example, when I come across someone who has gotten so close to a problem that they can't see the forest for the trees, I ask them how to eat an elephant. They look at me weirdly, and I explain, "To eat an elephant, first cut it up into very, very tiny pieces." After a few times, I expect each of my developers to know and recite back to me that answer - their doing so tells me that I have instilled these values in ourselves and our corporate culture.

Reviews

Another one of those rather unusual things we do is a quarterly review instead of an annual review.

New Employees

I touch base with a new employee every day the first week, and at the end of each week for the first month to make sure we are all set. Remember how you had a set of expectations for a new employee when you were interviewing them? Guess what? We've written these things down, and those are some of the things they should be expected to do after they start. Checking in with them on a regular basis - are they getting done what they are supposed to be doing, do they have any questions, problems, concerns, and - as important - has this job turned out the way you expected, based on the interviews you had here?

All Employees

At the end of each quarter, we review expectations that had been set for the quarter and what has actually been accomplished. If the two diverge badly, we need to examine why, and what we can do to improve things. This is not rocket science, of course, but the trick for us is to do this on a quarterly basis and not wait till the end of the year.

Why Quarterly?

In section three, we talked about tracking people's time. This means measuring the dollars they are bringing into the firm and the bugs they are producing and fixing. As I like to say, "What gets measured, gets done." This is all fine and good, but what use is all of this information if the developer never gets any feedback? Or worse, they get feedback on something that happened so long ago that it's of no practical use? Most firms schedule an annual review, and to my way of thinking, it's one of the stupidest things companies do. No one can remember what they did 11 months ago.

Second, the idea of a review is to provide the opportunity to take corrective action. If they have started screwing up on something 11 months ago, then they've had 11 months to get really good at screwing it up, right? It's a lot easier, and much more effective, to make smaller mid-course corrections than to try to make a big move once a year.

Part of the reason big companies use annual reviews is that they are tied to compensation. You don't have to do it this way. You needn't talk about dollars every time a review comes around, and, in fact, given the way we compensate developers, the compensation sort of runs along-side performance all the time.

Of course, you should be giving slight nudges on a daily, weekly, and monthly basis. We've found that a quarterly review gives us a formal place to do a reality check. If I need to talk to you about something or nudge you along this line or give you a pat on the back for something else you have done, I can do this at any time. But a formal meeting every three months makes sure I don't get so caught up in the day to day thing, that suddenly it's been seven months and that issue I wanted to mention has now become a real problem.

Furthermore, quarterly reviews lets the employee know that you are really interested in helping them do a better job - that your admonitions about "Our employees are our most important assets" aren't just lip service. This is a coaching session to say, "This is where we are at - and three months ago this is where we said we wanted to be. How are we doing?" If there is a difference, what can we do to make some corrections?

Another advantage to quarterly reviews is that in a fast-paced business, the environment could well have changed and therefore things that we thought were going to be relevant a while back are no longer important. If you only do this once a year, by this time the business has changed three times over, and it has been far too long.

In a larger company, you may feel that there is too much work involved in quarterly reviews. If you had 90 employees, you may feel that 90 reviews would be unmanageable. On the other hand, one person wouldn't be doing all of them, so again, you can cascade the requirements of who is doing what over a period of a couple of weeks. The bottom line is that if you do them at approximately the same calendar time, the benefit is everyone is hearing the same story instead of one person hearing the story the first of June and someone else hearing it the end of July.

By the way, it might sound like I am constantly crabbing about things employees may do wrong. But I'm not really. First, the developer is being paid to do X and we're simply taking action if X hasn't been done. If X has been done, then we're in great shape! Second, while I've been mentioning mid-course corrections, those aren't necessarily due to employee problems. The business plan might have changed, the customer requirements might have changed, or a host of other factors could have gotten involved. The key is that more regular, formal communication can provide substantial benefits. Finally, a quarterly review is also an opportunity to praise - to "catch them being good." I do try to find and note that as well. People need to hear that they're doing a good job - regularly - and you're the one person from whom praise means the most.

Not Keeping (Firing)

Sigh... Firing someone is one of the more uncomfortable tasks a business owner has to face. The first time I had to fire someone, it probably took me a month to admit that I had to do it, and another two weeks to garner up the courage to actually go about it. This was partly due to the pain I went through, and the subsequent guilt due to the fact that I screwed up the exit interview and made the other person feel uncomfortable. Therefore, I decided that I would have to create some sort of process to make parting ways less painful.

I'm reminded of the Cheers episode where Norm Petersen was given the job of hatchet man for the company. He was so unhappy about the job that he couldn't get around to actually performing the act. He took the soon-to-be-unemployed person out to lunch, then to a ballgame, then to a movie, and finally ended up at the bar seven or eight hours later, still not having delivered the bad news. When he finally got around to it, he was so broken up about it that the other person had to comfort Norm, attempting to cheer him up. "I'm young, Norm, I can find another job easily! And my wife has wanted to move to another city for years - maybe now is the time to make that move. And don't you worry, we've got some money saved up - we'll be fine!"

While this type of exchange might be a bit too much to hope for, an exit interview should not be a hostile, surprising encounter, any more than the actual job offer should be. If the groundwork has been laid properly, the exit interview should be a formality, rather than a shock.

It makes complete sense to me to approach the termination of an employee in this manner. First, it's less stressful on all parties involved. You don't need additional ulcers; bug-ridden development tools and irate customers churn up enough stomach acid as it is. Second, if you've done your job correctly, there is much less likelihood of things coming back to haunt you - wrongful termination suits, vengeful ex-employees, and so on. Third, there is the role model you are providing to the others in the company. If they see that you are fair and pleasant about a potentially hostile action, they'll feel better about their own job and working for you. I think this attitude is just one more part of providing a good environment for your people and allowing them to feel comfortable and happy.

Laying the Groundwork

Remember those quarterly review meetings we talked about earlier? The issues raised in these meetings become the genesis of an employee termination. If an employee regularly does not meet their goals, and is unable to formulate a plan or follow a plan laid out for them, then termination is one possible path.

However, it's not the only path. Let's suppose that a developer just isn't cutting the mustard. What could they be doing wrong? Well, let's set aside some of the more blatant problems - swinging at customers, arriving at work brandishing an automatic weapon, groping other employees in public or stealing office equipment. Those types of concerns should be addressed by any standard employment manual and are really out of the scope of this book. As they say, "See your lawyer."

But what about the situation when a developer's bug count is stubbornly high, and in spite of all attempts to bring it down - training, code reviews, automated tools, team coding - it stays way up in the stratosphere?

Section 4.3 Keeping People

Do you just walk into their office one day, swing your thumb over your shoulder like a baseball umpire and scream, "You're outta here!" I don't think so!

Here's how I approach this. At the onset of a problem, I like to make corrections so that we can possibly solve it immediately. And don't forget to document. If the problem does not remedy itself, I will take as much corrective action as needed till it's solved. And don't forget to document. Since you're reading this chapter, either you have a natural tendency to investigate the morbid, or you're past the point of no return. However, you should still have documented the difficulties you've been having throughout this whole process.

There are three possibilities for having problems with an employee.

Problem employees. First, the employee could be one of those "problem" types - despite having sky-high bug counts, they insist they don't have a problem, that the problems are all someone else's, and that if only "X" would change, they'd be at the top of the heap. Incessant denial of a problem and refusal to make modifications make this person a problem, and termination may be the only route.

Well intentioned, poorly skilled. The second case is when an employee is, again, having problems that can't be solved, but is trying to make things happen. The real problem may be that the person simply doesn't have the skills to do the work. This sometimes happens - bugs slip through the hiring process just as they slip through everywhere else, and it's possible that an employee can't hack the work. In this case, however, I try to evaluate what the person CAN do, and try to figure out what I can do to either change the job, or find a new position for that person. I've already invested a lot in this person, and hate to lose them unless absolutely necessary. Sure, if you've got four people on board, and this person isn't working out, it may be unreasonable to think that you can simply turn the company around on its ear just to accommodate one person. It doesn't make sense to bankrupt a company in an effort to keep one person employed. On the other hand, think outside the nine dots for a minute, and see if there isn't some creative solution to this situation.

No other options. The third possibility is when the person is just not cut out for the position, and there are no other openings.

In each of these cases, let the person know, in advance, what they've got to do in order to keep their job. This sounds a little harsh, and I don't really like this language, but you've got to make it clear to them that this is not simply a cosmetic matter, but rather, it's serious. You have to make sure they understand the gravity of the situation. You don't have to be mean about it, of course, but you do have to be firm.

The first quarterly review might consist of identifying a number of potential problem areas, and then documenting the plan to resolve those problems. The plan has to include both 1) actions that the employee (and perhaps the employer) has to take and 2) the way that the results will be measured in order to determine if the employee has gotten back on track. If there isn't a concrete measuring stick, the potential for conflict increases, and that's when things get ugly.

In the next quarterly review meeting (if not earlier), the progress made is reviewed and the level of the progress made is evaluated. In order to protect yourself, as well as to give the employee the best possible chance at sticking around, you need to make regular attempts to correct the problem. If repeated tries don't work, then the best solution is to part ways.

Document, document, document. And talk to your lawyer. This process is never a pleasant one, but it can be conducted civilly and properly if care is taken.

Appendix

The full text of each of these can be found on www.hentzenwerke.com.

Remember that I Am Not A Lawyer, nor have these documents been written or approved by a lawyer. They are not to be copied verbatim, but are provided to help you generate ideas for your own methodology. Please consult a lawyer before writing up and sending out your own documents.

Engagement Letter

April 1, 1997

Michael Austin-Thor
The Very Large Manufacturing Company
The Very Large Office Building
Milwaukee WI 53200

Dear Mike,

I am pleased to present this letter of engagement regarding custom database software development services for your firm. The ultimate intent is to completely replace and significantly enhance the functionality of your time and billing database system with a new one written in Visual FoxPro 7.0. For the purpose of this letter, this new system will be referred to as TABET (Time and Billing Entry and Tracking.)

The purpose of this letter is to outline the functionality of the system and describe the services we propose to provide toward the development of the system.

The Very Large Manufacturing Company is in the business of design, development and installation of automated manufacturing software. The Very Large Manufacturing Company has offices throughout North and South America and does business throughout both continents and the Pacific Rim.

The current time and billing system is an antiquated DOS-based application that has a number of deficiencies in its multi-user and multi-tasking capabilities. The purpose of TABET is to provide a simple, "on-demand" tool for employees to enter time spent on various jobs, and to provide automated billing and management reports across multiple offices. TABET will be completely multi-user across LANs and WANs and will be a completely native Windows application so that the user does not have to exit their current work in order to access the time and billing functions.

Specific functionality includes the ability:

- For a developer to record time spent against Customer/Project/Module/Task and Activity.
- To maintain Customers, Projects, Modules, Tasks, and Activities.
- To create Invoices Master and Invoice Detail output.
- To create Backlog and History reports against various entities (Company, Customer, Project, Developer).
- For a developer to track their "To Do" list.
- To track and compare time spent against time estimated for entities down to the Task level.

The system will be written using Visual FoxPro 7.0, will include a multi-user, security-enabled foundation and menuing system, maintenance (add/edit/delete/search) screens for each table and data structure, a flexible reporting utility for user-configurable reports, on-line help for each function in the system and system and maintenance utilities. The system will be developed using industry-standard, state of the art software development techniques including data normalization, professional code documentation and discrete alpha and beta testing to assure the production of a solid application that will require minimal maintenance. Installation and training at The Very Large Manufacturing Company will be included.

Development of custom software applications is done in two stages. The first is the system analysis and design, with the resulting product being a Functional Specification and an accompanying prototype. The Functional Specification is a written document that serves as the "blueprint" of the system. It consists of the following items:

Overview
* Purpose of the entire system and how it integrates into the business
* Description of the functionality of each module in the system

Technical Specifications
* Application Architecture (File Structure, Directory structure, Original Data and Logon)
* General Interface (Maintenance Screens, Common Buttons, Toolbars, Listbox Controls, and Notes Buttons)
* Menu layouts (File, Edit, Process, Reports, Utilities, Developer, and Help)
* Screen descriptions (Purpose, Access, Usage and Objects)
* Report and output layouts ((Detail entities, Filter, Order/Group, Fields, Calculated Fields)
* Data Structure (data dictionary, entity relationship diagrams)
* Test Data Set Requirements
* Environment and system requirements (definition of the network, what hardware and software the system will be working with, and what, if any, additional hardware or software will be required)
* Throughput analysis (for example, how many transactions would be entered into the system on a daily basis, how many users, etc.)

Implementation
* Installation
* Deliverables
* Testing methodology
* Test plans
* Modifications
* Milestones and Delivery

It is important to note that this Functional Specification will contain a fixed price and delivery quote for the system as described in the Specification. Thus, it is important that the Specification clearly describe the functionality and operation of the system as The Very Large Manufacturing Company requires. Changes to the system after the completion of the Functional Specification may result in additional costs and delays in delivery.

The second stage is to use the Functional Specification to code, test and install the system. The Functional Specification will cover this process in detail.

During the development of the specification, I will meet with you and other members of the firm involved with the system multiple times in order to determine the specific requirements (functions, data elements, operational procedures, user access, etc.) of the system. We'll outline the rules for data importing and validation, create prototypes of the menus and screens, and mock up the reports that make up the system. At each meeting we will review the progress made and view prototypes as they've been developed.

The development of complex software systems is an iterative process through which discovery of new requirements is a normal and expected part. As a result, the scope of the system will change during the specification process. Accordingly, it is not possible to provide a fixed cost or even a reasonable timeframe at this point.

Development of this Functional Specification is done on a time and materials basis. Rates for various Hentzenwerke personnel range from $<rate> to $<rate> per hour, depending on the experience of the individual. My time is billed at top rate; other developers range from $<rate> - $<rate> and administrative and testing personnel cluster at the low end. Time includes time spent meeting with you and other members of your staff and other firms involved in the production of the system, preparation for meetings and work resulting from meetings, including the design of the prototypes, and travel and phone time. Materials include straight reimbursement of long distance phone charges and mileage between Hentzenwerke's offices in Milwaukee and your offices at the standard IRS rate. All billable personnel track their time against specific modules and invoices reflect this level of detail.

At this point, the proposed deliverables include the following items:

Screens

Customer maintenance

Project maintenance
Module maintenance
Task maintenance
Activity maintenance
Application Feedback maintenance
Change Order maintenance
Invoice maintenance
Developer maintenance
Common Lookup maintenance
Time Entry
To Do list maintenance
Herman (current billings)
WIP (work in progress)

Reports

Invoices
Daily/weekly To Do List
Outstanding work/customer
Outstanding work/developer
Cumulative billings
Change Order status
Application Feedback status

I estimate that, based on these deliverables as well as our experience with other systems of similar magnitude and scope, the development of the Functional Specification will take between 120 and 150 hours and the Implementation of the system will take an additional 800 and 1000 hours. Please note that this time estimate is framed in terms of working hours and not in calendar terms.

These figures are estimates, not caps. However, you will be informed in writing should it appear likely that the estimate will need to be exceeded in order to finish the development of the specification.

Option I <start>

An initial retainer in the amount of <Amount> is required to start work, time will be posted against the retainer as noted above, and monthly statements will be rendered. Invoices will be used for replenishing the retainer as necessary.

Funds remaining at the end of the development of the Functional Specification will be returned to The Very Large Manufacturing Company or applied toward the implementation of the system as requested by The Very Large Manufacturing Company The Functional Specification and prototype tables, menus, screens, and report layouts are the property of The Very Large Manufacturing Company as delivered.

Option I <end>

Option II <start>

You will be invoiced every two weeks for work completed to that point; invoices are due in 10 days. Work will be stopped in the event an invoice becomes past-due. The Functional Specification and the prototype tables, menus, screens & report layouts [but not the supporting libraries and design tools] become the property of The Very Large Manufacturing Company upon payment. We can begin work immediately upon of receipt of a signed copy of this letter and the attached customer set up form.

Option II <end>

The terms in this engagement letter are good for 90 days as of the date of this letter. If this letter is not accepted in this period, we reserve the right to requote.

Software development is a complex process that, due to the ethereal nature of the product, lends itself to misunderstandings and miscommunication. Attached to this engagement letter is a document that describes my view of the software development process and explains how we handle issues that typically arise during the custom software process. If you have any questions or differences of opinion, please feel free to bring them up with me.

Option I <start>

To confirm that these arrangements reflect your understanding, please sign one copy of this letter return to me together with the attached Customer Information sheet and the aforementioned retainer in the amount of <amount>.

Option I <end>

Option II <start>

To confirm that these arrangements reflect your understanding, please sign one copy of this letter return to me together with the attached Customer Information sheet and a company purchase order if required.

Option II <end>

We can begin work within a week of receipt. We're all looking forward to working with your company. If you have any questions, please call me at your convenience.

Sincerely,
Hentzenwerke Corporation

Whil Hentzen
President

____________________________________ ______________

Accepted by Date

Customer: The Very Large Manufacturing Company, Inc.
Vendor: Hentzenwerke Corporation
Custom Software Development Issues

General

The Very Large Manufacturing Company, Inc. ("Customer") is looking for a vendor that will perform software development services for internal computer systems that will run on a PC platform due to the shortage of time and personnel at Customer, and has approached Hentzenwerke Corporation ("Vendor") to do so.

The purpose of this document is to spell out the terms and conditions of this working arrangement to ensure that the expectations of both parties are understood up front.

Services

Vendor agrees to perform for Customer services ("Services") to generally include, but not be limited to, design, development, coding, testing, documentation, installation, training and maintenance of software programs ("Programs") as specified in this or a future Proposal.

Customer is hereby contracting with Vendor for these Services and Vendor reserves the right to determine the method, manner and means by which the Services will be performed. Vendor is not required to perform the Services during a fixed hourly or daily time or at a specific location. If any or all Services are performed at Customer's premises, then Vendor's time spent at the premises is to be at the discretion of Vendor.

Vendor shall take appropriate measures to ensure that its staff who perform Services are competent to do so and that they do not violate any provision of this agreement or subsequent Proposals.

Vendor shall supply all equipment, software, peripherals, and supplies required to perform Services, with the general exceptions of installation and training, and when requested otherwise by Customer.

Vendor represents that it is an independent contractor and as such agrees to indemnify and hold harmless Customer from any and all liabilities for claims, judgments, or losses and all law suites including the costs, expenses, and attorneys' fees of any judgment for injuries to or property damage of any person or persons including parties hereto and their employees or agents, and third parties, arising from or caused in whole or in part by any operation incidental to the performance of the contract performed by Vendor for Customer under the terms described herein.

As a condition of this contract, Vendor agrees to carry the statutory Worker's Compensation coverage on any employee engaged in work on the premises of Customer within the purview of this agreement.

Support

Vendor will make its best effort via alpha testing, integration testing, beta testing and Customer testing to provide a bug-free application. Customer is responsible for providing a Test Suite of Data (with the assistance of Vendor) that accounts for all scenarios and cases of data that the system may process.

Vendor warrants that Customer will not be charged for fixing "bugs" that slip through the testing phase. A bug is defined as an operation that does not perform as specified in the written specifications and/or change notices, or an error that causes the program to stop and display an error message that says "An application error has occurred" and must be reproducible. Non-inclusion of options, behavior not specifically delineated in the written specifications, and operating system and environmental problems are not considered to be bugs. If the problem can be resolved without changing application code, if it is not reproducible upon demand, or if it occurs in a module which has been working for three months and which has not been changed, then it is not considered to be a bug. This does not mean that Vendor will not resolve these issues; this means that Vendor will not resolve them without charge. Note that Vendor reserves the right to interpret interface and performance issues that are not specifically described in a written specification as it sees fit.

Customer will be charged on a time and materials basis at Vendor's rates then in effect for time spent to investigate perceived bugs and to repair the problem if indeed the problem is not a bug as defined above.

Customer will be charged on a time and materials basis at Vendor's rates then in effect for services outside the scope of the proposal, including but not limited to:

* Additional training,
* Modifications to the system, such as screen or report layouts, after they've been accepted by Customer personnel,
* Modifications to formulas or calculations to account for scenarios or cases that were not part of the proposal or Test Suite of Data,
* Any services relating to modifications made to the application by non-Vendor personnel.

Ownership

Except as specifically set forth in writing and signed by both Customer and Vendor, Vendor retains all copyright and patent rights with respect to all materials as described in "Deliverables" developed under this Agreement and all subsequent Proposals to Customer. Therefore, Vendor grants to Customer a permanent, non-exclusive license to use and employ such materials within their business. Customer further agrees to execute a non-exclusive license agreement should Vendor deem that said execution is necessary.

In addition, Vendor agrees not to resell, duplicate to any significant degree, or otherwise infringe on the investment Customer has made in the development of Programs. This includes not approaching competitors of Customer with the intent of duplicating Programs.

Confidentiality

Each party shall hold in trust for the other party, and shall not disclose to any nonparty to this Agreement or subsequent Proposals, any confidential information of the other party. Confidential information is information which relates to research, development, trade secrets or business affairs, but does not include information which is generally known or easily ascertainable by nonparties of ordinary skill.

Vendor acknowledges that during the performance of this Agreement, Vendor may learn or receive confidential Customer information and therefore Vendor hereby confirms that all such information relating to Customer's business will be kept confidential by Vendor.

Customer Representative

Customer shall designate one employee to represent Customer during the performance of this Agreement. Said employee will be the primary contact for this Agreement, and will be authorized to make financial and legal commitments on the part of Customer. No other Customer employees will be authorized to act in such a capacity unless such authorization is made in writing to Vendor.

Disputes

Any dispute that arises between the parties with respect to the performance of this Agreement and subsequent Proposals shall be submitted to binding arbitration by the Better Business Bureau's Good Sense Arbitration Program, to be determined and resolved by said association under its rules and procedures in effect at the time of submission and the parties hereby agree to share equally in the costs of said arbitration. Arbitration will be undertaken and concluded within 15 days of commencement.

Liability

Vendor warrants to Customer that the material, analysis, data, programs and services to be delivered or rendered hereunder will be of the kind and quality designated and will be performed by qualified personnel. Special requirements for format or standards to be followed shall be included in a specific Proposal. Vendor makes no other warranties, whether written, oral or implied, including without limitation warranty of fitness for purpose or merchantability. In no event shall Vendor be liable for indirect, incidental, special, or consequential damages, whether or not the possibility of such damages has been disclosed to Vendor in advance or could have been reasonably foreseen.

Vendor's liability for Customer's actual damages will be limited to the actual amount paid by Customer for aforementioned Services. This limitation shall apply regardless of the form of action, whether such liability arises from a claim based on contract, warranty, tort or otherwise, including negligence. This limitation does not include liability due to claims by Customer for bodily injury, damage to real property, or damage to tangible personal property for which Vendor was found legally liable.

<End>

Customer Setup

1. Please provide the name and address where invoices should be sent:

Name ______________________________

Company ______________________________

Address 1 ______________________________

Address 2 ______________________________

City/State/Zip ______________________________

2. Please provide the name and phone number of the person to contact in the event of a question regarding an invoice:

Name ______________________________

Phone ______________________________

Available Hours ______________________________

3. Is a Purchase Order Number required on invoices? ___ Yes ___ No

If Yes, please provide the PO # for this project: ______________

4. Work is invoiced every two weeks and our terms are net 10 days. Work will be stopped in the event an invoice becomes past due.

5. Our Federal ID # is <number>. We are a Wisconsin Corporation.

______________________________ ______________

Authorized by Date

Functional Specification

April 1, 1997

Michael Austin-Thor
The Very Large Manufacturing Company
The Very Large Office Building
Milwaukee WI 53202-4104

Dear Mike,

We are pleased to present this quote for the Time and Billing Entry and Tracking (TABET) System.

Attached is the Functional Specification for TABET. This includes (1) the TABET main application, including the foundation directory structure, login and user and group permission maintenance, and the TABET functionality and (2) the TABET Reports. This Specification contains discrete descriptions of the functionality of each piece but each description references the other when applicable.

The total for the entire application is <$amount>. As requested, I've broken out the price and delivery for each piece separately. The Reports module can be viewed as an "add-on" to the main system, but can't be provided independently.

Main Application $
Reports $

If this quote is accepted within 15 days, the price is subject to a 6% <$amount> discount, resulting in an early acceptance price of <$amount>. We reserve the right to requote price and delivery after 60 days.

We can begin work on this project within <TimeFrame> weeks of acceptance. The final system can be delivered approximately <TimeFrame> working weeks later.

This is a fixed price quotation for the functionality described. Please read carefully and confirm that the functionality described meets your requirements. It is extremely important that every function and operation you are expecting is listed here; this document supersedes all verbal discussions - any modifications or changes requested after acceptance will alter price and/or delivery and will require written confirmation by both parties via the change order process described in the appendices to the specification.

Note that this is not an estimate but has been determined using our Action Point Counting system. Many software development companies use unreliable or seat-of-the-pants techniques to produce a rough approximation that is then bumped up by some arbitrary factor of safety to produce a price. Our methodology requires an accurate specification of functional capabilities for the system in question and relies on statistical analysis of historical performance to determine actual costs for each component of the system.

Payment terms consist of invoices rendered every two weeks for the work completed to that point, payable 10 days after presentation subject to a 1.5% discount. Work will be stopped in the event an invoice becomes past due. For specific information on how the work completed is broken into discrete deliverable components, see the section on Milestones at the end of the specification.

In order to accept this proposal, please sign one copy of this letter and return it to me. I'm looking forward to working with you and the rest of the crew at your firm on this system. If you have any questions, please call me at your convenience.

Sincerely,
Hentzenwerke Corporation

Whil Hentzen
President

Accepted By ____________________ Date ____________

Executive Overview

General Description

The purpose of TABET is to provide a centralized repository for time and billing records for all employees at the company that will be used for billing, backlog projections and "To Do" list maintenance.

We propose to provide a multi-user database system that will replace the current paper-based systems being maintained by various individuals and the administrative personnel at the company. In addition, TABET will create a database of data points of actual time spent to produce application components. This data will be used to fine-tune future project cost analysis.

Functionality

The major functions of TABET include the ability:

- For a developer to record time spent against Customer/Project/Module/Task and Activity.
- To maintain Customers, Projects, Modules, Tasks, and Activities.
- To create Invoices Master and Invoice Detail output.
- To create Backlog and History reports against various entities (Company, Customer, Project, Developer).
- For a developer to track their "To Do" list.
- To track and compare time spent against time estimated for entities down to the Task level.

Technical Specifications

Application Architecture

The majority of the cost of a custom software application is not in it's initial price but in the maintenance costs over the life of the system. Maintenance costs of 400% of the initial cost are often quoted in industry literature. Accordingly, a basic tenet of the design of this system is keeping maintenance costs down by providing user configurability and data-driven functionality whenever possible. A well-designed, maintainable system will provide substantial benefits over the life of the system.

Directory Structure

In order to avoid the difficulties encountered by having hundreds of files in a single directory as commonly practiced, the files for this application are broken out into multiple directories by function.

TABET will be loaded onto the network in a series of directories structured like so:

```
FPAPPS
  COMMON27  <Hentzenwerke-designed system-wide functionality files>
  THIRDP27  <third party system-wide functionality files
  TABET
    <TABET executable files - production version>
    APPFILES  <user-modifiable data-independent files >
    MDFILES   <data dictionary - not modifiable by user>
    SOURCE    <source code - used during testing>
    TESTDATA  <data set used for testing>
    LIVEDATA  <production version of data>
```

File Structures

The primary entities of TABET consist of a parent-child hierarchy chain of tables. The top-level entity is a Customer. A Customer is a physical billing location. If invoices are sent to more than one location or individual of a company, each is set up as a separate Customer.

A Customer may have one or more Projects. A Project is a discrete entity that is billed against; typically, each Project for a company will have it's own PO Number, as well as additional attributes such as PO amount and time-to-date hours and dollars.

A Project is made up of one or more Modules. A Module is a discrete component of a Project. Depending on the application, a Module may be a single screen or process, such as "Doctor Maintenance" or "Import Inventory from AS/400", or it may consist of a group of tasks to be done, such as "Additional Modifications."

A Module is made up of one or more Tasks. A Task is a description of work to be done to complete the Module. A Task is made up of one or more Activities. An Activity is a discrete action that can be accomplished in a single period of time. For instance, a Module could be "System Design" and Tasks for that Module would include "Design Meetings", "Specification Write-up" and "Prototype Demonstration Meetings." Activities for the Task of "Design Meetings" would be each individual meeting. There might only be a single Activity for the Task of "Specification Write-up" - Specification Write-up.

The Time entity is used to assign a block of time to a Task. All the Time spent on an Activity is attached to the Activities' Task.

A Time record contains a span of time - either a block of hours or a span of time - and is attached to a Developer. A Developer is an employee of the company. Each Developer has a default billing Rate in the Developer table, but they can also have multiple Billing Rates, and these rates can be attached to specific Customers, Projects or timespans.

Invoices are summaries from time entries for a single Customer. Invoice IDs are entered into time records so that they can be tied back to create invoice detail.

Original Data

TABET will initially be populated with the test data that is described later in this Specification.

Logon

In order to access the system, the user will select an icon in Windows to load the application. The user will enter their logon name and password. If the logon parameters are valid, the application will load and display the TABET main menu. If the parameters are not valid, the user will have two more attempts and then will be returned to Windows. In order to enhance security, the user will not be informed which piece of data is incorrect.

General Interface Notes

The following rules apply to the entire application. Exceptions are noted in the particular screen, process or report.

All screens are set up to be equally friendly to the keyboard and mouse users. For example, all objects can be operated with a keyboard shortcut as well as the mouse, the focus is automatically moved to the next appropriate object when a field is left, and so on.

All screens and menus provide visual clues to the user as to what operations are allowed through the use of enabled and disabled controls. All potentially destructive actions must be affirmatively confirmed.

All picklists feature changeable incremental search capability based on the column the user is in. In other words, when the user is in Column A, the picklist will be ordered on Column A and incremental search is active. When the user moves to Column B, the picklist changes sort order so that it is in order on the contents of Column B, and incremental search is functional on Column B.

Entry into any field where a code is entered (as opposed to picking from a listbox, pulldown, etc.) will validate the code and present a picklist with incremental search capability when an incorrect choice is selected. In most cases, the English description of that code will be displayed next to the code field.

Double-clicking on any listbox in the system will bring forward an editing dialog where the user can edit existing records and, if appropriate, add and delete records as well. Empty listboxes will contain a "<None>" entry. When the "+" button is pressed, a screen will display and allow the user to add records. When the "-" button is pressed the user will be prompted to answer "Yes" if they want to delete the record that was highlighted in the listbox. The listbox will be refreshed after adding or deleting a record.

All dates are stored internally in CCYYMMDD format so that dates after the year 2000 are handled correctly. Dates will be shown on the screen with the century (for example, 07/27/1996), but the user need only enter the year (for example, 07/27/96) for dates in the twentieth century.

Maintenance Screens

A maintenance screen is used to add, edit and delete data in a specific table. A maintenance screen may also be used to access child records related to the parent table in a parent-child relationship.

All maintenance screens have similar functionality; instead or repeating the same information for each screen, the following describes the common functionality across all maintenance screens.

Depending on the version of FoxPro used, the navigation and query access mechanism is either a set of buttons contained in the screen (FoxPro 2.6 for DOS and Windows) or an independent toolbar (Visual FoxPro 3.0 and 5.0).

Common Maintenance Buttons

The Next and Back buttons allow the user to navigate forward and back through the records of the current filter. (See the Find and Sort functions for more information on the "current filter.")

The List button lists the records of the current filter in the current order. By default, all fields are displayed; the user can select certain fields by selecting the Fields option and using the Mover to select which fields are to be browsed.

The Find button will display a dialog by which the appropriate records can be selected. The criteria by which records will be searched depends on the entity being searched. The user can set a filter in lieu of finding a specific record by selecting the Fields option. The set of records displayed will then be subject to the filter created by that search action. The user can remove the filter by selecting the Remove Filter pushbutton from within the Find screen.

The Sort button will display a dialog that displays the various sort orders the records can be displayed in. The user can choose whether to sort Ascending or Descending, and whether to stay on the current record or go to the top of the file.

Add will change the screen into a state where a new record can be entered. Otherwise, the screen is in an edit state where fields can be changed. Once a change in a field is made and the user tabs out of the field, the Save button becomes enabled. The user can Save or Revert their changes at any time.

The Done button will close the screen without affecting the data or the operation of the screen whenever it is enabled.

Anytime a user modifies data, they will be prompted to save or cancel their changes when they attempt to execute another action.

Toolbar

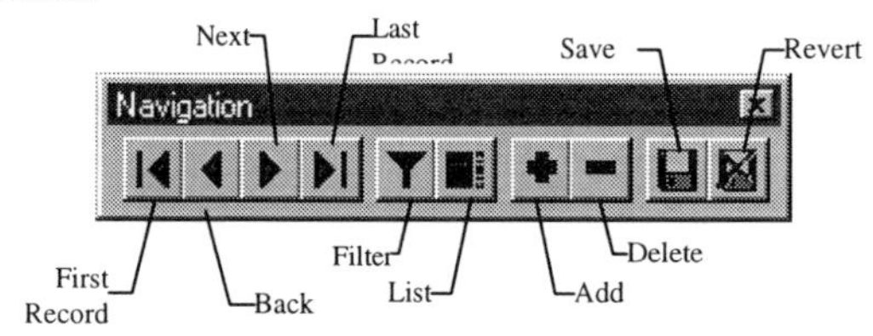

The First Record, Next, Back and Last Record buttons allow the user to navigate forward and back through the records of the current filter. (See the Current Filter for more information)

The Filter button will display a dialog by which the appropriate records can be selected. The criteria by which records will be searched depends on the entity being searched. The set of records displayed will then be subject to the filter created by that search action. The users can remove the filter by selecting the Remove Filter pushbutton from within the Search screen.

The List button lists the records of the current filter in the current order. By default, all fields are displayed; the user can select certain fields by selecting the Fields option and using the Mover to select which fields are to be browsed.

All screens are in live edit mode by default. Add (+) will blank out all fields on the screen and allow the user to add a new record. Once a change in a field is made and the user tabs out of the field, in either Add or Edit mode, the Save button becomes enabled. The user can Save or Revert their changes at any time. Delete (-) will delete the current record after prompting the user to confirm their choice.

Each button has a Tool Tip associated with it which is used to provide a text description of the button. This can be seen when the user pauses the mouse pointer over the button.

Specific functionality for each screen is described below. When it is in conflict with the above description, the functionality for the specific screen takes precedence.

Listbox Controls

A listbox is used to provide navigation through sets of child records in some situations. The listbox displays more information about the set of records to be transferred but is not editable. The fields on the same screen as the listbox are editable; the Add button provides the ability to add child records while the Delete button removes the currently highlighted record. Save and Revert operate in the same manner as the regular maintenance screen.

Notes button

Many screens contain a "Notes" button that provides access to a free-form memo field. The prompt of the button changes to indicate whether there is data in the memo field. If the button displays "Add" then no record for that Item exists and by selecting the button, the user can add information. If the button displays Edit then a record does exist and by selecting the button, the user can edit the information.

<u>Main Menu</u>

The Main menu contains six menu pads for the user: File, Edit, Process, Reports, Utilities, and Help, and one for developers: Developer. The menu is disabled once a user brings a screen forward. The menu options under each menu pad are described below.

<u>Main Menu - File</u>

The File menu pad contains options for each data entry screen in the system, and exiting the system. It also contains a Lookup Maintenance option that provides the ability to add, edit and delete data in the system's lookup tables. It is only accessible to selected system personnel according to the group they belong to.
Each user will also have the ability to select a dataset to work with, independent of other users under the Change DataSet option.

The menu choices under File are as shown:

File menu - Enter Time

Time Entry

Next | Back | List | Fields... | Find... | Sort... | Add | Delete | Save | Revert | ? | Done

Developer: WH

Customer: Hentzenwerke

Project: Writing/Speaking

Module: [PVFP3 - Ziff-Davis

Task: Chapter 23

Dupe Last Record

Mark Task as Done

Type of Work: Writing

Date of Activity: 03/18/1995

Time Span: 09:30 21:30

Actual Hours: 12.00

Billable Hours: 0.00

Billable Amount: 0.00

Override Rate

Include Hours in Calc

Put Description on Invoice

Mark Item as N/C on Invoice

Flat Amount

Chapter 23
- outline chapter
- write page frames section
- create sample code for page frames
- write option group section

Purpose

The purpose of this screen is to allow the user to enter and edit time spent on company projects - both billable and non-billable.

Access

This screen is accessed through the Enter Time menu option under the File menu pad.

Usage

When a Time record is entered into the system, the user selects a Customer, Project, Module, and Task. The system uses the Developer ID to determine the current rate per hour for this task. First, if the Customer or Project is marked as non-billable, the Rate is set to zero. Otherwise, the rate from the Developer table is used as a default. Then, a rate for the Developer without a Project or Customer is sought in the Rate table for the current date of activity. If found, this rate overrides the default rate from the Developer table. Then, a rate for the Developer for the current Customer is sought in the Rate table, and if found, overrides the Developer/Rate rate. Finally, a rate for the Developer for the current Project is sought in the Rate table, and if found, overrides the Developer/Project rate.

If upon saving an entry, the user has not provided the following information the user will be notified and the record will not be saved until such information is provided.

- Customer
- Project
- Module
- Task

Only users with a Supervisor Permission level will be able to Add, Edit or Delete time for users other than themselves. All other users will be able to Add, Edit or Delete time for themselves only.

Screen Objects

All fields are editable and no validation is performed except for the following rules:

The Developer dropdown is automatically populated based on the user who logged into the application.

The Customer dropdown is populated based on the contents in the Customer table. The Project, Module and Task dropdowns are all populated based on the selection made in the previous table in the hierarchy. All dropdowns are populated with the active values placed in front of non-active values. Non-active values are bracketed.

The time spans are validated so that the user can't enter a second time earlier than the first one. All times are entered in 24 hour HH:MM format. Leading zeros are required.

The actual time is the difference between the first and second times. The billable time is defaulted to the same but can be overridden.

The current rate per hour for the selected Developer/Customer/Project hierarchy is displayed in the box next to the Override Rate text box and is multiplied against the billable time to determine the billable amount.

The Mark Task as Done pushbutton sets the flag of the currently Task to inactive.

The Dupe Last Record allows the user to easily make multiple duplicate entries of the current record.

The Override Rate checkbox is used to override the rate per hour calculated as described below. Checking this box enables the textbox next to it.

The Include Hours in Calc checkbox is checked by default. In order to not include the hours for the current time entry, uncheck the box.

The Put Description on Invoice checkbox is checked by default. In order to inhibit the display of the description, uncheck this box. A developer may wish to inhibit the display if multiple blocks of time are spent on the same task in order to complete.

The Mark Item as N/C on Invoice checkbox is unchecked by default.

The Flat Amount checkbox is used to create an invoice item for a flat amount, such as an item that is purchased on the behalf of a customer, or certain expense items such as hotels or phone charges.

The edit box in the bottom of the screen is used to enter a long description of the work done that will appear on the invoice.

Main Menu - Edit

The Edit menu pad contains Windows-standard options for editing - Undo, Redo, Cut, Copy, Paste, Select All and Find. These functions are available whenever the cursor is in an edit field.

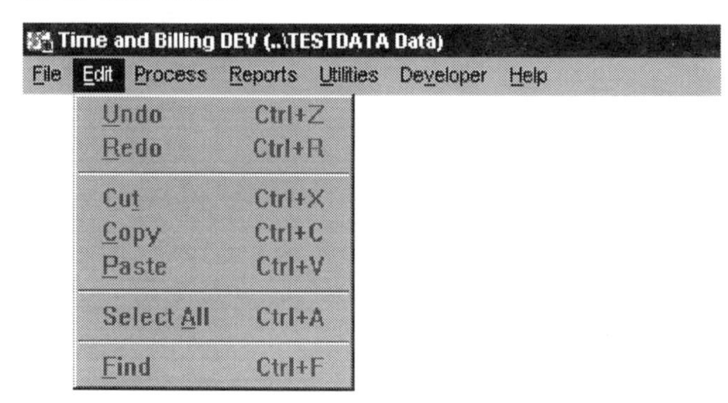

Main Menu - Process

The Process menu pad contains menu options for operations that are not file-centric, such as importing and exporting.

The Export Invoices to Quicken produces a Quicken-readable file. The user can specify the name of the file and select the range of invoices to export.

Main Menu - Reports

The Reports menu pad contains options to produce output from the system. The Reports menu option brings forward Foxfire!, a utility from which standard reports can be run and custom reports can be created. The Herman screen is the companies' specific name for current activity and recent billing history. The Backlog screen produces a variety of permutations of work in progress.

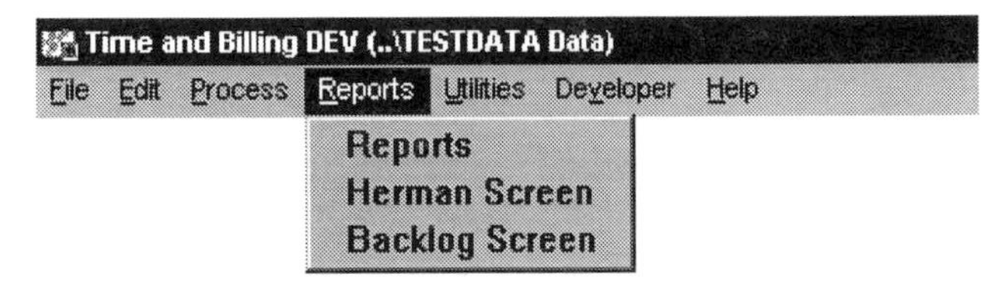

Herman Screen

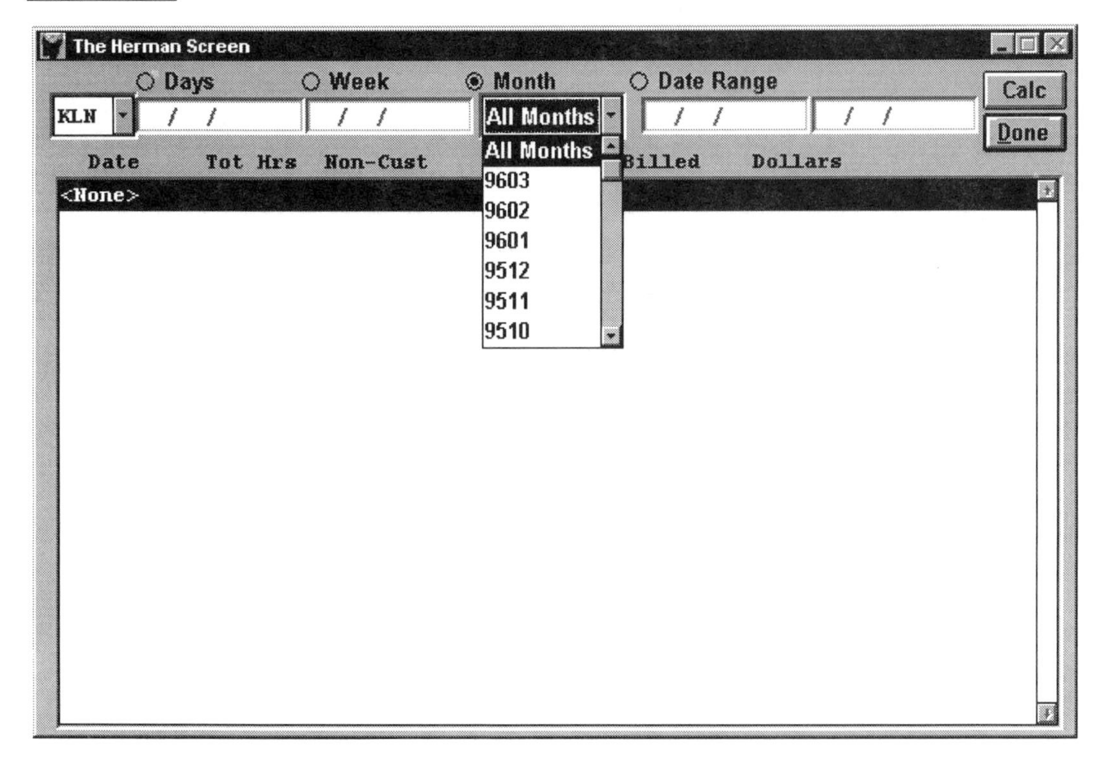

Purpose

The purpose of this screen is to allow a developer to track their billable and non-billable hours on a daily, weekly, or monthly basis, or select a range of dates to report upon.

Access

This screen is accessed through the Herman Report menu option under the report menu pad.

Usage

The user selects which grouping to report on and enters a starting date for which the report is to be generated. The values are defaulted to approximately 20 rows of data - for example, selecting the Days radio button on the 30th of the month will generate data for the past 20 days.

No special rules are in effect for this screen.

Screen Objects

The dropdown listbox is used to select Employee to report on.

Reports

Reporting will be done through Foxfire!, a third-party ad-hoc report utility. The following reports will be provided:

Open Task List By Customer:

Purpose: This report will list all tasks for a specific customer which are to be completed within the user specified time frame.

Detail Entity: Tasks

Filter: Tasks for a user-selected customer with due dates that fall within user-defined date range and that have not been finished.

Order/Group: Group by project, then module within project, then due date within module.

Fields: Customer, Project, Module, Task Description, Task Due Date, Task Scheduled Date, Developer Responsible.

Calculated Fields: None.

Samples of these reports are attached to the end of this document.

The ability to modify existing reports and create new reports will be allowed based on the permission level of the user.

Since the appropriate appearance of reports is a highly subjective and personal matter, it is possible to make modifications to reports ad infinitum. Since this is a fixed price proposal, we will create data items for the detail fields listed above, produce the data file to populate the report, and mock up a sample report layout based on the examples provided. Additional modifications to reports can be made by customer through the Foxfire! utility or by vendor at additional charge.

Main Menu - Utilities

The Utilities menu contains options for setting user preferences, changing the current data set (from TEST to LIVE, for example), and changing one's own password. It also contains an Administrator menu option and a User Maintenance option that are only accessible to selected system personnel according to the group they belong to.

Utilities Menu - Preferences

The preferences submenu allows the user to set specific options for their personal session.

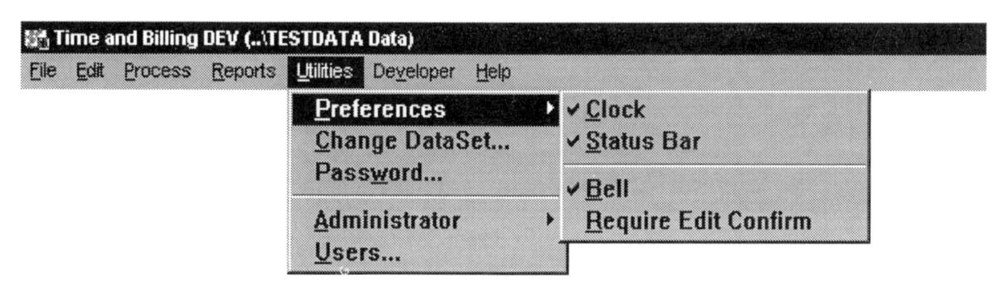

Utilities Menu - Administrator

The Administrator menu option brings forward a submenu that contains various system maintenance options.

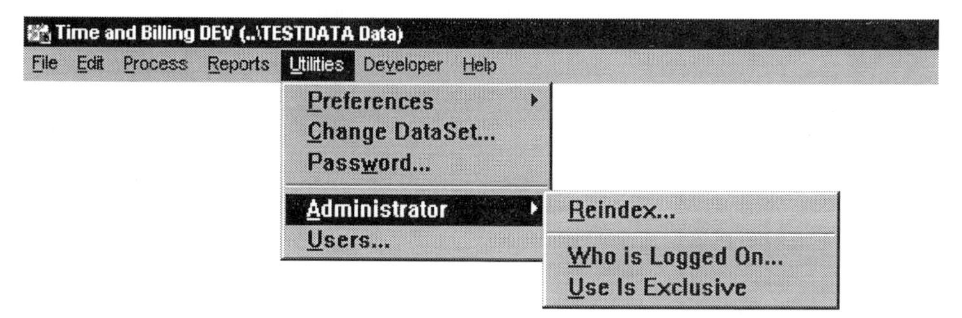

Change DataSet

Each user has the ability to select a dataset to work with, independent of other users. This capability is useful for training new users on test data and for testing new segments of the application without disturbing modules that are already installed. It is also useful for testing against large data sets in anticipation of growth of the application.

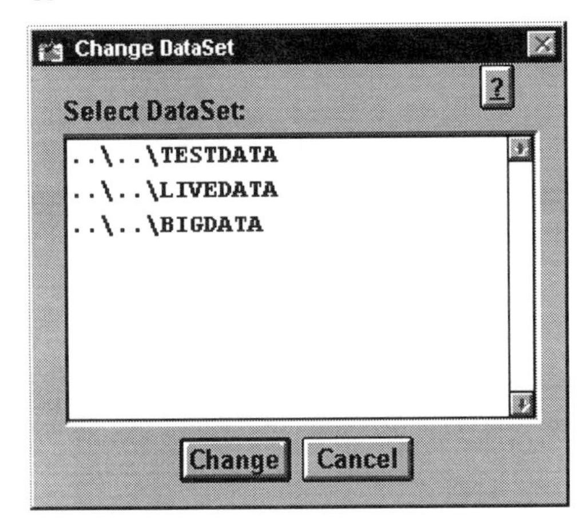

Password

Each user has the ability to change their own password through the Change Password screen under the Utilities menu pad. Passwords do not ever expire and can be reused. The user must enter their original password and then enter the new password twice. Passwords are case-sensitive.

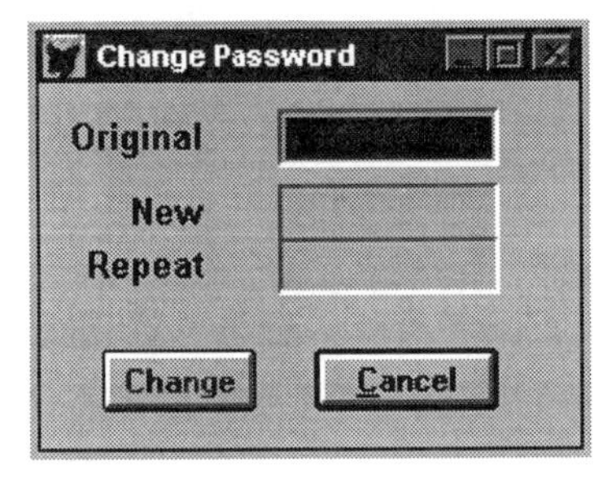

User Maintenance

Users are added, deleted and edited through the User Maintenance screen found under the Utilities menu pad. This is also used to flag existing users as Active or Inactive and to assign a user to a Permission Level. When a new user is added, their default password is the same as their username. The username can be characters or numbers and has a maximum length of 10.

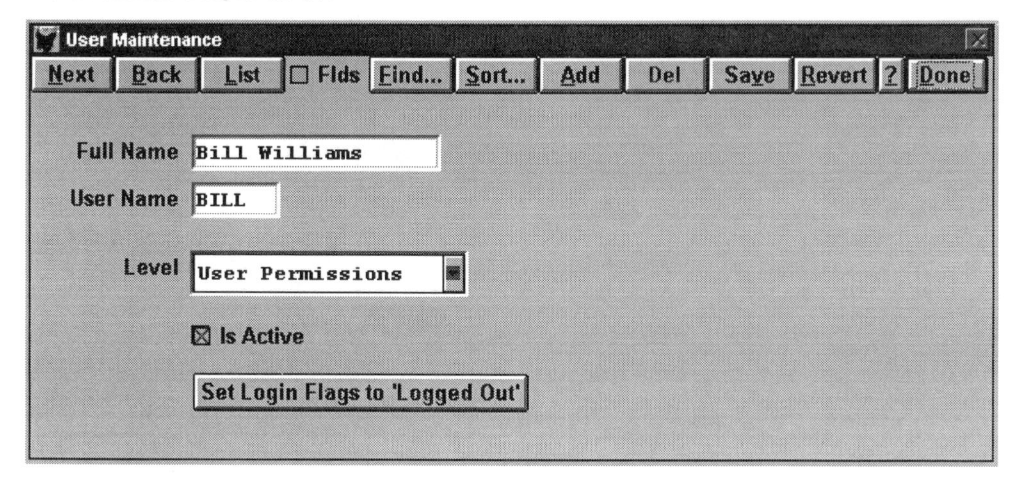

Permission Levels are:

- Supervisor — Write All, Read All, Delete All, Reindex, Maintain Users, Change Help
- Manager
- Super User — Write All, Read All, Delete All
- Regular User — Read All

Users are assigned a Permission Level which allows the user Add/Edit/Delete permissions in all screens in the system, unless otherwise noted. Users assigned a Supervisor permission have complete rights throughout the system. Users assigned a Manager permission have complete rights except to maintain Users and execute System Administration functions (described in the Utilities section of this Specification.) Users assigned a Super User permission have complete add/edit/delete rights to all data unless described differently later in this Specification. Users assigned a User permission have read-only rights throughout the system.

Main Menu - Developer

The Developer menu dropdown contains options that the system developer can use during the development and testing of the application. The entire pad is only available when a developer logs on to the application.

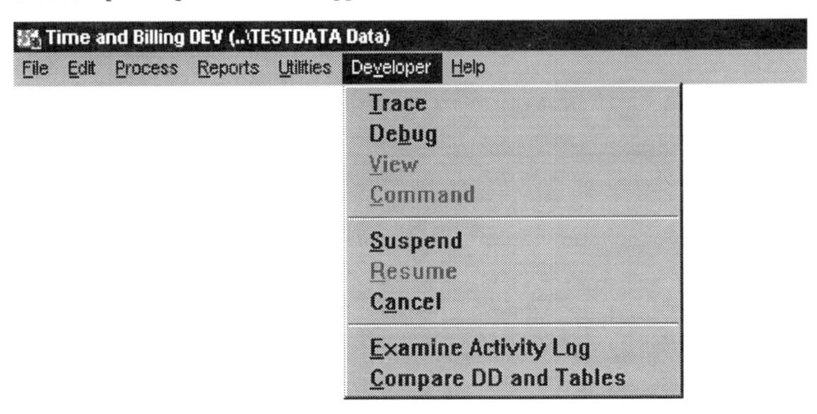

Main Menu - Help

On-line help contains topics for every menu option (screen and process) in the system. Pressing F1 when a screen is active will bring forward the help topic for that screen; otherwise, a list of help topics will be displayed from which a specific topic can be selected.

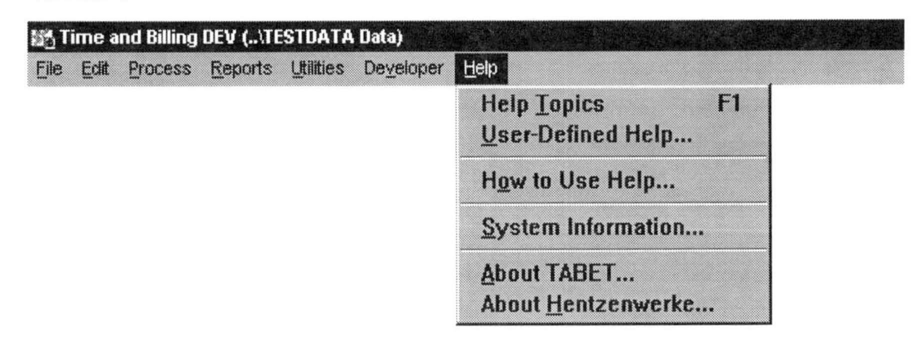

User-Defined Help

Users can add custom help to any screen by pressing F2 when the screen is active, or by selecting the User-Defined Help menu option and selecting the desired topic.

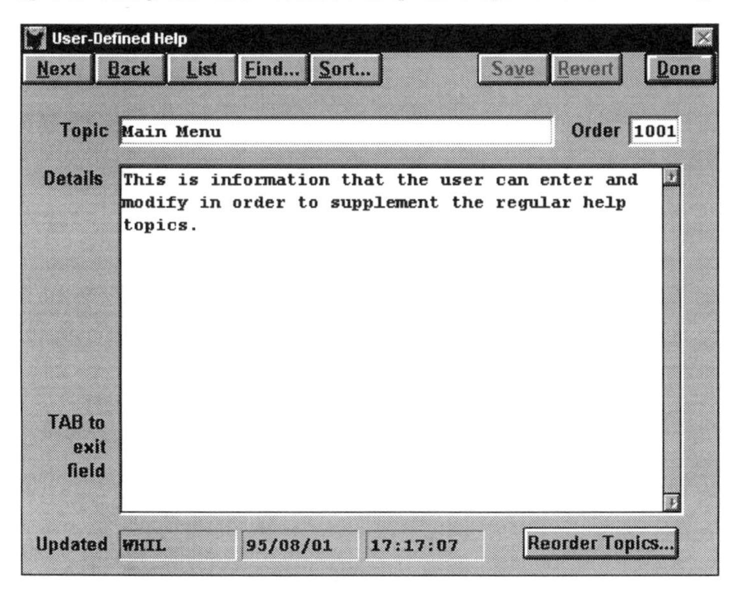

System Information

The System Information screen can be used for remote analysis of the hardware and software environment that the application is running. This information can be helpful in resolving problems encountered during regular operation of the application.

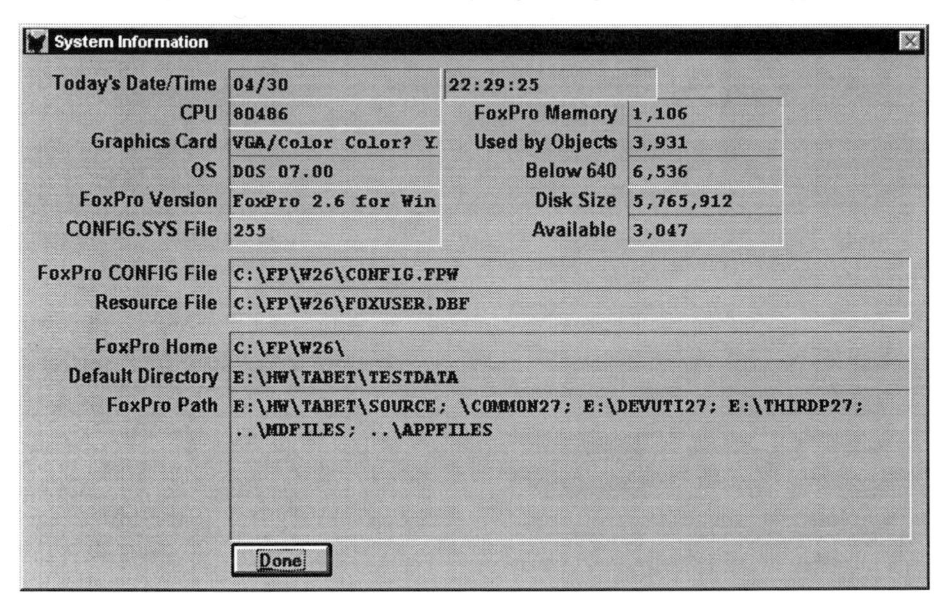

Data Structures

Identical field names indicate the same attribute (data element) in different tables. For example, the CIDFa field in the FACILITY table represents the same data element wherever CIDFa is found.

All fields that begin with "CID" are unique, primary keys or foreign keys. All keys are system generated and hidden from the user.

All fields that are named "NLMOD" or "CLMOD" are audit fields that track the date and time of the last edit of the record.

The first character of each field name represents the type of data - C for character, N for numeric, D for Date, L for Logical, and M for memo. The following characters indicate more specifically what the field represents. For example, "NO" represents a number, "TY" represents a type, "CD" represents a code, "NA" represents a name, etc.

Instead of storing repetitive data (Container Types, etc), each data element is stored in a single lookup table along with a code. This code is stored in the appropriate primary entity.

The associative tables are listed. Each "many-to-many" relationship has one of these tables that includes the Ids from each table.

The data dictionary tables that make up the foundation are not listed because they are not customized for this system.

DEV.DBF

Field	Field Name	Type	Width	Dec	Description
1	CIDDEV	Character	5		PK
2	CNAF	Character	10		First Name
3	CNAL	Character	15		Last Name
4	CINITIALS	Character	3		Initials
5	NRATEDEV	Numeric	6	2	Default Rate/Hour
6	LISACTDEV	Logical	1		Is Active
7	CIDA_US	Character	5		FK to A_USER
8	CLMOD	Character	10		User stamp
9	NLMOD	Numeric	15	2	Time stamp
** Total **			71		

Test Data Set Requirements

Customer will provide the current live data from their current application to use for testing.

Environment

If the system must run on 16 bit operating systems, FoxPro 2.6 will be used. If the system will only run on 32 bit operating systems, FoxPro 5.0 can be used if desired.

This system will be written entirely in FoxPro for Windows, version 2.6, and will be compiled to a runtime .APP to run under FoxPro on the LAN. However, it is advisable to have FoxPro installed on the LAN during development instead of relying on run-time files. This will provide for easier debugging and other modifications that could be made on site. Third party software is limited to JKEY, an incremental search routine for use within Browse windows, Foxfire!, a reporting utility, and KeyMask, a password masking utility.

Operation of System will be performed on equipment purchased, owned, and maintained by Customer. The system will run on Novell Netware 3.1x, DOS 5.x or later, and Windows 3.1, Windows for WorkGroups 3.11 or Windows 95. The workstations will be IBM PC compatibles containing a minimum of 486 processors with 8 MB. Machines with less than 16 MB may not work reliably as far as moving data between System and other Windows applications.

All will be equipped with monitors capable of VGA color display and all will have hard disks with several megabytes of disk space available. A mouse is required. Some Windows functions may not be available without a mouse. Data backup will be done according to standard internal MIS procedures independent of System.

Printing will be directed to generic dot matrix and HP LaserJet printers via parallel ports or network connections.

The equipment may be used for purposes other than running System, but System will take precedence in terms of use, access by Customer and Hentzenwerke personnel, and setup parameters. In addition, Customer personnel will take reasonable precautions that equipment is protected from outside interference including, but not limited to, virus infection and use or access by non-authorized personnel.

System will not perform environment checking such as looking for the existence of fonts, non-FoxPro-specific system files, or available memory and diskspace. Time spent on the resolution of problems causes by the alteration of the environment once the System has been installed is not included as part of this proposal and will be billed on a time and materials basis.

Throughput Analysis

Table	Original Load	Weekly Load
CUST	50	1
PROJ	125	2
MOD	490	4
TASK	2900	30
ACT	7500	100
TIME	5000	50
INV	750	5

Implementation

Installation

System will be installed on the office server and on one PC that represents the standard configuration throughout the office. Time spent configuring System to run on additional configurations, if any, is not included as part of this proposal and will be billed on a time and materials basis.

Customer will provide remote access through modem dial-in software in order to facilitate long distance support.

Deliverables

Customer will provide ...

- All equipment and supplies necessary for the operation and maintenance of the System.

- A test suite of data to use for development and testing. The test suite should include a variety of data sets that fairly represent data on the system and represent all possible cases of variance. Hentzenwerke will assist in the development of an acceptable set of data.

Hentzenwerke will provide ...

- DOS and/or Windows executable software programs that perform the functions listed in this Functional Specification.

- Run-time versions of third-party utilities JKEY, Foxfire! and KeyMask.

- All source code and associated design surfaces used to generate the executable.

- Installation instructions including a description of the environment required for operation of the program, a list of the files that make up the system and how they are installed for use (audience: systems).

- Technical documentation, including fully commented and indented source code (audience: programmers and analysts).

- On-line help sufficient to assist in the operation of the system for a user in the department already familiar with the business operations of the company.

- Training for one or two Customer personnel to the extent necessary for proper operation of the Programs.

Test Methodology

Hentzenwerke uses three distinct testing phases during system development. The first phase consists of testing each action in the system (menu choices and screen objects) to verify that it operates without adverse effects. The second phase consists of verifying that each function point in the system (menu choices, screen actions, screen data fields, and report objects) performs the function or contains the data it is supposed to. The third phase consists of checking that the business rules of the system (logic and branching, algorithms, special cases) are carried out through the operation of the system.

Each phase of testing is planned prior to the testing by the Software Developer. This is referred to as the Test Plan. Upon completion of the Test Plan, the Application Tester will perform the Test according to the plans and record the results. This process will be followed for each Deliverable. Hentzenwerke will perform all testing for each of these phases before delivery of any working prototypes or final programs.

Test Plan

In order to test the system, Hentzenwerke's QA department will perform the following functions:

- Enter a new customer into the system.
- Enter a new project and multiple modules for the new customer.
- Enter multiple tasks for more than one module.
- Enter time against several tasks in several modules.
- Run all reports and verify that new information has been recorded and categorized correctly.

Modifications

The menus, screens, reports, table structures and functionality described in this Functional Specification are final.

It is not uncommon for modifications to be requested after such a point. Depending on the type of modification and the stage of during development when that modification is requested, the amount of work that the modification requires may range from the trivial to the substantial.

Estimates for such modifications will be provided in writing on a Hentzenwerke Corporation Change Order form and will need to be signed off on before they are incorporated into the system.

Customer agrees not to modify the source code and/or design surfaces during the development of the System.

Hentzenwerke reserves the right to interpret interface and performance issues that are not specifically described in this Functional Specification as it sees fit.

Milestones and Delivery

Upon acceptance of this proposal, we will schedule our first meeting to finalize the data structures and related menu and screen details. At that time, we will schedule delivery milestones. At each milestone, Hentzenwerke will provide the version of the system developed to that point, including source code and documentation. Screens and functions will either be completely operational, working but in testing stage, or stubbed out if under development.

Delivery milestones will include the following:

Maintenance Screens
- Customer Maintenance
- Project Maintenance
- Module/Tasks Maintenance

Date Entry Screens
- Time Entry
- To Do Entry

Reporting Module

Upon delivery of each milestone, the customer will walk through the work delivered with Hentzenwerke personnel to verify that the work performs as specified. Upon acceptance the customer will be invoiced for that milestone. In the event that the walkthrough is either postponed for more than a week or canceled due to customer request, the milestone shall be considered accepted and will be invoiced.

Upon delivery of the final build the customer will be given a final build sheet. The customer then has one week after delivery to perform final internal testing and return the final acceptance sheet to Hentzenwerke. If the final build sheet isn't returned within one week, System will be deemed to have been accepted and the remaining balance due will be invoiced.

<END>

Cover Letter to Functional Specification

April 1, 1997

Michael Austin-Thor
The Very Large Manufacturing Company
The Very Large Office Building
Milwaukee WI 53202-4104

Dear Mike,

We are pleased to present this quote for the Time and Billing Entry and Tracking (TABET) System.

Attached is the Functional Specification for TABET. This includes (1) the TABET main application, including the foundation directory structure, login and user and group permission maintenance, and the TABET functionality and (2) the TABET Reports. This Specification contains discrete descriptions of the functionality of each piece but each description references the other when applicable.

The total for the entire application is <price>. As requested, I've broken out the price and delivery for each piece separately. The Reports module can be viewed as "add-ons" to the main TABET system, but can't be provided independently of the main system.

Main Application $
Reports $

The price for this application is effective for 15 days. After this period, the price increases by 7%. We reserve the right to requote price and delivery after 60 days.

We can begin work on this project within <TimeFrame> weeks of acceptance. The final system can be delivered approximately <TimeFrame> working weeks later.

This is a fixed price quotation for the functionality described. Please read carefully and confirm that the functionality described meets your requirements. It is extremely important that every function and operation you are expecting is listed here; this document supersedes all verbal discussions - any modifications changes requested after acceptance will alter price and/or delivery.

Note that this is not an estimate but has been determined using our Action Point Counting system. Many software development companies use unreliable or seat-of-the-pants techniques to produce a rough approximation that is then bumped up by some factor of safety to produce a price. Our methodology requires an accurate specification of functional capabilities for the system in question and relies on statistical analysis of historical performance to determine actual costs for each component of the system.

Payment terms consist of invoices rendered every two weeks for the work completed to that point, payable 10 days after presentation subject to a 1.5% discount. Work will be stopped in the event an invoice becomes past due. For specific information on how the work completed is broken into discrete deliverable components, see the section on Milestones at the end of the specification.

In order to accept this proposal, please sign one copy of this letter and return it to me. I'm looking forward to working with you and the rest of the crew at your firm on this system. If you have any questions, please call me at your convenience.

Sincerely,
Hentzenwerke Corporation

Whil Hentzen
President

____ ____________
Accepted By Date

Application Feedback Form

Application Feedback

Company/System: ______________________________
Today's Date/Time: ______________________________
Your Name: ______________________________
Hentzenwerke Developer: ______________________________

☐ Bug Is it reproducible? Yes No

Steps to reproduce:

What happened:

Expected:

☐ Enhancement Request (Please be specific)

☐ Question

Internal Use
☐Analysis ☐Design ☐Prog ☐Envir ☐Install ☐Train ☐Data ☐Unrepr

Hentzenwerke Resolution: By______________________Date____________
Client Informed of Resolution: By______________________Date____________

Change Order Form

Change Order Form

Order #: ______________________________
Date: ______________________________
Customer Name: ______________________________
System: ______________________________
Developer Name: ______________________________

1. Description of change request:

2. Steps Required:

3. Test Plan:

4. Ramifications:

5. Cost:

☐ No Charge
☐ Fixed Price price:
☐ Time and Materials estimate:

6. Customer Approval

☐ Accept ☐ Reject

SIGNATURE: ______________________________ Date: ______________

Customer please complete and fax to LINDA BOINSKI at Hentzenwerke (414)224-7650.

On-Site Activity Report

#

Purpose

DM=Design Mtg
PDM=Prototype Demo Mtg
BDM=Beta Delivery Mtg
FDM=Final Delivery Mtg
IT=Investigate/Troubleshoot

Company/System: ______________________

Today's Date: ______________________

Contact Name/Phone: ______________________

Hentzenwerke Developer: ______________________

Arrival/Departure Times: From: ____________ **To:** ____________

Agenda	Purpose/ Reference #	(Initial & Date) HW Inspect	(Initial & Date) Customer Accept

Issues to be resolved	Responsible	Due Date

Developer's Notes:

Customer Feedback

It is essential we know if our customers are satisfied with our services. Please take a moment to answer the following four questions. If you are dissatisfied with our services in any way, please note the reason(s) in the specified area below the questions. If you are unable to describe the reason(s) you are dissatisfied during the on site visit, please fax (414) 224-7650 or phone (414) 224-7654 comments to my attention within five days of the on site visit. If we do not receive your comments via fax or phone, I will contact you directly to discuss the situation. Thank you - Brenda Rave, Quality Assurance.

1) HW responded to my concerns within an acceptable time frame. ☐ Yes ☐ No
2) All agenda items were resolved to my satisfaction. ☐ Yes ☐ No
3) All of my questions were answered to my satisfaction. ☐ Yes ☐ No ☐ N/A
4) I am pleased with the outcome of the on-site visit. ☐ Yes ☐ No

The 17 Dreaded Questions

I've been interviewing of potential employees for a high level programming position lately. A lot of folk still have a dBASE III mindset, but label themselves as "experienced FoxPro 2.5 programmers" simply because they're writing dBASE III code inside FoxPro/Win. It's easy to spend a lot of time just separating the "pretenders" from the "contenders" - and time is not one of those abundant resources....

As a result, I put together a set of questions that were designed to determine where an individual stood on the ladder of FoxPro 2.x programming proficiency. Note that I chose those words very carefully. I'm not looking for a developer - but a programmer. And I'm not just looking for the highest score possible, but rather, I want to understand the breadth of that individual's skill set so I can better evaluate the likelihood of their fitting in as a cog in my development environment's machine.

These questions came about as a result of an evening's discussion at FoxTeach with Steven Black and Pat Adams, and then generated a lengthy thread on FoxGang afterward. The rationale behind the questions is in brackets behind each question.]

1. Versions of FoxPro. Name three major differences between 2.0 and 2.5. [How long have they been around?]

2. Language - Code a simple Foundation Read. Alternate: How do you get rid of the Command Window after you've put up a menu? [Are they still using DO WHILE? Have they even _heard_ of a FR?]

3. What is the difference between WHERE and HAVING? Describe how to implement an outer join in FoxPro. [A blank look here generates the prompt - "you know, in SQL" - which often leads to a "Oh, I only use FoxPro commands." And that's what I wanted to know <g>.]

4. Name five FoxPro third party products and what they do. [Do they insist on inventing everything themselves?]

5. What periodicals do you regularly read? What books have you read? What else do you do to learn? [Do they understand the availability of resources available, or do they try to learn it all themselves?]

6. Screen Builder. Describe the tradeoffs of desnippetizing. Where do you keep your code? Name two valid reasons for modifying the SPR [Ha! Trick question!]

7. What's the difference between a function and a procedure? [Let's not forget the basics...]

8. What does this line of code do: private all like j* [Are they familiar with safe programming techniques?]

9. Describe your naming conventions for tables, fields, variables, arrays, windows. [A true mark of differentiation between hacks and professionals.]

10. What technique do you use to integrate browses with READs. [The best answer here is "Ugh, I can hardly wait until they make it a true READ object..."]

11. Name each band in the RW and describe when it is executed. [Are they still hand coding reports? Don't laugh - it happens....]

12. Describe the Transport process. [We do a lot of xplat work - have they?]

13. Write out a command to find a record that is Rushmore optimizable. Write one that is not. [Critical to find out if they understand how to take advantage of FoxPro's speed.]

14. Describe an alternative to PACK, when you'd use the alternative, and why. [Tells me if they've done any serious multi-user work.]

15. Describe what Set Default and Set Path do. [These are fundamental concepts in our environment. A lot of programmers still just throw all the programs and tables in a single directory.]

16. What's the difference between Build Project and Rebuild All. [Have they ever used the PM? And for what?']

17. Tell me all you know about using Debug. [I _assume_ they've had bugs in their programs. Do they understand how to go about tracking them down efficiently?]

Again, this isn't intended to be the ultimate FoxPro certification test. The purpose is to weed out, over the phone, the amateurs from those who've a solid foundation of knowledge. I can deal with a few weak spots; gaping holes, on the other hand, well, I'll let them work for my competition.

The 17 Dreaded Questions: The Answers

By Jim Booth

(This response to "The 17" was posted by Jim Booth on CompuServe's FoxUser Forum.)

This is the answer sheet to Whil's 17 dreaded questions. Be sure to refer to these answers when scoring your potential employees.

1A. The runtime files got bigger.
1B. The memory footprint got bigger.
1C. The bugs changed.

2. You can eliminate the command window by creating an EXE and running that.

3. HAVING is what you got and WHERE is the place you got it.

4. FoxExpress: Mails your code to the client overnight.
FoxFire: Eliminates unwanted employees.
CodeBOOK: Decrypts encrypted EXEs.
Tom Rettig's Office: A nice place to work
dBASE IV: Makes code run slower so users can keep up

5A. Action comics and MAD magazine.
5B. All of Erma Bombeck's books.
5C. Make mistakes.

6. If one is desnippetized, it could take micro surgery for hours to reattach your snippet. Reason 1: I like pain. Reason 2: I am developing an SPR to SCX application and want to test it.

7. Spelling

8. Means you will need a key for things like jars, jaguars, and the john.

9. I have a random name generator that prevents duplicate names for anything.

10. If you hide behind the shelves you can often read a book while the store's staff thinks you are only browsing.

11. The Rolling Stones, the Who and Credence Clearwater. I don't think it is nice to execute the band even if you don't like their music.

12. Step onto one of the circles on the floor and say "Energize".

13. LOCATE WHAT I WANT REAL FAST
LOCATE WHAT I WANT REAL SLOW

14. Bring enough money to buy new clothes when you arrive. If you have alot of money and the trips expenses are tax deductible.

15. SET DEFAULT is used to control when the application will fault. SET PATH is used to find your way home from work.

16. BUILD PROJECT will build a single house. REBUILD ALL will tear down all the houses in the neighborhood and then build them again.

17. Since my code doesn't have bugs, I've never used it.

<EOF>

The 67 Dreaded Technical Questions

67 question test for interviewing prospective FoxPro 2.x programmers. These questions are based on the way we do things at Hentzenwerke Corp. They are not intended to be a thorough coverage of every feature in FoxPro. If, despite this caveat, you insist on whining about it, I will use you as the "BEFORE" speciman in a "Before and After" comparison" in my next book.

Purpose:
1. Determine your habits
2. Find out what you know and don't know
3. Demonstrate to you about the types of things we do here, so that you can understand what our expectations are

This test is not to beat up on you (unless you're arrogant <g>) but rather to give you a perspective on where you are and where you need to be in order to be productive here

You will have access to the LR but not a computer. We're not interested in how much syntax you have memorized, but we're also not interested in seeing what you can put together by trial and error. There is no time limit, but, on the other hand, efficiency is a positive attribute.

Your Development Environment

How is your FoxPro environment set up now? Where is FoxPro located, where are your apps located, what does your CONFIG.FP look like, what does DEFAULT.FKY contain, what else have you done to customize and tailor your environment?

How do you handle multiple versions of an app?

Describe some of the homegrown utilities that you've written.

Describe the data dictionary that you use. Do you use an existing product or have you rolled your own? How does it work and what do you use it for? How do you reconcile the contents of the data dictionary with the actual data structures?

Your Application Environment

How is a project of yours structured - where do you have the various components (menus, dbfs, prgs, screens, bitmaps, data, metadata, and so on) located?

How have you structured an application so that it is transportable? In other words, suppose you've developed the application under the "APPS" directory on drive S. How do you make sure that the application can be moved to the "SALES\FOXPRO" directory on drive C of a notebook?

How do you handle multiple data sets?

What environment settings have you customized for an application?

Suppose you're in directory XXX, and the following files are located in directory YYY: Y.DBF, Y.PRG, Y.MNX/T, Y.APP, Y.SCX/T, Y.SPR. Then, you issue the command

```
set path to YYY
```

Which of the following commands work, which don't, and why?

```
use Y
do Y
modi menu Y
do Y.APP
do Y.SPR
modi screen Y
```

Essential Programming

Describe your naming conventions for applications, directories, source code files, data files,
question about parameters - validating, types, checking, local, blah blah blah

An application contains programs A and B. A calls B. (Assume that NAMES exists and it contains the fields cNaF and cNaL). Running this will fail. Why?

```
* a.prg
use NAMES
scatter memvar
if empty(m.cNaF) and empty(m.cNaL)
  m.cNaF = "Herman"
  m.cNaL = "Werke"
  m.glWeAreDone = .f.
endif
do B with m.cNaF, m.cNaL

* b.prg
parameter m.tcNaF, m.tcNaL
public m.glWeAreDone
if !empty(m.tcNaF) and !empty(m.tcNaL)
  report form NAMES
  m.glWeAreDone = .t.
endif
if m.glWeAreDone
  return
endif
```

Program X calls program Y which calls program Z. What are the values of m.nA, m.nB, and m.nC at each set of "?"s? (Write the answers next to the ???s)

```
* x.prg
m.nA = 10
m.nB = 50
m.nC = 99.00
do y.prg
? m.nA + m.nB + m.nC
return

* y.prg
private m.nA, m.nB
m.nA = 11
m.nB = 51
m.nC = 99.1
? m.nA + m.nB + m.nC
do z.prg
? m.nA + m.nB + m.nC
return

* z.prg
m.nA = 12
m.nB = 52
m.nC = 99.2
? m.nA + m.nB + m.nC
return
```

How would you create a memory variable that is "local" to a program - that is, it's scope is specific to the program it's in and any manipulation to it in that program is unseen by calling or called programs?

The following segments of code are two different ways of providing access to variables m.cA and m.cB in program X. When is each method preferable?

```
***** method 1
m.cA = "Herman"
m.cB = "Werke"
do X.PRG with m.cA, m.cB
```

```
* x.prg
parameter m.cA, m.cB
wait wind "What is " + m.cA + m.cB

***** method 2
m.cA = "Herman"
m.cB = "Werke"
do X.PRG

* x.prg
wait wind "What is " + m.cA + m.cB
```

What is wrong with the four following pieces of code:

```
***** sample 1 *****
m.cA = "Herman"
m.cB = "Werke"
do X.PRG with m.cA, m.cB

* x.prg
parameter m.tcName, m.tcAddress
private m.tcName, m.tcAddress
wait wind "What is " + m.tcName + m.tcAddress

***** sample 2 *****
m.cA = "Herman"
m.cB = "Werke"
do X.PRG with m.cA, m.cB

* x.prg
parameter m.tcA, m.tcB, m.tcC
private m.tcA, m.tcB, m.tcC
display memory

***** sample 3 *****
m.cA = "Herman"
m.cB = "Werke"
m.cC = "Esq."
do X.PRG with m.cA, m.cB, m.cC

* x.prg
parameter m.tcA, m.tcB
private m.tcA, m.tcB
display memory

***** sample 4 *****
<assign values to m.cA, m.cB, m.cC>
do X.PRG with m.cA, m.cB, m.cC

* x.prg
parameter m.tcA, m.tcB, m.tcC
private m.tcA, m.tcB, m.tcC
wait wind "What is " + m.tcA + m.tcB + m.tcC
```

Given a program that contains at least some of the following memory variables:

memvar	size/type	sample data
m.cNaPrefix	c 20	Mr.
m.cNaFirst	c 20	Herman
m.cNaMiddle	c 20	A.B.
m.cNaLast	c 20	Werke
m.cNaSuffix	c 20	Esq.
m.dBirth	d 8	{2/29/01}

Write a reusable routine that is passed these memvars values returns a string like:

Mr. Herman A.B. Werke, Esq. Was born on February 29, 1901

like so:

```
m.cNaFirst  = "Ted"
m.cNaMiddle = "T."
m.cNaLast   = "Turner"
```

```
m.cNaSuffix = "Esq"
m.cFullString = <call to your program>

m.cNaPrefix = "Ms."
m.cNaFirst  = "Sally"
m.cNaLast   = "Fields"
m.dBirth    = {2/2/36}
m.cFullString = <call to your program>
```

Menus, projects, etc.

How do you make a menu option disappear based on the user who has logged into the application?

Suppose you've created a project and added program X, menu HERMAN, and screens A, B and C. Program X calls the menu, and menu options call the screens. Then you add program Y, and want to make that the main (top most) program, because it has a call to X. How do you do this?

You make some changes to a program (.PRG) file that's part of a project and then run it again. The changes don't appear to have taken effect. Why might this have happened?

A reasonably sized project may have hundreds of files in it. How do you keep the various files straight in the Project Manager?

How do you prevent the Fox logo from displaying when an application built with the Project Manager is run?

Functions

Given the following array consisting of the following columns:
column 1: a concatenated string consisting of values from columns 3, 4, and 5
column 2: a primary key value
column 3: first name
column 4: last name
column 5: birth date

```
aEmployee[4,5]
Herman Werke  February 2, 1934     AAAA1     Herman  Werke     {1/2/34}
Art Hritis    September 19, 1906   AAAB7     Art     Hritis    {9/19/06}
Ben Dover     May 6, 1978          AAARe     Ben     Dover     {5/6/78}
Eileen Dover  June 1, 1961         AALL3     Eileen  Dover     {6/1/61}
```

Write a generic expression that returns the element in column 1, given a value in column 2. In other words, I'm looking for the text string that corresponds to the key value I'm passing.

```
m.cID = "AAAB7"
m.cRetVal = YourFunc(m.cID)
* m.cRetVal should be "Art Hritis Sept     September 19, 1906"
```

The concatenated string is used to populate a listbox via array. Write a generic expression that returns the key, given a selected value in the list box. In other words, when the user selects "Ben Dover   May 6, 1978", the expression should return "AAARe"

Write code that would sort this array by the date of Birth.

Write code to redefine the array to include a sixth column and place the day of the week (Monday, Tuesday, etc.) of the date in that column.

This array is created with the code

```
select "", cIDEmployee, cNameF, cNameL, dBirth ;
  from EMPLOYEE ;
```

```
    where dBirth < {1/1/79} ;
    into array aEmployee
```

Assuming that the EMPLOYEE table contains the appropriate fields, what conditions would cause this code to break?

When would you use DIMENSION and when would you use DECLARE?

Describe a scenario where you would use the keyword "external"

Suppose you keep the "Last Invoice Number Used" and the "Last Quote Number Used" in a table like so:

cDescription	nValue
INVOICE	10034
QUOTE	34901

Write a routine that returns the "next highest value" if you pass it the value "INVOICE" or "QUOTE."

How do you handle the issue of multiple users trying to access this table? How do you handle the issue of a user getting a new Invoice number, and then deciding not to add the Invoice after all, possibly leaving a hole in the string of Invoice numbers?

Given the following table structure:

```
  dBirth     D 8
  cSex       C 1  (can be M, F, or U)
  nAge       N 3
  cUnique    C 5
  dEnrolled  D 8
  cType      C 1  (can be A or B - first of this month or first of next month)
```

- Write an expression that orders the table on the enrollment date.
- Write an index expression that orders the table on sex, and then on birthdate within sex.
- Replace dEnrolled with the first day of the current month of cType = "A" or the first day of the next month of cType = "B"
- The following code place a unique value in the field cUnique. What is wrong with it.

```
  replace cUnique with string( recno() ) all
```

Data Design

Normalize the following file. Each record consists of a medical claim (date, amount, whether paid or not) and also has a patient name and address, a doctor name, and the procedure done.

Patient First Name
Patient Last Name
Patient Address
Date of Birth
Doctor Name
Doctor Tax ID #
Claim Date
Claim Amount
Procedure Code
Procedure Description
Claim Was Paid (Y/N)
Doctor Address

Design the tables for this situation: One person can belong to one or more organizations. An organization can have one or more employees. A phone number may belong to a person only (such as a mobile phone), to a company but not any one person, such as a main switchboard, or to a person at a company (such as a direct dial number). Of course, a person may have any number of phone numbers, such as home, work, fax, mobile, CIS, Internet, car, direct dial, switchbaord, home fax, and so on.

Data Manipulation

You've got a fixed length text file that consists of purchase order info from the mainframe. You're going to bring it into a DBF of POs. Some of the POs in the text file might already be in the DBF, others are not. If a PO is already in the DBF, you'll overwrite the information with new information from the text file, otherwise, you'll add the PO as new. Write the routine that does so. Document any assumptions.

You've got several hundred TXT files of length from 5K to 50K in a directory. You want to bring them into a DBF, storing the text file in a memo field in the DBF. Write the code that does so.

You are importing a customer contact list from the mainframe into a DBF. All records are new. You have normalized the customer DBF so that customer type, headquarters (the address to which a contact is attached), and other replicated information are stored in lookup tables. For example, the customer DBF contains a foreign key to the "customer type" value in the lookup table. Discuss the tradeoffs between doing seeks in the lookup table or doing lookups in an array in order to grab the foreign key for each new record.

Suppose you have a screen with twenty memory variables that all map to fields in a table. If you wanted to update the entire table with values from the screen, you could use the command GATHER MEMO MEMVAR. How would you update only certain fields from the screen instead of all of them?

Error Handling

Describe two types of expressions you can put in the left side of a debug window.

You have a number of expressions in the left panel of the debug window, and as your program runs, values do not show up in the right side. Why?

What is a breakpoint?

What happens when you delete a CDX from a disk and then try to open the DBF? How would you trap this? How would you fix it?

Create an error handling routine that handles all 'out of memory' errors.

What causes 'too many files open' and how do you fix it? How would you trap for it?

Screen Builder

Discuss desnippetizing.

Format a social security number.

What customary font should be avoided on a screen. Why?

What does the "Windows Only " checkbox in the extended screen design dialog do?

Describe three ways to design a query screen where the user can search for a name, then compare and contrast each of the three ways.

How would you populate a listbox from only a subset of values in a table. For example, suppose you have a list of properties in a table, and each property is marked as "Summer", "Fall", "Winter" or "Spring." The user selects which season from a group of radio buttons. Populate the listbox with the properties for the season that they selected.

Discuss the tradeoffs between using listboxes and picklist browses when providing the user with the ability to make a choice from a list.

Queries

Number of distinct visits: You have a claim file and a patient file. There are many patients, each with an ID number. The claim file contains a record for each procedure done for a patient on a given day. Thus, if a patient goes to a doctor and has three things done, there are three claims, each with the same patient ID and date, but a different procedure code. Write a SQL SELECT that shows how many visits each patient made between two dates.

Describe a situation that requires an outer join

Values in one but not in the other: Table 1 has 300 procedures. Table 2 has 450 procedures, some of which are also in table 1. Of the 450, 250 are in table 1, and the other 200 are not. Write a SQL SELECT that contains a list of all of the procedures in table 2 that are not in table 1.

Last Question

What question should be on this test" that wasn't?

The Job Offer

<Date>

Dear <name>:

I am pleased to extend an offer of employment as a Software Developer at Hentzenwerke Corporation to you. As we discussed earlier today, here are the terms:

Job description: Design, write, test, install and maintain custom database software using desktop application packages including FoxPro, Visual Basic, Delphi and other tools as they become available.

Annual base salary, paid every two weeks is $<amount>.

Tuition reimbursement will be 100% for an A, 90% for a B, 80% for a C, no reimbursement otherwise. Reimbursement paid upon receipt of grades.

Monthly insurance premiums will be 50% paid. Details of insurance coverage to be determined as we are in the process of converting individual plans to a group plan at the company, but coverage will be comparable to coverage that others at the company are receiving.

Parking within one or two blocks of the shop will be 50% paid.

Bonuses are paid quarterly based on amount actual billings exceed quarterly targets.

You are expected to take two weeks of vacation per calendar year; this equivocates to approximately one week for 1996. The shop is closed on the following dates: New Year's Day, Bill Gates' birthday (Thursday/Friday of third week of March), Good Friday, Memorial Day, Fourth of July, an additional day to round out a four-day weekend if 7/4 falls on a Tuesday or Thursday, Labor Day, Thanksgiving and the day after Thanksgiving, Christmas Eve, Christmas Day. Salary is paid through all holidays and vacations.

Hours are up to your discretion, given the requirements that our customers and other employees have in terms of your availability to them.

You will have a private office with a workstation of your choice and a personal computer with the following specifications: P90, 32 MB RAM, 2 GB local hard drive, CD-ROM, 17" monitor, tape backup. Printing is done over local area network to laser and dot matrix printers. You will have access to most any software you need. Resources include all industry books, magazines and newsletters.

You will receive an individual CompuServe account; monthly fees plus all business-related charges will be reimbursed monthly.

The company provides all the soft drinks and other beverages during the workday.

Dress code at the shop is casual but not "grunge"- jeans, t-shirts, shorts and the like are acceptable as long as clothes are not dirty, torn, or disorderly. The purpose is to present a comfortable, productive atmosphere and environment while not offending our customers or projecting an unprofessional appearance. We often "dress up" for meetings with customers; for men, that means suits and ties, for women, that means skirts/dresses, hose and jackets or sweaters.

You will have a one month training period during which you will be doing primarily billable work, albeit at a reduced or discounted rate in order to compensate for the expected learning curve. At the beginning of your second month, it is our intent for you to be far enough along the learning curve that you can bill approximately 30 hours a week.

Your expected start date is Monday, <date>.

We are all absolutely thrilled to have you join us at the shop and are looking forward to seeing you shortly!

Sincerely,
Hentzenwerke Corporation

Whil Hentzen
President

Bibliography

Required Reading

The following books have changed my life. They will change yours as well.

Parker, Jr, John L., *Once a Runner,* Cedarwinds Publishing, ISBN 0-91597-01-9

Pirsig, Robert M., *Zen and the Art of Motorcycle Maintenance,* Bantam, ISBN 055327-7472

Rand, Ayn, *Atlas Shrugged,* New American Library, ISBN 0451132157

Strongly Suggested Reading

The following books should be on every developer's bookshelf - after you're finished reading them.

Brooks, Frederick P., *The Mythical Man-Month,* Addison-Wesley, ISBN 0-201-006-50-2

Constantine, Larry L., *Constantine on Peopleware,* Yourdon Press ISBN 0-12-331976-8

Cringely, Robert X., *Accidental Empires: How The Boys Of Silicon Valley Make Their Millions, Battle Foreign Competition, And Still Can't Get A Date,* HarperBusiness ISBN 0-88730-621-7

DeMarco, Tom and Lister, Tim, *Peopleware,* Dorset House, ISBN 0932633145

Demarco, Tom, *Why Does Software Cost So Much?,* Dorset House ISBN 0-932-633-34-X

Dreger, Brian J., *Function Point Analysis* , Prentice Hall, ISBN 0-13-332321-8

Eisenberg, Arlene; Murkoff, Heidi; Hathaway, Sandee, *What to Expect When You're Expecting,* Workman Publishing Company, ISBN 1563058723

Freedman Daniel P. And Gerald M.Weinberg *Handbook Of Walkthroughs, Inspections, And Technical Reviews,* Dorset House, ISBN 0-932633-19-6

Freedman, Daniel P. and Weinberg, Gerald P., *Handbook of Walkthroughs, Inspections and Technical Reviews,* Dorset House. ISBN 0-932633-19-6

Grady, Robert B., *Practical Software Metrics for Project Management and Process Improvement,* Prentice-Hall, ISBN 0-13-720384-5

Humphrey, Watts S., *Managing the Software Process* ,Addison Wesley, ISBN 0-201-18095

Humphrey, Watts S., *A Discipline for Software Engineering,* Addison, Wesley, ISBN 0201546108

Jones, Capers, *Applied Software Measurement,* McGraw-Hill, ISBN 0-07-032613-7

Kernighan, Brian and Plauger, P.J., *Elements of Programming Style,* McGraw Publishing Company, ISBN 0070342075

Kidder, Tracy, *Soul of a New Machine*, Avon, ISBN 038071115X

Maguire, Steve, *Debugging the Development Process,* Microsoft Press, ISBN 1-55615-650-2

Maguire, Steve, *Writing Solid Code,* Microsoft Press, ISBN 1-55615-551-4

Marinaccio, Dave, *All I really need to know I learned from watching Star Trek,* Crown Publishers, Inc. ISBN 0-517-59798-5

McCarthy, Jim, *Dynamics of Software Development*, Microsoft Press, ISBN 1-55615-823-8

McConnell, Steve, *Code Complete,* Microsoft Press, ISBN 1-55615-484-4

Metzger, Philip W., *Managing a Programming Project*, Prentice Hall, ISBN 0135542391

Moore, Geoffrey A., *Crossing The Chasm,* Harper Business, ISBN 0-88730-519-9

Moore, Geoffrey A., *Inside The Tornado,* Harper Business, ISBN 0-88730-765-5

Norman, Donald A., *The Design Of Everyday Things,* Bantam Doubleday Dell Publishing Group Inc. ISBN 0-385-26774-6

Pascal, Zachary G., *Show Stopper,* Free Press Inc. ISBN 0-02-935671-7

Ruhl, Janet, *The Computer Consultant's Guide*, ISBN 0-471-59661-2

Ruhl, Janet, Th*e Computer Consultant's Workbook*, ISBN 0-9647116-0-5

Weinberg , Gerald , *Secrets of Consulting*, Dorset House Publishing Company, ISBN 0932633013

William, Perry, *Effective Methods for Software Testing*, John Wiley & Sons, ISBN 0-471-06097-6

Yourdon, Edward, *Structured Walk Throughs,* Yourdon Press, ISBN 0-13-855289- 4

50% Charter Discount
for the
1998 DEVELOPER'S GUIDE

The 1997 DEVELOPER'S GUIDE is an ongoing concern. The print was barely dry on the 1997 Edition before we started compiling additional material to be included in the 1998 Edition. Changes, corrections, expansion of existing material as well as brand new material, and, of course, feedback to the ever popular "Reader Mail" - there'll be plenty to look forward to.

Send us this card (sorry, snail-mail only) and you'll receive a 50% discount off of the regular price of the 1998 DEVELOPER'S GUIDE.

Name:____

Company: _____________________________________

Address:______________________________________

C/S/Z: ____

Phone:______________ Fax: ______________

E-mail:____________________________

Number:______________
Hentzenwerke use only